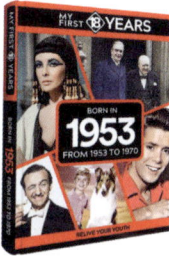

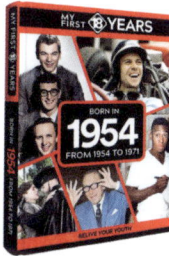

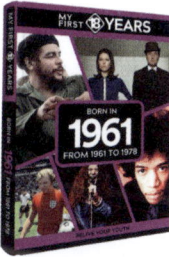

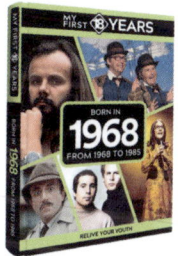

MY FIRST **18** YEARS

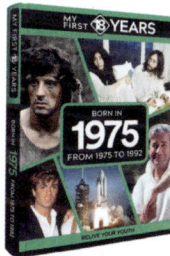

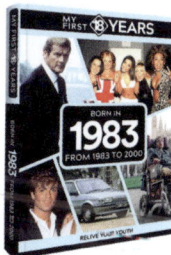

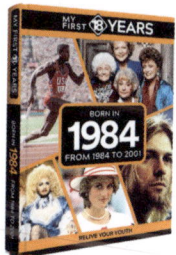

BORN IN
1953
FROM 1953 TO 1970
RELIVE YOUR YOUTH

MY FIRST **18** YEARS

BORN IN
1954
FROM 1954 TO 1971
RELIVE YOUR YOUTH

BORN IN 1955 FROM 1955 TO 1972
RELIVE YOUR YOUTH

MY FIRST **18** YEARS

BORN IN
1961
FROM 1961 TO 1978
RELIVE YOUR YOUTH

MY FIRST **18** YEARS

BORN IN
1962
FROM 1962 TO 1979
RELIVE YOUR YOUTH

MY FIRST **18** YEARS

BORN IN
1963
FROM 1963 TO 1980
RELIVE YOUR YOUTH

MY FIRST **18** YEARS

BORN IN
1964
FROM 1964 TO 1981
RELIVE YOUR YOUTH

MY FIRST **18** YEARS

BORN IN
1967
FROM 1967 TO 1984
RELIVE YOUR YOUTH

MY FIRST **18** YEARS

BORN IN
1968
FROM 1968 TO 1985
RELIVE YOUR YOUTH

MY FIRST **18** YEARS

MY FIRST **18** YEARS

BORN IN
1973
FROM 1973 TO 1990
RELIVE YOUR YOUTH

MY FIRST **18** YEARS

BORN IN
1974
FROM 1974 TO 1991
RELIVE YOUR YOUTH

MY FIRST **18** YEARS

BORN IN
1975
FROM 1975 TO 1992
RELIVE YOUR YOUTH

MY FIRST **18** YEARS

BORN IN
1976
FROM 1976 TO 1993
RELIVE YOUR YOUTH

MY FIRST **18** YEARS

BORN IN
1981
FROM 1981 TO 1998
RELIVE YOUR YOUTH

MY FIRST **18** YEARS

BORN IN
1982
FROM 1982 TO 1999
RELIVE YOUR YOUTH

MY FIRST **18** YEARS

BORN IN
1983
FROM 1983 TO 2000
RELIVE YOUR YOUTH

MY FIRST **18** YEARS

BORN IN
1984
FROM 1984 TO 2001
RELIVE YOUR YOUTH

MY FIRST 18 YEARS

18

BORN IN

1951

FROM 1951 TO 1968

My First 18 Years is a brand of TDM Publishing.
The image, brand and logos are protected and owned by TDM Publishing.

www.mijneerste18jaar.nl
info@mijneerste18jaar.nl

My First 18 Years idea and concept: Thars Duijnstee.
Research and text: Lucinda Gosling, Stephen Barnard, Jeffrey Roozeboom, Katherine Alcock.
Composition and image editing: Jeffrey Roozeboom.
Design: Ferry Geutjes, Boudewijn van der Plas, Jeffrey Roozeboom.
Proofreading: Alison Griffiths.

Every effort has been made to trace the rights holders of all images. If you believe an image has been incorrectly credited, please contact the publisher.

Photos: Sound & Vision, National Archives, Getty images, Mary Evans Picture Library, Shutterstock, BNNVARA, AVROTROS, Veronica, KRO-NCRV, KIPPA, *Mijn eerste 18 jaar* archives.

In writing this series, the authors drew from the following sources: view from 1963-1999, NTS / NOS Annual Review, nueens.nl, vandaagindegeschiedenis.nl, beleven.org, IMDb, Wikipedia, Eye Filmmuseum, Rollingstone.com, image & sound, National Archives, Onthisday.com, Parlement.com. *Complete Book of UK Hit Singles, First Hits 1949-1959* (Boxtree Books), Billboard Books, *Reader's Digest* Music series 1950s-1970s, British Library Newspaper Archive, rogerebert.com

Thanks to: Spotify, Rick Versteeg, Rik Booltink.

The Top 10 list for each year is compiled by Stephen Barnard and is a personal selection of best-selling hits, radio favourites and lesser-known tracks that reflect the popular artists and styles of each year. Some are universally regarded classics, others will be less remembered yet are equally emblematic of the tastes of that year. Each list should provoke many 'Ah yes!' moments, particularly those almost forgotten treasures that are rarely heard even as 'golden oldies' yet tickled the ears in their day.

How to use Spotify playlists:

1. Open Spotify.
2. Click search (the magnifying glass in the image).
3. Click scan (the camera in the picture).
4. Point your camera at the Spotify code in the book.
5. After that, you can play the selected list.

ISBN 978 94 9331 760 4
NUR: 400

SPORT

Sugar Ray's sweet victory
14th February 1951 In a bruising encounter later re-created very graphically in the film *Raging Bull*, Sugar Ray Leonard takes the world middleweight title from one of the most resilient sluggers in boxing, Jake LaMotta. Five months and nine fights later, Robinson sensationally loses his title to British underdog Randolph Turpin (photo), though he reclaims it from the same fighter in New York in September.

Spurs are champions
28th April 1951 Tottenham Hotspur win the First Division title for the first time in their history, just a year after celebrating promotion from football's second tier. Former Spurs captain Arthur Rowe only joined the club as manager in 1949 and made the crucial signing of future England manager Alf Ramsey to implement his favoured 'push and run' style.

Stirling effort
27th May 1951 Making his World Championship Grand Prix debut in Switzerland is a motoring legend in waiting. Twenty one- year-old Stirling Moss, driving for Hersham and Walton Motors (HWM), finishes in a deeply impressive eighth place in what is effectively a Formula Two car. He will go on to win sixteen Grand Prix races in his illustrious career. The future is equally bright for HWM, who are awarded the sought-after Aston Martin franchise later in the year.

First slam for 'Little Mo'
5th September 1951 Set to become a nine-time Grand Slam winner before a life-changing riding injury cuts short her career, sixteen-year-old tennis sensation Maureen 'Little Mo' Connolly wins her first US Open title. She defeats her fellow American Shirley Fry in three sets.

The one day game is born
Though its importance isn't realised at the time, the first match of the All India Pooja Cricket Tournament is a milestone in the sport's history. As a day-long match limited to 50 overs, it marks the birth of one-day cricket, a concept that will reach England in more developed form in 1962.

100 hundreds
16th July 1951 Having played with typically rugged determination in the recent Test series in Australia, England's cricket captain-in-waiting Len Hutton hits the 100th century of his career playing for Yorkshire versus Surrey at the Oval. He is only the thirteenth player to do so.

10 JAN 1951	15 FEB 1951	10 MAR 1951
UN headquarters opens in New York.	Membership of UK trade unions reaches an all-time high of over 9.3 million.	Ireland wins the Five Nations Championship with a 3-3 draw against Wales.

3

1951

DOMESTIC NEWS

X-rated movies!
January The 'X' rating is introduced for the first time in the UK, replacing the old H rating. The British Board of Film Censors state that films rated X are 'extremely graphic, only those aged 16 and over can be admitted'. This would rise in 1970 to age 18, before the X rating was replaced in 1982.

Nation takes on steel
15th February 1951 The Iron and Steel Corporation of Great Britain is created to take control of 80 steel and iron companies brought under national ownership. The nationalisation of steel proves controversial in the Commons, and Conservatives soon seek to reverse the process.

Atlantic Crossed
21st February 1951 The English Electric Canberra becomes the first jet to cross the Atlantic without stopping to refuel. Taking off from RAF Aldergrove in Northern Ireland, it takes just 4 hours and 37 minutes to arrive safely at Gander in Newfoundland.

HMS *Affray* lost
17th April 1951 The disappearance of the submarine HMS *Affray* becomes headline news, and the papers flood with conspiracy theories. Missing with 75 souls on board, including several trainee officers, the *Affray* had been engaged in exercises in the Channel. Once it fails to return to port, a search is launched, with the wreck discovered two months later in June. The exact cause of the sinking remains disputed.

The Glorious Glosters
22nd-25th April 1951 The Battle of the Imjin River in the Korean War leads to the famous last stand of the 1st Battalion Gloucestershire Regiment, 'the Glorious Glosters' under Lieutenant-Colonel Carne. Trapped on Hill 235 and outnumbered 18-1, the Glosters fight bravely, losing 620 men and having 522 taken prisoner. Despite ultimate defeat, their courage would become the stuff of military legend.

Missing diplomats
26th May 1951 Two British diplomats, Guy Burgess and Donald Maclean, disappear in mysterious circumstances, leading to speculation that they may have been Soviet spies. A worldwide manhunt is launched, and whilst the truth would not be known for some time, suspicion is naturally cast on their close associates, people who would one day be recognised as members of the Cambridge Five Spy Ring.

11 APR 1951
President Truman sacks his Commander in Chief Douglas MacArthur for insubordination.

15 MAY 1951
Roberta Cowell was the first known British trans woman to undergo sex reassignment surgery.

11 JUN 1951
Mozambique becomes an oversea province of Portugal.

Festival of Britain

3rd May 1951 King George VI opens the Festival of Britain to nationwide excitement. Officially commemorating 100 years since the Great Exhibition of 1851, it is designed to give post-war Britain something to celebrate. Special commemorative stamps are released, new buildings including the Royal Festival Hall are opened and the Festival ship, *Campania*, cruises the ports.

Situation in Suez escalates

18th October 1951 Following a deteriorating political situation and rioting in the Suez Canal Zone, British paratroopers move quickly to seize key points of control around the Canal. By the 19th they are in full control of the area with only a handful of casualties, but the situation deteriorates over the next month with fighting in the streets, and by 20th November the families of British servicemen are evacuated from the area. By December there is open conflict and fierce fighting in the area.

Colliery explosion

29th May 1951 Easington Colliery experiences a huge explosion when firedamp ignites killing all 81 men inside the shafts that night. A rescue mission led by Frank Leadbitter, who enter the mines at great personal risk, also loses two men who are overcome by the noxious gases trying to save their comrades.

Austin A30

17th October 1951 Austin release their A30 model, announced as the 'new' Austin 7 and created to compete directly with the very popular Morris Minor. It has a top speed of 62 miles per hour, and can do 0-50mph in 29 seconds, all whilst undercutting the Minor in price by £62.00. This competition is brought to an end just a month later, when Austin and Morris announce their merger to form the British Motor Corporation Limited.

Zebra crossing

31st October 1951 The very first zebra crossings are introduced to the UK on Slough High Street. Designed to stop people ignoring the existing Belisha beacons, the idea to paint the road black and white is credited to George Charlesworth, Head of Traffic at the Road Research Laboratory.

10 JUL 1951
Peace talks open to end the Korean War.

14 AUG 1951
Death of US newspaper magnate William Randolph Hearst.

20 SEP 1951
Old adversaries Turkey and Greece join NATO.

1951

O and A

The Higher School Certificate is replaced with new qualifications, the GCE 'Ordinary' and 'Advanced' Levels. Initially these result in either a distinction, pass or a fail, with later years introducing the current A*-O grades. Ordinary Levels are later replaced with GCSEs, graded 1-9.

ROYALTY & POLITICS

Bevan resigns

23rd April 1951 Minister of Labour Aneurin Bevan resigns from Clement Attlee's Cabinet in protest at government plans to introduce charges for false teeth and spectacles. The charges are a sign of the financial pressures now being faced by Bevan's creation, the infant National Health Service.

A Palace operation

23 September 1951 The King undergoes a successful three-hour operation at Buckingham Palace to remove his left lung. The British people are not told of his cancer diagnosis but only that the operation is to address 'structural abnormalities' in his respiratory system.

Margaret comes of age

24th August 1951 Princess Margaret celebrates her 21st birthday at Balmoral where she is presented with a 30lb zodiac-style cake brought up by train from London. Her parents' gifts comprise a string of 21 pearls and a pair of diamond earrings. Now she has come of age, Margaret is entitled to £6,000 a year from the Civil List. Press speculation continues about her romantic life and the possibility of an engagement announcement, though her growing closeness to her father's now divorced equerry, Peter Townsend, goes unnoticed for the moment.

Winston is back

26th October 1951 Called by Clement Attlee a month earlier, the General Election sees 76-year-old Winston Churchill lead the Conservative Party to victory and replace Attlee as Prime Minister. The Conservatives win a working majority of seventeen seats but curiously have a lower share of the overall popular vote than Labour.

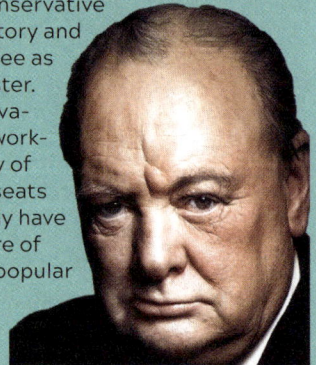

19 OCT 1951

US President Harry Truman formally ends state of war with Germany.

20 NOV 1951

Snowdonia follows the Peak District and Lake District in gaining National Park status.

31 DEC 1951

Expiry of the Marshall Plan that granted $13bn of post-war aid to Europe.

Final broadcast

25th December 1951 An ailing King George VI makes what will prove to be his last Christmas radio broadcast to Britain and the Commonwealth. Because of his delicate condition, his speech is pre-recorded for the first time in his reign. His voice controlled but a little unsteady, he thanks 'my people in these islands and the British Commonwealth and Empire' for their 'support and sympathy'.

FOREIGN
NEWS

Porsche dies

10th January 1951 Ferdinand Porsche, renowned designer of high-performance cars, dies in Stuttgart aged 75.

United Nations opens HQ

8th January 1951 Though construction is as yet unfinished, the United Nations headquarters are officially opened in Midtown Manhattan, New York City, with an initial complement of 3,300 staff. The design of the complex is the work of the architectural firm Harrison and Abramovitz with input from Oscar Niemeyer and Le Corbusier.

Spies on trial

6th March 1951 The trial of married couple Julius and Ethel Rosenberg begins in the US. Both are accused of passing on information about the atomic bomb to the Soviet Union. Their conviction and death sentence sends a shock wave through the Western world. President Truman will not even accept a plea for clemency from the Pope. The electric chair awaits the Rosenbergs in 1953.

Seoul recaptured

15th March 1951 In the Korean war, United Nations forces recapture Seoul. This is the fourth and final time in which the city will change hands during the conflict.

Coffee grinder

State of war ends

9th July 1951 The UK and Australia become the first countries to formally end the state of war with Germany. Canada follows in July and the US in October. In San Francisco during September 48 countries sign a treaty to end the war in the Pacific.

1951

Artificial heart

30th August 1951 In an important development in cardiac surgery, Dutch professor Jacob Jongbloed demonstrates an artificial heart machine at a meeting of the Congress of Surgeons at the Sorbonne in Paris.

Nobel Prize for Medicine

The Nobel Prize for Medicine goes to South African virologist Max Theiler, who in 1939 discovered a vaccine against yellow fever, a fatal disease transmitted from animals to humans by mosquitoes.

Nuclear energy

20th December 1951 Electricity is generated from nuclear energy for the first time in the Experimental Breeder Reactor 1 in Idaho. The next day, the reactor produces enough power to light the entire building. Three years later, a nuclear power plant in the Soviet Union supplies electricity to a closed electricity grid for the first time.

ENTERTAINMENT

Welcome to Ambridge

On 1st January, listeners tune in for the first time to hear the daily ups and downs of the inhabitants of Ambridge. Billed as 'an everyday story of country folk', *The Archers* was originally broadcast on the Midlands Home Service and told the tale of three farmers, including Dan Archer and family of Brookfield farm, as a vehicle for promoting good agricultural practice. The success of the pilot leads to a permanent serialisation. *The Archers* will go on to be the longest-running radio serial in the world, with guest appearances over the years from notable figures including Judi Dench and Princess Margaret.

Blown away

General Electric introduces the bonnet hair dryer to consumers. An inflatable cap, fed hot air from the dryer through a tube, it allows a hands-free hair styling experience from the comfort of your own home.

THE NEW SUPER-COLOUR WEEKLY FOR EVERY GIRL

Girl

SISTER PAPER TO EAGLE.

Girl power

Girl comic is launched by Hulton Press on 2nd November as a sister paper to the popular boys' title, *Eagle*. The cover strip of its early issues features the in-flight adventures of Kitty Hawke and her all-girl air crew.

I spy with my little eye

I-Spy books, pocket-sized spotter guides, are published by the *News Chronicle* in which kids have to tick off things they see on myriad themes from the seaside to dogs. Once completed, books can be posted to 'Big Chief I-Spy' and spotters receive a reward for their eagle-eyed diligence.

What's My Line

Described by the *Radio Times* as 'a beat the panel entertainment' *What's My Line* is broadcast for the first time on 16th July, with the likeable Eamonn Andrews 'seeing fair play'. Among the panellists who are tasked with guessing what each contestant did for a living are stage favourites Frances Day and Dorothy Dickson.

Men only

23rd January BBC radio announces cuts to the number of announcers, keeping men only, and none with 'dialect voices' The corporation claims, in a display of undisguised misogyny 'People do not like momentous events such as war or disaster to be read by a female voice'!

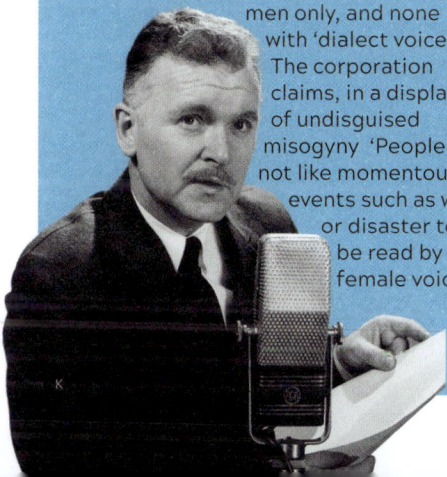

The arts come to the South Bank

The Royal Festival Hall opens as part of the redevelopment of London's South Bank for the Festival of Britain, intended as a permanent arts venue. The royal family attends a dedication ceremony on 3rd May, followed by a concert of British music. A short distance along the riverbank, Queen Elizabeth lays the foundation stone for the National Theatre on 13th July, although plans for the building have changed so often, she jokes that perhaps the stone should be on castors. The National Theatre finally opens in 1976!

Enter the Goons

28th May 1951 Spike Milligan, Peter Sellers, Harry Secombe and Michael Bentine perform together in *Crazy People*, the radio show that would eventually evolve into *The Goon Show*. Its seventeenth episode, two million listeners are tuning in to chuckle at their surreal brand of absurd comedy.

Teenage tale

J. D Salinger's *The Catcher in the Rye* is published by Hamish Hamilton in the UK.

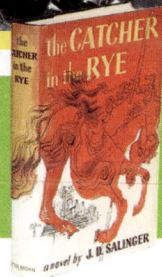

9

Deliquent diva
Joan Collins, aged nineteen, appears in
I Believe in You as a wayward girl to Celia
Johnson's probation officer. In her first
major film role, the London *Evening News*
compares her to Jane Russell, while the
Daily Mirror is unabashed, declaring her
'a saucy and sexy lass'.

Prized pastries
John Gregg opens a bakery shop in
Gosforth High Street, Newcastle-up-
on-Tyne, the first in what is to become
Britain's favourite chain of sausage roll
and pasty purveyors, Gregg's.

Earl and the girl
The Pool of London from Ealing Studios
gets mixed reviews in the press, but most
single out the outstanding performance
of Earl Cameron, a Bermudian actor, whose
character, a sailor, falls in love with a
white girl during his two days' shore leave.
Cameron is one of the first black actors
to take a lead role in a British film since
before the war in a storyline tackling race
relations.

MUSIC

Mob mayhem
Ealing Studios
score another hit
with their film
*The Lavender Hill
Mob*, in which Alec
Guinness stars as a
bank clerk turned
criminal, partner-
ing with Stanley
Holloway to hatch
an audacious plan
to smuggle stolen
gold bullion out
of the country.
Filling a small part
in this crime caper is an early-career
Audrey Hepburn in the role of Chiquita.

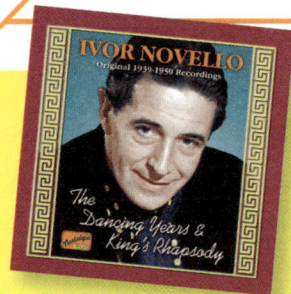

Novello's final curtain
6th March 1951 Cardiff-born composer and
actor Ivor Novello dies shortly after performing in his musical *King's Rhapsody*
at London's Palace Theatre. Loved and
loathed in equal measure for the self-writ-
ten and decidedly florid Viennese-style
operettas in which he also starred, his
name will be immortalised by the Ivor
Novello Awards launched in 1955 to honour
excellence in British songwriting.

Festival Pleasure Gardens

Battersea Park is transformed into the fantastical Festival Pleasure Gardens with fun fair, tree walks and a railway designed by Roland Emmett. Girl orange-sellers mimic Nell Gwynne and echo the time of Charles II.

Coward's commentary

24th May 1951 Ever the pin-sharp commentator, Noel Coward responds to the opening of the Festival of Britain with the tongue in cheek and not wholly supportive *Don't Make Fun of the Fair*. He has written the song for Ian Carmichael to perform in the topical revue show *The Lyric Revue* at the Hammersmith theatre of the same name.

Doris weds Marty

3rd April 1950 Film and record star Doris Day (real name Doris Kappelhoff) celebrates her 27th birthday by marrying movie producer Marty Melcher in Los Angeles. Although she is specialising in effervescent movie musicals, Doris takes on her first dramatic role this year in *Young Man with a Horn*, as the true love of a troubled jazz musician played by Kirk Douglas.

Judy is back

April-July 1951 After being sacked from her movie contract by MGM and with her divorce from Vincente Minnelli finalised, Judy Garland is determined to re-launch her career with a four-month tour of the UK and Ireland. The tour includes a month-long residency at the London Palladium that closes with what the theatre's manager calls 'the loudest ovation I have ever heard'.

Home-made magic

In his own self-built studio at the home he shares with his wife Mary Ford, Les Paul multi-tracks Mary's voice and his own guitar playing to create the almost other-worldly *How High the Moon*, one of the most sophisticated and technically advanced recordings to date. Paul has also designed and patented the solid body electric guitar that bears his name.

A new orchestral sound

In Decca Records' studio in North London, bandleader Annunzio Mantovani and his arranger Ronald Binge create a whole new approach to light orchestral music by bathing the 1920s ballad *Charmaine* in lush cascading strings. Likened by Binge to a gently tumbling waterfall, it will be the basis of the shimmering Mantovani sound for the next 30 years.

1951

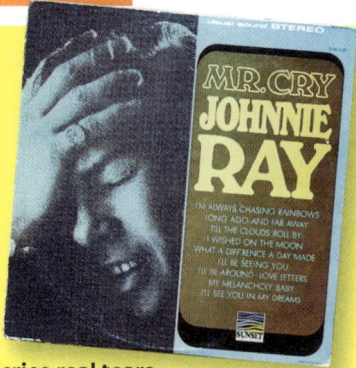

He cries real tears

Atmospheric and echo-laden, Johnnie Ray's melodramatic recording of *Cry* marks the true start of the teenage music revolution to come. The bridge between the post-war Frank Sinatra-led heart-throb years and hip-swinging Elvis-inspired rock'n'roll, Johnnie's emotional delivery and ability to summon on-stage tears will earn him such nicknames as 'the Nabob of Sob', 'the Prince of Wails' and 'the Cry guy'.

Feline fun

The prize for funniest record of the year has to go to *I Taut I Taw a Puddy Tat* by Mel Blanc, the multi-talented voice of all the great characters in Warner Brothers' *Looney Tunes* and *Merrie Melodies* cartoons. *Puddy Tat* finds Blanc voicing the plucky pint-sized canary Tweetie Pie and his perpetual would-be predator, the sibilant, ever-ravenous Sylvester the Cat.

Black Dyke win again

27th October 1951 Held annually at the Royal Albert Hall, the National Brass Band Championships is a British institution in which every major band in the country participates. This year's winner - for the fourth time in five years - is Bradford's Black Dyke Mills Band, which was founded for the welfare of local mill workers in 1855.

MY FIRST 18 YEARS TOP10 1951

1. **Mel Blanc** *I Taut I Taw A Puddy Tat*
2. **Mario Lanza** *Be My Love*
3. **Libby Holman, Josh White** *On Top of Old Smoky*
4. **Guy Mitchell** *The Roving Kind*
5. **Jo Stafford** *Shrimp Boats*
6. **Les Paul and Mary Ford** *Mockin' Bird Hill*
7. **Tennessee Ernie Ford** *Shotgun Boogie*
8. **Mantovani and his Orchestra** *Charmaine*
9. **Debbie Reynolds** *Aba Daba Honeymoon*
10. **Nat King Cole** *Too Young*

Open | Search | Scan

Callas at La Scala

7th December 1951 After understudying several roles, the 20th century's greatest soprano, Maria Callas, makes her stunning official debut at La Scala in Milan in Verdi's opera *I vespri siciliani*. Such is her reception that she will regard La Scala as her spiritual and artistic home for the rest of her career.

SPORT

Winter gold

17th February 1952 British figure skater and reigning European Champion Jeannette Altwegg wins the gold medal in the women's singles at the Winter Olympics in Oslo. She retires immediately and swaps the ice rink for a position at Pestalozzi Children's Village in Switzerland.

Workington at Wembley

19th April 1952 Workington becomes the first club outside Lancashire or Yorkshire to win rugby league's Challenge Cup Final. The match at Wembley against Featherstone Rovers is the first televised final.

Fiery Fred's debut

5th June 1952 Fast bowler Fred Trueman makes his Test match debut for England against India at Headingley. Trueman takes seven wickets in an England win - an impressive figure for someone who is currently doing his National Service at RAF Hemswell in Lincolnshire and has had limited opportunities to play for his native county of Yorkshire this season. Fred will be an England regular for thirteen years, playing in 67 Tests and taking 307 wickets.

Olympic heights

19th July-13th August 1952 At the Olympic Games in Helsinki, 257 British athletes take part across 127 events in eighteen disciplines. Their medal haul is skimpy - one gold, two silver and eight bronze - with the gold coming in the last event on the last day, to Harry Llewellyn, Duggie Stewart and Wilf White in the equestrian show jumping team event. The highlight of the whole games is without doubt the performance of Emil Zatopek, the Czech long-distance runner whose three golds include the marathon, an event in which he had never competed before.

Loch Ness tragedy

29th September 1922 Former RAF Squadron Leader John Cobb, who has held the world land speed record since 1947, is killed while attempting to claim its water speed equivalent on Loch Ness. Reaching over 200mph, his jet-powered boat *Crusader* loses stability and disintegrates.

26 JAN 1952	15 FEB 1952	14 MAR 1952
Fierce rioting erupts in Egypt against Britain's military presence.	The Austin and Morris motor companies merge to form the British Motor Corporation.	New transmitters at Kirk O'Shotts and Wenvoe bring television to Scotland and Wales.

1952

DOMESTIC
NEWS

Turing on trial

31st March 1952 Alan Turing, the mathematician and computer scientist credited with breaking the codes of the German Enigma machines, is found guilty of gross indecency after admitting to a consensual homosexual relationship. To avoid imprisonment, he agrees to undergo 'chemical castration'. In 2017 the 'Turing Law' retroactively pardoned all men cautioned or convicted of consensual homosexual acts. Turing's image is now on the £50 note.

TV detector vans

1st February 1952 The first TV detector vans are launched by the General Post Office to clamp down on those families not paying the £2 licence fee. Hillman Minx and Morris Oxford vans kitted out with special equipment are despatched to roam the streets looking for the estimated 150,000 families using television sets without a licence.

Eastcastle Street robbery

21st May 1952 £287,000 is stolen (equivalent to over £10 million in 2024) in Britain's largest post-war robbery. At 4:20am a Post Office van is held up in Eastcastle Street in London by seven masked men who use two cars to trap the van and steal it from its attendants. Despite a large investigation and manhunt, no one is ever caught.

ID cards abolished

21st February 1952 Compulsory Identity cards, first introduced in September 1939 with the outbreak of the Second World War, are abolished. Citizens will no longer have to carry cards detailing their identity, address, and occupation, or present them to police officers when challenged.

Farnborough Air Show crash

6th September 1952 31 people are killed as a prototype de Havilland DH110 jet fighter disintegrates in the air over the crowd at Farnborough Air Show in Hampshire. A failure of the aircraft's wing during an aerial manoeuvre is to blame, ripping the aircraft apart and sending its engines hurtling into observers. Following this tragedy, stricter rules regarding crowd safety are introduced at air shows.

Britain has atomic bomb

29th February 1952 Winston Churchill announces that Britain has developed an atomic bomb and is capable of manufacturing them.

15 APR 1952

Franklin National Bank issues the first bank credit card.

18 MAY 1952

Stonehenge is dated back to 1848 BC by Professor Willand Libby.

14 JUN 1952

Jim Peters runs a world record marathon 2:20:42.2.

Goodbye to London's trams!

6th July 1952 The very last of London's trams takes its final passengers into New Cross Depot. Since October 1950 the tram network had been steadily replaced by new diesel buses as the capital updated its transport infrastructure.

Devastating rail crash

8th October 1952 A collision between two trains at Harrow and Wealdstone station kills 112 people. The 7:21am commuter train to Euston, London, is struck from behind by an express train from Perth, sending wreckage flying onto the platform and across the lines, causing a third train to strike the debris and derail.

Lynmouth flood

16th August 1952 On the night of the 15th-16th August, 34 people are killed in a flash flood in the village of Lynmouth in Devon. Following a huge storm, water and debris are brought rushing down from the surrounding moorland, demolishing 100 buildings and sweeping 38 cars out to sea. Boulders and uprooted trees devastate the village, and 420 people are made homeless. The village was later rebuilt, and the river Lyn diverted.

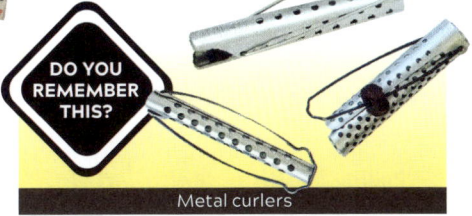

DO YOU REMEMBER THIS?

Metal curlers

Tea off the ration

5th October 1952 Tea rationing finally ends after thirteen years, marking yet another step in post-war economic recovery. Brits are finally able to indulge in as many cups as they like, reigniting the nation's love affair with a good brew.

The Great Smog

4th December 1952 An anticyclone settles over London, causing a dense fog which mingles with the city's pollution to create a poisonous smog. Exhaust fumes, coal fires, industrial chemicals, and soot cling to the moisture in the air, which is then breathed in by millions of the Thames Valley's inhabitants. The smog is so dense that the London ambulance service halts operations, as does most public transport, with visibility limited to a metre or so ahead.

5 JUL 1952

Maureen Connolly (US) wins Wimbledon for the third time in a row.

3 AUG 1952

Ferrari driver Alberto Ascari wins his first Formula 1 World Drivers' Championship.

19 SEP 1952

Farnborough Air Show crash kills 31.

ROYALTY & POLITICS

The last goodbye

30th January 1952 Having attended a performance of *South Pacific* the night before, the King and Queen are driven to Heathrow to wave off Princess Elizabeth and the Duke of Edinburgh on what is planned to be a six-month royal tour of the Commonwealth. It is the last time that the King will see his daughter.

The Queen's Speech

The new Queen makes her first Christmas broadcast, speaking to the Commonwealth from the study at Sandringham House and using the same chair and desk her father, George VI, and grandfather, George V, had used for the same purpose.

Death of the King

6th February 1952 The King is found dead in his bed at Sandringham around 7am, having suffered a coronary thrombosis in his sleep. He was 56 years old. Princess Elizabeth and Prince Philip are now in Kenya and only receive the news after some delay. BBC radio reveals the King's death to a shocked nation at 11:15am. Princess Elizabeth is officially proclaimed Queen at a ceremony in St James's Palace that afternoon and returns to the UK two days later.

A family affair

14th August 1952 Opinion has it that Foreign Secretary Anthony Eden will be Winston Churchill's successor as Prime Minister when the time comes. Now the relationship between the two politicians has become even closer with Eden's marriage to Winston's niece, Clarissa Spencer-Churchill.

3 OCT 1952

The UK tests its first atomic bomb in Australia's Monte Bello Islands.

13 NOV 1952

The first set of false fingernails is sold.

30 DEC 1952

Introduced to combat wartime wood shortages, the utility furniture scheme ends after ten years.

Granville defects

8th January 1952 With only nine seats in the new Parliament, the Liberals suffer another blow with the defection to Labour of former MP and party heavyweight Edgar Granville. He has campaigned alongside Megan Lloyd George for the party to reassert what he calls the radical tradition of Liberalism. Granville will accept a Labour peerage in 1967 before gravitating towards the political right and support for Margaret Thatcher.

FOREIGN NEWS

They like Ike

4th November 1952 Standing on the Republican ticket, Dwight D. Eisenhower, nick-named Ike, is elected 34th President of the United States.

Von Braun predicts space travel

22nd March 1952 Wernher Von Braun, the German scientist who developed rocketry for the Nazis in the Second World War, publishes the first in a series of articles called *Man Will Conquer Space Soon.* Now working for the US government, he predicts that regular flights to the Moon and Mars will be possible before the end of the century.

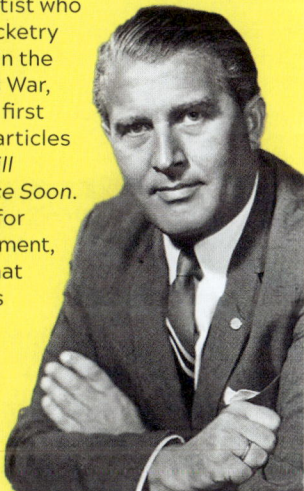

Nelson Mandela

26th June 1952 The African National Congress (ANC) launches a non-violent resistance campaign after the apartheid regime in South Africa denies basic rights for blacks. At 33 years old, Nelson Mandela is appointed as chief volunteer and travels across the country to incite supporters to civil disobedience. Mandela is arrested in July for alleged violations of anti-communism legislation. Later in the year, he starts the first law firm for black Africans oppressed by apartheid laws, in the heart of Johannesburg.

Miss Universe

28th June 1952 Seventeen-year-old Armi Kuusela of Finland becomes the very first Miss Universe in a contest held in Long Beach, California. In addition to a very expensive crown and the promise of eternal fame, she receives a multi-year film contract with Universal Studios.

Treaty of Paris

23rd July 1952 After the signing of the Treaty of Paris in 1951, the European Coal and Steel Community (ECSC) becomes a reality. Jean Monnet, one of the leading advocates of the European Community, will become the first President of the High Authority, the executive body of the ECSC.

5 PESOS CORREOS
EVA PERÓN
ARGENTINA

Evita is dead

26th July 1952 Eva Perón, First Lady of Argentina, dies of cancer. A former actress, she married Juan Perón in 1945 and assisted his rise to the presidency a year later. Through her philanthropy and espousal of causes such as women's suffrage, Eva has built a following among the ordinary population or 'shirtless ones' comparable to that of Perón himself. Although allegations of corruption persist, she has almost achieved the status of sainthood within Argentina itself. Her life will be dramatised a quarter of a century later in the musical *Evita*.

Airbag patented

5th August 1952 US engineer John Hetrick applies to patent his 'safety cushion' invention for cars - an airbag. He encounters widespread indifference among vehicle manufacturers. Only years later, after the patent has expired, do car brands start to install the safety airbag as part of a car's standard equipment.

ENTERTAINMENT

Mandy

A tender and thoughtful drama from Ealing Studios, *Mandy* is a revealing study of the challenges facing a young deaf girl and is pioneering in sharing the learning techniques at the Royal Residential Schools for the Deaf in Manchester. The performance of Mandy Miller in the title role was so convincing, many assume she is deaf herself. The juvenile cast also includes Jane Asher in her first role.

The Way of Wisdom

The Way of Wisdom, a vehicle for comedian Norman Wisdom, is shown on BBC TV on 27th February. With his endearing haplessness and a knack for performing pratfalls and physical contortions, Wisdom is well on his way to success as one of Britain's favourite entertainers. He also performs at the Royal Variety Show for the first time this year.

Hydrogen bomb

1st November 1952 On the tiny atoll of Enewetak, part of the Marshall Islands in the Pacific Ocean, the US tests a hydrogen bomb detonation for the first time. Exploding at a force of 10.4 megatons of TNT, larger than all the Allied bombs in the Second World War combined, the bomb creates a crater almost two kilometres in diameter and a mushroom cloud ten kilometres high with a diameter of 161 kilometres.

Dimbles bimbles?
On 29th February, Richard Dimbleby invites viewers to join him for the first time for a programme that 'journeys to people and places of yesterday and today'. In *About Britain*, Dimbleby, dressed like a rather austere bank manager, explores different regions and traditions around the country, from Irish ceilidhs to a hot penny-throwing ceremony in Rye.

Saturday matinees
The average weekly attendance at children's cinema matinees around the country is over 1,016,000, with more than 1,700 cinemas around the country holding either morning or afternoon programmes especially for youngsters.

Killer heels
Vogue makes its first mention of the stiletto this year, the vertiginous shoe with the slender heel, named after a deadly Italian dagger. Stilettos increasingly become part of the film star-inspired, ultra-feminine fashions of the 1950s.

Spinning a tale
Charlotte's Web by E. B. White is published with illustrations by Garth Williams. It's a heart-warming story set on an American farm about Fern and Wilbur, the little pig she rescues, and Charlotte, the wise spider who befriends them. *The Sphere* magazine, enchanted by its cross-generational appeal, thinks, 'it is a great too good for children'.

The boy who never grew up
Billy Bunter of Greyfriars School, based on the stories by Frank Richards in *The Magnet*, is adapted for television with the first episode broadcast on 19th February. In the title role is 29-year-old Gerald Campion, playing a schoolboy roughly half his age. By the time the series ends in 1961, Campion is 40. Among his more age-appropriate school chums are the actors Michael Crawford and Melvyn Hayes.

Hidden lives
The Borrowers, Mary Norton's delightful tale of tiny people who live hidden in a house and borrow from the big people, is published by Dent and wins the Carnegie medal that year.

Singin' (and Dancin') in the Rain

Gene Kelly makes cinema history with his soggy, sploshy, feel-good dance routine in *Singin' in the Rain*. Co-directed and choreographed by Kelly, the film initially has only modest box office success and is overlooked for an Academy Award. But in time, this joyful musical, good-humouredly navigating the transition from silent movies to 'talkies', will consistently be included in the 'top ten' best films of all time.

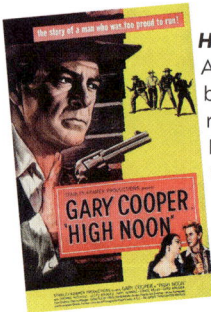

High Noon shootout

As a popular singing cow-boy star with hit movies and records to his name, Tex Ritter is an obvious choice to sing the western-style *Ballad of High Noon* over the opening sequence of the Gary Cooper film. The hit version and over three million sales, however, go to Frankie Laine, who brings a trembling nobility to the tune. Composers Dmitri Tiomkin and Ned Washington win the Academy Award for best movie song of the year.

Pottering about

Bill and Ben the Flowerpot Men, the little chaps at the bottom of the garden who speak complete gobbledegook, make their TV debut on 18th December, joining the *Watch with Mother* family.

Record-breaking whodunnit

The Mousetrap, the latest play by Agatha Christie, opens at the New Ambassadors Theatre in London's West End on 25th November with Richard Attenborough and his wife Sheila Sim filling the leading roles of Detective Sergeant Trotter and Mollie Ralston. Christie gave the rights to the play to her nine-year-old grandson Mathew Prichard, unaware that this whodunnit would go on to become a record-breaking phenomenon, still running seven decades later.

MUSIC

Ink Spots split

There are now officially two sets of Ink Spots! The black American vocal four-some famous for *Whispering Grass* and *If I Didn't Care* has officially split in two. Only the courts can determine which of them can carry on with the name.

Steve Conway dies

19 April 1952 Singer Steve Conway overcame debilitating rheumatic fever to earn his chance at the big time but its lingering effects have led to his death at just 31. His voice lives on, however: for the next 30 years his recording of *At the End of the Day* will be heard on Radio Luxembourg as the station closes down each night.

Barber recruits Colyer

British jazzman Chris Barber forms his own band and enlists trumpeter Ken Colyer, who has recently been deported from New Orleans, the birthplace of Dixieland jazz, where he reported his exploits in letters to *Melody Maker*. Barber calls his new outfit the Ken Colyer Jazz Band in deference to his colleague. So passionate is Colyer about playing the Dixieland way that he and Barber soon part company, each claiming to have sacked the other.

Buried in her ball gown

6th September 1952 Rodgers and Hammerstein's *The King and I* has been lighting up Broadway for well over a year. Now comes the news that the star for whom they wrote the show, Gertrude Lawrence, has passed away at the age of 54. Her grief-stricken co-star Yul Brynner, who was virtually unknown before the show, is one of her pallbearers and she is buried in the sumptuous ball gown she had worn every night on stage.

The policeman laughs his last

17th November 1952 Music hall star Charles Penrose dies in London aged 79. Although he made the record in 1922, when performers had to shout into the microphone to make themselves heard, his unfailingly mirth-inducing *The Laughing Policeman* is still played regularly on BBC radio.

Jo at the Palladium

11th April 1952 In a bumper year for American stars appearing at the London Palladium, Jo Stafford takes to its famous stage with her new husband Paul Weston supervising her accompaniment. Because of its references to places in which they are stationed, her version of the yearning *You Belong to Me* is a huge favourite with British forces serving overseas.

Anyone for doughnuts?

15th October 1952 The very first seven-inch 45rpm records to be manufactured and marketed in Britain go on sale, courtesy of industry leader EMI. They are nicknamed 'doughnuts' in the trade for their squat appearance compared to the breakable 78s that everyone is used to.

THE NEW MUSICAL EXPRESS

Britain's first record chart

20th November 1952 Britain's very first chart based on record sales (a Top 12) is launched by *New Musical Express*. The very first No. 1 is *Here In My Heart* by Al Martino, one of ten American stars to feature, the only British names being Vera Lynn and Max Bygraves. The chart's accuracy is doubtful as only twenty shops were canvassed, but within a year or so it will be regarded as a useful barometer of changing tastes. Martino will remain at the top for nine weeks.

1952

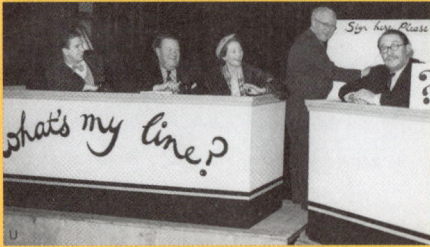

Gilbert and Gingold together

The often-outrageous British cabaret star Hermione Gingold is forging a new career in revue in New York but finds time to record a classic comedy duet during a visit to the UK. Her singing partner on *Takes Two to Tango* is none other than the grumpy TV personality Gilbert Harding (photo on the right), who is known as 'the rudest man in Britain' because of his outbursts on *What's My Line*.

MY FIRST 18 YEARS
TOP10 1952

1. **Unforgettable** *Nat King Cole*
2. **Singin' in the Rain** *Gene Kelly*
3. **Four Legged Friend** *Roy Rogers*
4. **Outside of Heaven** *Eddie Fisher*
5. **I Went to Your Wedding** *Spike Jones*
6. **Sugarbush** *Doris Day & Frankie Laine*
7. **Isle of Innisfree** *Josef Locke*
8. **Down Yonder** *Del Wood*
9. **Here in My Heart** *Al Martino*
10. **Blue Tango** *Les Baxter and his Orchestra*

Open | Search | Scan

Fisher flies in

6th December 1952 Top American bal-ladeer Eddie Fisher flies into the UK in the middle of the worst smog conditions that London has ever seen. With no other transport available, he is forced to take a crowded tube train into central London to book into his hotel. Eddie is still officially a member of the US Armed Forces Special Services until the new year, but records like *Outside Of Heaven* and *Any Time* keep him firmly in the public eye.

They've got rhythm

22 December 1952 The Modern Jazz Quartet make their recording debut in New York. Formed out of the rhythm section of Dizzy Gillespie's former big band, they mix cool jazz and bebop with classical touches to make a clean, sophisticated sound that's more at home in the concert hall than the smoky nightclubs of New York or Paris.

A double first for Vera

After a public row with the BBC that prompts her to move her popular radio show to Radio Luxembourg, Vera Lynn switches her attention to the US. She becomes the first British artist to top the US charts with *Auf Wiederseh'n Sweetheart*, a Cold War companion to her Second World War classic, *We'll Meet Again*. It also reaches No. 1 in the newly instituted British charts, making it the first disc to top both charts simultaneously.

SPORT

The Matthews final

2nd May 1953 An unforgettably topsy-turvy Wembley cup final finds Blackpool facing Lancashire neighbours Bolton Wanderers. All attention is on Blackpool's Stanley Matthews (see cigarette card) who at 38 is aiming to win a Wembley winner's medal for the first time. Coming from 3-1 down, Blackpool win 4-3. The match will always be remembered as 'the Matthews final', even though another Stan - his teammate Stan Mortenson - scores a hat trick.

Pinza wins the Derby

6th June 1953 Just days after the Coronation, the Queen watches her horse Aureole take second place in the Epsom Derby behind joint favourite Pinza, owned by Sir Victor Sassoon. Pinza's victory is a personal triumph for the newly knighted Sir Gordon Richards, who wins the Derby for the first and only time after 27 years of trying.

England regain the Ashes

19th August 1953 In one of cricket's most memorable summers, England beat Australia by eight wickets to regain the Ashes for the first time since 1934. With all three previous Tests drawn, the series goes to an electrifying fourth match at a packed Oval and ends with Denis Compton striking the winning four off the bowling of Arthur Morris.

Humbled by Hungary

25th November 1953 Hungary give England a hard footballing lesson as they win a pulsating match 6-3 at Wembley. At a time when the Football Association is sniffy about English participation in European competitions, the myth of the supremacy of the English game is spectacularly blown apart. The architect of Hungary's victory is the brilliant Ferenc Puskas who scores twice while midfielder Nandor Hidegtuki bags a hat trick. Six of the England team never play for their country again.

Fastest man alive

26th September 1953 A new world air speed record is set by Vickers test pilot Mike Lithgow, beating the record set two weeks earlier by fellow Brit Neville Duke. Flying a Supermarine Swift F4 near Tripoli, Libya, he reaches a speed of 735.7mph.

TURF CIGARETTES

Lt/Cmdr. MIKE LITHGOW

1953 Set up World Speed Record of 735.7 m.p.h.

Supermarine Swift

50 FAMOUS BRITISH FLIERS No 50

---

31 JAN 1953

Extreme storm winds flood the Netherlands, drowning 1,835.

12 FEB 1953

USSR breaks off all relations with Israel.

26 MAR 1953

Dr Jonas Salk announces that he has successfully tested a vaccine to prevent polio.

1953

Wales beat the All Blacks
19th December 1953 With centre Gareth Griffiths suffering a dislocated shoulder but insisting on playing on, Wales beat New Zealand 13-8 at Cardiff Arms Park during the All Blacks' winter tour of Britain, France and Ireland. Although this marked the first Welsh victory in this fixture in eighteen years, no Welsh team has beaten New Zealand in the seven decades since.

Car ferry disaster
31st January 1953 The car ferry MV *Victoria* sinks in the Irish sea after gale-force winds and failure to close the guillotine doors cause water to enter the car deck. Rescue attempts are hampered by bad weather and confused information, and 135 people are killed.

DOMESTIC NEWS

Laura Ashley launches
Inspired after a visit to the Victoria and Albert Museum, Laura Ashley designs and launches her very first products. These Victorian-style headscarves are made on a £10 screen printing frame by her husband, Bernard, and become enormously popular. Her scarves, available by mail-order or in retail stores such as John Lewis, launch what will become a household brand.

10 Rillington Place murders
24th March 1953 The discovery of eight bodies at the home of John Christie reveals not just the actions of a terrible serial killer, but also an awful miscarriage of justice. Two of the bodies are the wife and daughter of Timothy Evans, who had been hanged for their murder in 1950. Christie is found guilty and hanged in July at Pentonville Prison.

DNA is a double-helix!
28th February 1953 Cambridge University scientists Francis Crick and James D. Watson announce that they have discovered DNA has a double-helix structure. This research will later earn them, and fellow scientist Maurice Wilkins, a Nobel Prize. Their discovery rested heavily on X-ray diffraction data provided by Rosalind Franklin, who died from cancer before the prize could be awarded.

8 APR 1953	4 MAY 1953	24 JUN 1953
Crash on Central Line near Stratford tube station kills 12.	Ernest Hemingway wins the Pulitzer Prize for Literature for *The Old Man and The Sea*.	Uprising in East Germany against communist rule is suppressed.

North Sea flood
31st January 1953 Enormous storm surges, hurricane-force winds and high tides lead to major flooding in the North Sea. England sees 307 casualties in Norfolk, Suffolk, Essex and Lincolnshire, and 19 people are killed in Scotland as lives are lost across the coasts of the Netherlands and Belgium. A corvette and submarine sink in the docks at Sheerness and several lives are lost at sea. Thousands are left homeless and rescue operations are launched for the hundreds stranded on rooftops and high points across the country.

Korean War Ends
27th July 1953 The Korean War finally comes to a formal end with the signing of an armistice after two years of off-and-on negotiations.

Everest conquered!
29th May 1953 Edmund Hilary and Sherpa Tenzing Norgay become the first people to conquer Everest. They have climbed the mountain as part of the British expedition led by John Hunt, and news arrives back in the UK on the day of the Queen's Coronation, marking a double celebration.

Good Samaritans
2nd November 1953 The Reverend Chad Varah launches the telephone line which would become the charity Samaritans, providing emotional support and counselling to those in need. He is drawn to this work after presiding over the funeral of a 14-year-old girl who had committed suicide, and by a desire to assist those in emotional distress.

Roll On Roll Off!
30th June 1953 The first 'roll-on roll-off' channel ferry crosses from Dover to Boulogne, opening the continent to Brits who want to travel abroad in their cars for the first time.

Matchbox toys
December 1953 Lesney Products of London launches the Matchbox toy, which quickly becomes one of the country's most popular. It is invented after co-owner Jack Odell discovers his daughter's school only allows children to bring in toys that fit inside a matchbox. The initial range features a road roller, dump truck and cement mixer, and is available to purchase in matchbox-style packaging.

18 JUL 1953
Elvis Presley records his first demo, at Sun Studio in Memphis.

8 AUG 1953
USSR announces possession of hydrogen bomb.

12 SEP 1953
Senator John F. Kennedy marries socialite Jacqueline Bouvier.

1953

G-Plan Furniture

E. Gomme capitalises on the end of the Utility Furniture scheme in 1952 and launches G-Plan Furniture. This modern, exciting range was for the whole house and could be bought piece-by-piece. Consumers could purchase what they could afford and then save up to complete the set over several years.

Television takes over

25% of British households now own a television set, with a huge upsurge in sales thanks to the decision to tel-evise the Queen's Coronation. Fami-lies huddle around their neighbours' sets to see the young Queen in all her glory, and wave goodbye to the austerity of the war years.

Queen Mary dies

24th March 1953 Queen Mary dies at her Marlborough House home at the age of 85 with her daughter Mary, the Princess Royal, by her side. She was the widow of King George V, the mother of the late King George VI and grandmother of Queen Elizabeth II, who leads the nation's mourning at the funeral service in St George's Chapel, Windsor, seven days lat-er. One of her sons, the Duke of Windsor, also attends but is not accompanied by the Duchess. Over 4,000 join a memorial service held on the same day at St Paul's Cathedral.

ROYALTY & POLITICS

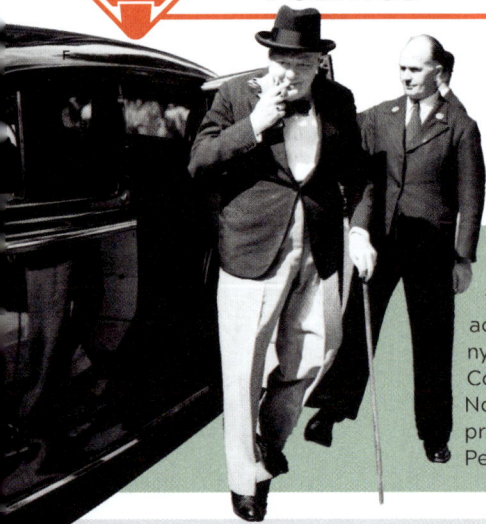

Churchill is knighted

24th April 1953 Having declined a dukedom after the Second World War, Winston Churchill finally accepts a knighthood from the Queen at a ceremo-ny in Buckingham Palace. His official title is Knight Companion of the Order of the Garter. Awarded the Nobel Prize for Literature in December, he expresses private disappointment that it was not the Nobel Peace Prize.

19 OCT 1953

The first Miss World beauty contest is held in London.

2 NOV 1953

The Samaritans charity is founded by Rev. Chad Varah.

24 DEC 1953

Tangiwai railway bridge collapses in New Zealand during royal tour, killing 151.

Britannia rules the waves

16th April 1953 The Royal Yacht *Britannia* is launched by the Queen. Built in the John Brown shipyards in Dundee for the royal family's use, the ship is 412 feet in length and has a maximum speed of 21.5 knots (24.7mph). By the time of her decommissioning in 1997, she will have travelled over one million miles on royal service across the world.

UK backs Iranian coup

15th August 1953 Churchill authorises British involvement in CIA plans to overthrow the elected government in Iran. The US and UK fear that the new Iranian government under Mohammed Mossadegh will nationalise the Anglo-Iranian Oil Company and jeopardise oil supplies. The resulting coup boosts the dictatorial power of the monarch, the Shah of Iran, who will rule with US support for the next 26 years.

The Queen is crowned

2nd June 1953 Queen Elizabeth II is crowned at Westminster Abbey. An estimated three million people pour into London to witness the Coronation procession, while millions more follow the proceedings via radio and television. At 5.40pm, the Queen makes the first of six appearances with her family on the balcony of Buckingham Palace, as RAF jet fighters fly overhead in salute. A huge and lively crowd remain outside the Palace until well after dark, while beacons are lit from Cornwall to John O'Groats.

War on 'male vice'

25th October 1953 In the House of Commons, Home Secretary Sir David Maxwell-Fyfe speaks out against homosexuality in virulent terms. His call for 'a drive against male vice' triggers a new police clampdown on gay men's haunts and activities, resulting in thousands of arrests including the actor John Gielgud.

FOREIGN NEWS

Tito is President

13th January 1953 Former wartime partisan leader Josip Broz, better known as Marshal Tito, is elected president of the People's Republic of Yugoslavia. Although a committed communist, Tito's policy is to maintain independence for his country by advocating a 'third way' between Soviet communism and Western capitalism and backing the principle of non-alignment.

Death of a dictator

5th March 1953 Soviet dictator Joseph Stalin dies of a cerebral haemorrhage. The man who turned the Soviet Union into an industrialized world power, defeated the invading forces of Nazi Germany and consigned many millions of citizens and opponents to the gulag, starvation or murder, is no more. Millions of Russians take to the streets crying as soon as they hear the news. After three days of lying in state, he is buried with great pomp next to Lenin in the Kremlin mausoleum.

Hop-on-hop-off

30th June 1953 Motorists can drive their cars on to the ferry for the first time on the first roll-on-roll-off ferries that commute across the Channel between Boulogne and Dover. Modelled on landing boats from the Second World War, this new generation of ferries make the crossing much faster. The number of cars crossing the Channel increases massively, from approximately 10,000 in 1953 to several million by the 1990s.

Korean ceasefire

27th July 1953 US forces make a target of every North Korean building in which you can take shelter, bombarding the entire territory with more than 30,000 kilos of napalm bombs which kill half a million people. But the impasse continues as United Nations forces fire six times more ammunition at the North as communist forces fire at the South backed by a constant threat of nuclear attack. After Stalin's death, negotiations lead to a ceasefire and the guns fall silent. But it is only an armistice: North and South Korea will never make peace.

Diving record

1st August 1953 Swiss inventor Auguste Piccard designs a new type of bathyscope that can dive up to 4,000 m below sea level. In September he dives to 3,150 m off the island of Ponza, and his son Jacques Piccard breaks all records with a depth of 10,916 m in the Mariana Trench in 1960.

ENTERTAINMENT

Wheel wait

The hypnotic Potter's Wheel interlude film is introduced by the BBC on 16th February to fill time between programme and studio changes.

Cotton club

The Queen packs several dresses from Horrockses fashions for her Common-wealth tour cementing the success of the firm's printed cotton frocks, a look that is to define the early 1950s.

DO YOU REMEMBER THIS?

Baby pram

Coronation fever

Coronation celebrations dominate magazines this year, with knitting patterns for regally-themed cardigans and sweat-ers, and a splendid St. Edward's Crown centrepiece suggested by the makers of Chiver's jelly!

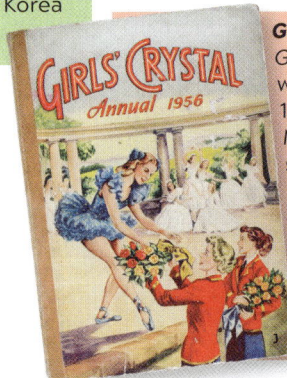

Girl's Crystal

Girl's Crystal story paper, which has been going since 1935, relaunches on 21st March with a change of style in order to compete against the popular *Girl* magazine. It concentrates on picture stories with the cover featuring Merle's Voyage of Mystery, set on a cruise ship.

TV nation

Sales of television sets rise sharply in the weeks leading up to the Coronation. Meanwhile, the *Radio Times* 31st May Coronation edition sells a record 9,012,358 copies.

A Star is Born

Although she has had roles in the West End and bit parts in several British films, Audrey Hepburn is comparatively un-known when she is cast opposite Gregory Peck in director William Wyler's *Roman Holiday* as a princess eager for freedom in the Eternal City. Hepburn lights up the screen, wins an Academy Award and the on-screen princess quickly graduates to Hollywood royalty.

Peter Pan

It was only a matter of time before Disney studios adapted J. M. Barrie's magical tale of the boy who never grew up, but this 1953 release actually comes fifteen years after development first began. Work was mothballed due to the war while Disney focused on producing films for the US government.

Sweet release

Sweet tooths rejoice as sweet rationing ends on 5th February - hooray! Newsagents and sweet shops are inundated and the makers of sugary treats such as Rowntree's Fruit Gums and Spangles place colour adverts in the press.

Gloriana

Benjamin Britten's coronation opera, *Gloriana*, is performed at the Royal Opera House for the first time on 8th June in the presence of the Queen and royal family. A glittering occasion, the au-dience attends in full evening dress.

Blondes have more fun?

Marilyn Monroe teams up with Jane Russell in the film adaptation of Anita Loos's novel, *Gen-tlemen Prefer Blondes*, a movie that will turn her into a phenome-non. Diana Dors, Britain's own blonde bomb-shell, never quite emerges from Marilyn's shadow.

Just for kids

The Stolen Plans is the first release from the Children's Film Foundation. The organisation, fund-ed by a tax on box office receipts, had been founded three years earli-er, aiming to create quality films for children to be shown in cinemas at Saturday matinees.

Live from the BBC

BBC Television Theatre opens in the former Shepherd's Bush Empire which had originally been built as a variety theatre in 1903. The theatre becomes the setting for some of the BBC's best-loved shows including *Crackerjack, This is Your Life, The Old Grey Whistle Test* and *Wogan*.

Airfix legends
Airfix launch a kit of the famous 'BTK' Spitfire, the first of their many Spitfire kits. The company had created their very first kit, the *Golden Hind*, the previous year, which is sold for two shillings in Woolworths.

The third dimension
Taking fright at television's encroachment, the movie industry revives 3-D films. In London, cinema-goers can get the 3-D experience at the Telecinema on the South Bank, but soon other cinemas show 'the Deepies'.

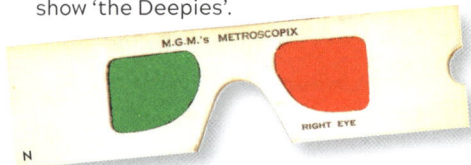

Rag, Tag and Bobtail
Rag, Tag and Bobtail, a hedgehog, mouse, and rabbit respectively, appear on television screens for the first time. The glove puppets tell a gentle tale every Thursday in the *Watch with Mother* slot.

From Here to Eternity
Scooping no fewer than eight Academy Awards at the 1954 Oscars, *From Here to Eternity*, starring Burt Lancaster, Montgomery Clift and Frank Sinatra as three soldiers stationed in Hawaii prior to Pearl Harbor, is adapted from the racy novel by James Jones. Although necessarily toned down, that scene, with Burt Lancaster and Deborah Kerr writhing around in the surf, goes on to becomes one of the most memorable moments in cinematic history.

Teens on the telly
The BBC attempts to cater to Britain's youthful demographic with *Teleclub*, a magazine programme featuring an audience of teenagers, a dancefloor and even a soda fountain. The rather middle-aged choice of Max Robertson (who was also the presenter of *Panorama* that year) slightly diluted the happening vibe.

MUSIC

Hank passes on
1st January 1953
Once described as 'the hillbilly Shakespeare', maverick country star Hank Williams dies in the back seat of a car in freezing night in West Virginia. Hank's heavy drinking and pill taking were matched by a messy private life, but he was a charismatic performer with an international following. His gritty true-to-life songs have become known well beyond country circles thanks to cover versions.

Stars in his eyes
6th February 1953 It was only a matter of time before the genial, ever-mellow Perry Como would top the newly instituted British record chart. Today's he's achieved it with the finger-wagging *Don't Let The Stars Get In Your Eyes*, just weeks after hitting No. 1 in the US with the same song.

Faith and Frankie
19th June 1953 Frankie Laine's (photo) brooding *I Believe* makes history by spending 18 consecutive weeks at the top of the UK record chart - an achievement never equalled or beaten. While *Answer Me*, another Laine song with religious overtones, is banned by the BBC, David Whitfield's version avoids such a fate by replacing the words 'my Lord' with 'my love'.

Brits at No. 1
10th April 1953 Six months after its launch, Britain's record chart finally has a home-grown act at No. 1. *Broken Wings* is by the Stargazers, who are best known for their appearances with the BBC Show Band. Their leader is Cliff Adams, who will recruit a new group of singers for the long-running singalong radio show *Sing Something Simple* later in the decade.

Roger bonds with Dorothy
6th July 1953 A big-voiced, straight-from-the-heart singer from the Welsh valleys, Dorothy Squires ends her on- and off-stage partnership with pianist-composer Billy Reid and marries a little-known actor named Roger Moore. He is twelve years her junior. Reid's parting gift to her is *I'm Walking Behind You*, which gives her the biggest hit of her career and is the first Frank Sinatra song to be released as a single by Capitol Records.

Dance hall danger
Saturday night dancing at the local ballroom has been part of everyday life for decades. Now it is under threat from television and from the increasing numbers of Teddy boys - teenage boys in Edwardian gear - disrupting the genteel conventions. Teddy boy taste is for gutsy records like Tennessee Ernie Ford's *Shotgun Boogie* and Hank Williams' *Move It On Over* that hint at the rock'n'roll explosion to come.

Frank is back!
Frank Sinatra's comeback is well underway after a period of falling sales and negative publicity around his divorce from first wife Nancy and his pursuit of second wife Ava Gardner. Now he is at Capitol Records singing the kind of songs he adores in a swinging new style, while his supporting role in the movie *From Here to Eternity* wins him an Academy Award and puts his Hollywood career back on track. His sensitive treatment of classic songs from the 1930s and 40s is unmatched by any of his singing rivals.

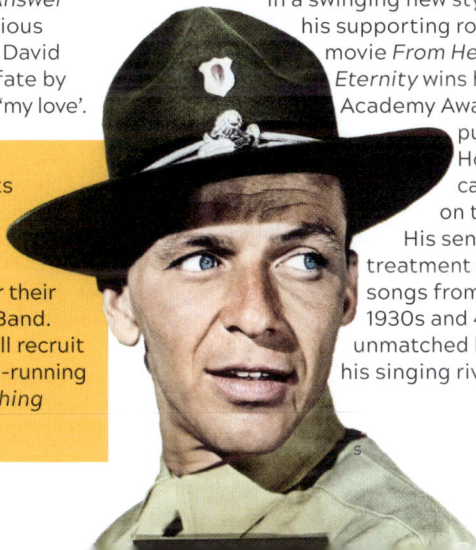

Kathleen Ferrier dies

9th October 1953 A former telephonist from Lancashire who conquered the worlds of opera and oratorio, Kathleen Ferrier dies of cancer at a London hospital. A true people's favourite, her beautiful contralto voice was never better showcased than on her spirited record-ings of north country songs like *Dance to thi' Daddy* and *Blow the Wind Southerly*.

A boom in baby songs

Who will win the battle of the 'doggie in the window'? American Patti Page has the original version, but former Ted Heath singer Lita Roza takes *How Much is That Doggie in the Window?* to No. 1 in the UK. The current popularity of children's songs like this is a sign of the post-war baby boom: there are simply more young children than ever before.

MY FIRST 18 YEARS
TOP10   1953

1. **The Ugly Duckling** *Danny Kaye*
2. **Theme from 'Moulin Rouge'** *Ron Goodwin*
3. **Crying in the Chapel** *Lee Lawrence*
4. **Settin' the Woods on Fire** *Hank Williams*
5. **Little Red Monkey** *Joy Nichols*
6. **Theme from 'Limelight'** *Ron Goodwin*
7. **Broken Wings** *The Stargazers*
8. **The Dummy Song** *Max Bygraves*
9. **I Believe** *Frankie Laine*
10. **In a Golden Coach** *Billy Cotton and his Band*

Open | Search | Scan

Sisters in harmony

6th December 1953 The year's big Christmas hit is *I Saw Mommy Kissing Santa Claus* by the Beverley Sisters, a close-harmony trio from East London comprising Joy, Babs and Teddie. Although the song has an Americanism in its title, it's the work of British comedy song king Tommie Connor, writer of the Gracie Fields masterpiece *The Biggest Aspidistra in the World*. Elder sister Joy Beverley will marry England's football captain Billy Wright in 1958.

Ol' big 'ead is back

BBC radio's *Educating Archie* has already made stars out of Tony Hancock, Harry Secombe and ventriloquist's dummy Archie Andrews. Now it's the turn of Max Bygraves, whose debut hits are *Ol' Big 'Ead* (named after his character in the show) and *The Dummy Song*. Rapidly developing into the best all-round enter-tainer in the country, former RAF ground crew man Max is set for a dozen more comedy hits before the decade is out, including the nonsensical *Gilly Gilly Oss-enfeffer Katsezellenbogen by the Sea* and the sugar-sweet *You're a Pink Toothbrush*.

Happy as Larry

The UK's top film of the year is the comedy caper *Genevieve*, with a theme tune composed and performed by the great harmonica player Larry Adler. Larry has made London his home since falling foul of Joseph McCarthy's anti-communist campaign in the US. The US print of the film omits Larry's name from the credits for fear of disrupting its chances, but his score will nevertheless win an Academy Award nomination.

SPORT

Tragedy at the Grand National
10th April 1954 The Grand National's reputation as the most gruelling and dangerous of horse races is demonstrated once again as four horses are killed or destroyed during the 108th running of the race at Aintree. It is the highest number of fatalities in the National's history and prompts questions in Parliament about the safety of the race.

A Derby first for Piggott
2nd June 1954 At 18 years old, future champion jockey and 'people's favourite' Lester Piggott becomes the youngest ever winner of the Epsom Derby, riding the American-bred colt Never Say Die.

The four minute mile
6th May 1954 Oxford University medical student Roger Bannister achieves an athletics feat long thought impossible and even potentially dangerous - the sub-four-minute mile. With Christopher Chataway and Chris Brasher acting as pacemakers, the 25-year-old breaks the seemingly impregnable 240-second barrier on a damp Oxford evening.

Another Hungarian humbling
23rd May 1954 In a friendly match in Budapest, the England football team is humiliated once again by its Hungarian counterpart. With memories of England's 6-3 defeat at Wembley a year earlier still very raw, England lose the return match 7-1 and throw their World Cup preparations into turmoil.

A record rugby league crowd
5th May 1954 If ever proof was needed of the depth of rugby league's popularity in the north of England, the events at Bradford's Odsal Stadium provide it. A world record crowd of 102,000 - and quite possibly thousands more - converges on the city to witness the Challenge Cup Final replay between Warrington and Halifax.

14 JAN 1954
Marilyn Monroe and baseball great Joe Di Maggio marry in San Franscisco.

2 FEB 1954
President Eisenhower announces the detonation of the first hydrogen bomb.

1 MAR 1954
Evangelist Billy Graham begins 12-week crusade in Britain.

1954

Diane dips under five

29th May 1954 Attracting rather less attention than Roger Bannister's achievement three weeks earlier, 21-year-old chemistry student Diane Leather becomes the first woman in the world to run a mile in under five minutes (4:59:06) at a championship meet in Birmingham.

World Cup controversy

4th July 1954 The second FIFA World Cup of the post-war era comes to a close with a 3-2 victory for West Germany over Hungary in Switzerland. Widely expected to win, Hungary are denied a potentially game-changing equaliser when Ferenc Puskas's 87th minute 'goal' is disallowed.

SWISS WORLD CHAMPION MATCH-BALL

Marathon heartbreak

7th August 1954 Possibly the most heartbreaking moment in the history of British athletics occurs as England's Jim Peters - easily the finest marathon runner of his time - fails to complete the course at Empire Games in Vancouver just 220 yards from the finish line. Seventeen minutes ahead of his nearest rival, he collapses with dehydration several times on the stadium track and is stretchered away in distress. He will never race again.

DOMESTIC NEWS

Comet grounded

10th January 1954 The fatal crashes of BOAC flight 701 in January, and South African Airways flight 201 on 8th April, ground the de Havilland Comet jet. Engineers find that the cause of both planes disintegrating in mid-air is metal fatigue in the aircraft, leading to changes in airworthiness requirements. 35 and 21 lives are lost respectively.

Smoking causes cancer!

12th February 1954 The British Medical Committee publish a report on their British Doctors Study, establishing a link between smoking tobacco and the development of lung cancer. This study vindicated doctors who had been reporting such links since 1950.

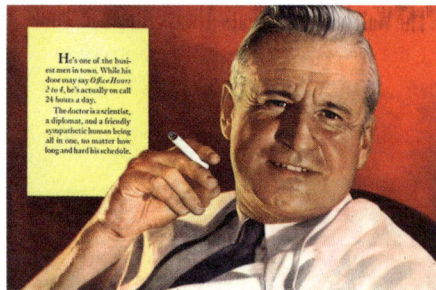

He's one of the busiest men in town. While his door may say *Office Hours 2 to 4*, he's actually on call 24 hours a day.

The doctor is a scientist, a diplomat, and a friendly sympathetic human being all in one, no matter how long and hard his schedule.

According to a recent Nationwide survey:

MORE DOCTORS SMOKE CAMELS THAN ANY OTHER CIGARETTE

---

13 APR 1954

Robert Oppenheimer, architect of the atomic bomb, has his clearance revoked in security probe.

17 MAY 1954

US Supreme Court rules that segregation of schools on racial grounds is unconstitutional.

7 JUN 1954

Scientist and mathematician Alan Turing commits suicide.

Lord Montagu's sexuality on srial
24th March 1954 The eight-day trial of Lord Montagu and others ends with a conviction for charges associated with homosexuality and a sentence of twelve months in prison. This widely publicised trial, along with others, leads to the establishment of the Wolfenden Committee which sits until 1957 and - in a landmark moment in Britain's LGBT+ story - issues a report that leads to the decriminalisation of homosexual acts between consenting adults.

Rationing ends!
4th July 1954 Rationing introduced during the Second World War finally comes to a complete end, as the very last restrictions on meat and housebuilding are scrapped. Brits can finally enjoy as much meat as they can afford!

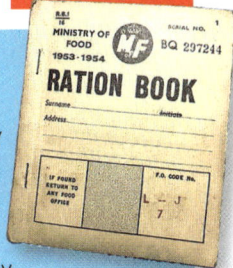

MINISTRY OF FOOD
1953-1954
RATION BOOK
Surname
Address
BQ 297244

Britain sees eclipse!
30th June 1954 Britain experiences an eclipse, its first since 1927. Children and adults alike are encouraged to create pinhole cameras from paper to witness the event, as the eclipse taking place over America casts its shadow across the country.

McGill guilty of obscenity!
15th July 1954 Donald McGill, the artist famous for his saucy seaside postcards, is found guilty of breaching the Obscene Publications Act 1857. His postcards, for which he created approximately 12,000 different designs, were extremely popular, but bring him under government scrutiny. Found guilty, he is fined £50 and postcards across the country are destroyed in a panic.

George, I've told you you were not to kiss me like that till we are married

Nuclear weapons in service
3rd August 1954 Britain's first nuclear weapon, the 'Blue Danube', is fitted to RAF Vickers Valiant aircraft and brought into service at RAF Wittering.

VICKERS VALIANT
V CLASS BOMBING

IRA resumes activity
12th June 1954 The Irish Republican Army launches a raid on Gough Barracks in Armagh. During the raid, IRA operatives make away with a truck filled with 340 rifles and other armaments, enormously embarrassing the British Army. The raid signals a return to activity for the IRA, which had appeared dormant since the 1940s.

Supersonic fighter plane flies
4th August 1954 The English Electric P-1, later known as the 'Lightning', makes its maiden flight from RAF Boscombe Down. The Lightning can reach speeds greater than Mach 2, or twice the speed of sound.

8 JUL 1954
Irish boxer George Gardner (77), the first World Light Heavyweight Champion dies.

3 AUG 1954
Death of novelist Colette in Paris, aged 81.

24 SEP 1954
London's classic red Routemaster bus debuts at Earl's Court Motor Show.

1954

Suez Canal occupation ends
19th October 1954 The British military occupation of the Suez Canal ends after the signing of a tentative agreement with the Egyptian government. It is agreed that the Canal Company will not be transferred to Egyptian control until 1968.

Churchill is 80
30th November 1954 Eighty years old today, Prime Minister Sir Winston Churchill is given a birthday presentation in Westminster Hall by members of both Houses of Parliament.

ROYALTY & POLITICS

Bevan v Gaitskell
14th April 1954 The divide in the Labour Party between the 'Bevanites' on the left and the 'Gaitskellites' on the right widens with Aneurin Bevan's resignation from the parliamentary party over leader Clement Attlee's policy on nuclear arms.

Will Margaret marry Peter?
July 1954 The debate rumbles on about whether Princess Margaret should be free to marry Peter Townsend, a royal equerry who is divorced with two children. He was dispatched to the British embassy in Portugal a year ago in the hope that the romance would cool down, yet rumours persist that they are in touch almost every day by phone call and letter.

The Queen Mother in America
November 1954 After her daughter's accession to the throne in 1952, there were concerns that the Queen Mother would no longer have a role in royal affairs or the life of the country. Those concerns are answered by the masterly way she handles her current North American visit, during which she stays at the White House as a guest of the Eisenhowers and accepts an honorary Doctor of Laws degree from New York's Columbia University.

Stately couture
Christian Dior stages a fashion show amid the magnificent splendour of Blenheim Palace in Oxfordshire. Princess Margaret, one of Dior's most prominent customers, attends the show which raises funds in aid of the British Red Cross.

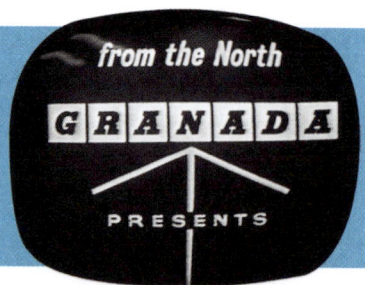

Parliament authorises commercial TV
30th July 1954 An Act of Parliament enabling the introduction of commercial television is given royal assent. The Act places the responsibility for awarding and overseeing regional franchises on a new authority appointed by the government. The way is now paved for a direct competitor to BBC television, breaking the monopoly on broadcasting that it has held since 1922.

from the North
GRANADA
PRESENTS

24 OCT 1954
West Germany joins NATO.

3 NOV 1954
Artist Henri Matisse dies in Nice aged 84.

23 DEC 1954
First successful kidney transplant performed in Boston, Massachusetts

FOREIGN NEWS

Changes in Crimea
19th February 1954 During celebrations to mark three centuries of Russian-Ukrainian unification and strengthen ties between the two Soviet republics, the ruling Politburo of the Soviet Union orders the transfer of the Crimean peninsula from Russia to Ukraine.

Fighting polio
23rd February 1954 During a frightening trans-global outbreak of polio that leaves many children and teenagers disabled for life, the US rolls out the first mass vaccination programme in Pittsburgh, Pennsylvania. Though the vaccine dramatically reduces numbers of polio cases over the next decade, the complete eradication of polio from the US is only confirmed in 1994 and from the UK in 2002.

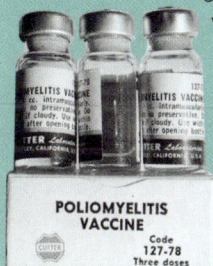

Boeing 707 takes to the air
14th May 1954 The new jet aircraft from Boeing makes its first flight. Since the troubles besetting the UK-manufactured de Havilland Comet, California-based Boeing has been able to steal a march on its UK rival and become the major global force in jet aviation.

Zipper creator dies
21st June 1954 Although never a household name, Gideon Sundbäck designed and developed an everyday item that in its small way enhanced the lives of millions. His invention was the metal zip fastener, for which he was granted a US patent in 1914. Sundbäck dies today in the US, having emigrated from his native Sweden in 1905.

French leave Vietnam
1st August 1954 The First Indochinese War ends when the French expeditionary force is overwhelmingly defeated by Hô Chí Minh's Viet Minh at the Battle of Điên Biên Phu. A humbled France withdraws from Southeast Asia, leaving Vietnam partitioned between capitalist and theoretically democratic South Vietnam and the communist North. But peace does not return. US President Eisenhower has announced that Vietnam must not be the next domino to fall to communism. A new conflict is brewing.

Transistor radio
18th October 1954 In the US, Texas Instruments launches the first transistor radio, the Regency TR-1. The transistor is much smaller and lighter than mains operated radios and is portable, cheap and liberating.

Nasser in power
26th October 1954 Egyptian Prime Minister Lt. Colonel Gamal Abdel Nasser survives an assassination attempt while his speech is being carried live on radio. Ordering a crackdown on his political opponents on all sides, he leaves the way clear for his own presidential bid and makes the removal of British influence and power in the region his priority.

POLIOMYELITIS VACCINE
Code
127-78
Three doses

B·O·A·C

📺 ENTERTAINMENT

Bentine's Bumblies

14th February Michael Bentine has parted company with his fellow Goons, but his next project is no less surreal. He creates and stars in his own 13-part children's programme, *The Bumblies*, featuring three little pear-shaped aliens who hope to learn the ways of Earthling children.

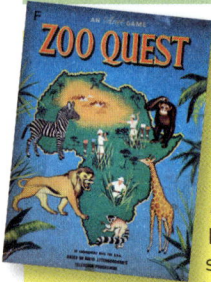

Attenborough's Ark

The first episode of *Zoo Quest* is broadcast on 21st December, with David Attenborough as he travels around the globe on animal collecting expeditions with staff from London Zoo. Watched by millions, *Zoo Quest* launches Attenborough as a wildlife presenter, a role which he continues, on and off, for the next seven decades.

James Stewart stars

James Stewart stars in one of the year's most successful films. In Hitchcock's (photo) stylish psychological thriller, *Rear Window*, he plays a wheelchair-bound voyeuristic photojournalist who seems more interested in the intrigues going on in the apartments surrounding him than his fashion model girlfriend Lisa (played with cool panache by Grace Kelly).

Jack and Jill

Amalgamated Press launch *Jack and Jill* comic on for younger children with picture stories about the antics of Harold Hare, Walter Hottle Bottle and Chalky the Blackboard Boy among others.

Early (weather) man

At 7:55pm on 11th January, George Cowling becomes the first televised weather presenter on the BBC. The tall and distinguished-looking Cowling, who had been a forecaster for the RAF during and after the war, stands with a pencil and rubber marking how the weather will change, and advises viewers, 'Tomorrow will be rather windy, a good day to hang out washing.'

Fast food first

Britons are introduced to a taste of America when the Wimpy Bar is opened in the J. Lyons Corner House at Coventry Street in the heart of London. It's a slick operation with their famous burgers as well as Torpedoes, Yankees, Aunt Mary's Cheesecake and Whippsy (a thick, cold milkshake) prepared at a central island and served by waitresses in uniforms designed by Hardy Amies.

Calamity Jane

'A fast-moving, bright and breezy musical with rousing songs' is how *Picture Show* magazine describes *Calamity Jane*, the latest comedy-romantic-Wild-West-musical, co-starring for the first time together, Howard Keel and Doris Day.

Teddy boys

The *Daily Express* coin the term 'Teddy boy' this year to describe working class teens whose style was a riff on Edwardian dandyism. With their slicked ducktail hair-cuts and sharply cut frock coats, the Teds are into rock 'n' roll and dancing.

Hell's belles

The Belles of St. Trinian's is released based on the Ronald Searle comic strip about a fictional girls' school where the pupils run amok and the headmistress who indulges them (Alistair Sim brilliantly dragged up as Miss Millicent Fritton). As wild and anarchic as Searle's original illustrations, *The Belles of St. Trinian's* spawns four more films in the series.

White Christmas

White Christmas, Paramount's tinselly, Technicolor festive hit starring Bing Crosby, Rosemary Clooney, Vera-Ellen and Danny Kaye, is the first movie to be filmed in wide-screen Vistavision. It's a box-office smash, especially in the US, aided of course by Irving Berlin's evergreen song which doubles as the film's title.

Doctor Dirk

Doctor in the House is the most successful film of the year at the UK box office and makes a star of its lead, Dirk Bogarde. Based on the 1952 novel by Richard Gordon (who co-wrote the film), it follows the misadventures of medical students at St. Swithin's Hospital including Bogarde as Simon Sparrow who regularly falls foul of the James Robertson Justice's intimidating chief surgeon, the spectacularly named Sir Lancelot Spratt.

DO YOU REMEMBER THIS?

Yoyo

Here is the news

'News is not at all an easy thing to do on television,' says the BBC Director General Sir Ian Jacob of the corporation's first news bulletins, which are presented by Richard Baker on 5th July. The concept of providing news as it happens is a novel one and some viewers think the programme 'ghastly' but it soon catches on.

Hancock's Half Hour

Tony Hancock takes to the airwaves on 2nd November for the first episode of *Hancock's Half Hour*, in which he plays a down-on his luck-comedian. Writers Ray Galton and Alan Simpson craft a situation comedy destined to become a classic.

Wild One & Waterfront

'I coulda been a contender', one of the most famous lines in film, is spoken by Marlon Brando in *On the Waterfront*, as Terry Malloy, the boxer turned longshoreman trying to break free of corruption in a New Jersey dockyard. Brando is at the height of his powers (and at his most handsome), and in the same year creates another iconic role in *The Wild One*, as leader of a motorcycle gang. British cinema audiences, however, must wait until 1967 to see it as the British Board of Film Censors refuse to give a certificate due to its 'unrestricted hooliganism'.

Judy reborn

A Star is Born, a remake of the 1937 original, is intended as Judy Garland's comeback after she was dropped by MGM five years earlier. She plays a waxing starlet married to James Mason's waning matinee idol, and despite her own struggles with drugs, gives the performance of a lifetime.

MUSIC

Golden Eddie

8th January 1954 A one-time amateur brass band musician from Lancashire, Eddie Calvert is a successful solo instrumentalist in a music scene dominated by vocalists and dance combos. Billed as 'the man with the golden trumpet', his soaring treatment of the 19th-century Yiddish ballad *O Mein Papa* stays at No. 1 for nine weeks.

Death of Noel Gay

4th March 1954 One of Britain's leading songwriters for over two decades, Noel Gay, dies suddenly in London aged 55. Gay's long list of cheery keep-your-chin-up hits includes *Leaning on a Lamppost, Run Rabbit Run, The Sun Has Got His Hat On* and *The Lambeth Walk*.

A rocking revolution

12th April 1954 Originally a country and western band who added saxophones and drums to play in a black-influenced rhythm and blues style, Bill Haley and his Comets make a disc that will revolutionise the record industry. *Rock Around the Clock* becomes a small hit on its first release but the best is yet to come. The song's inclusion in the film *The Blackboard Jungle* a few months later sends the track soaring to No. 1 in the US and UK, by which time their hit cover version of Joe Turner's blistering *Shake Rattle and Roll* has cemented the band's status as avatars of rock'n'roll.

Elvis in the studio

5th July 1954 A nervous 19-year-old truck driver named Elvis Presley makes his first professional recordings for Sun Records in Memphis, including both sides of his first single *That's All Right, Mama* (a blues song) and *Blue Moon of Kentucky* (a country number). Meanwhile, Presley's electrifying impact in live performance gets the attention of the wily self-styled 'Colonel' Tom Parker. Signed to Parker's management, Presley's destiny is sealed.

The first last night

18th September 1954 The last night of the Royal Albert Hall Promenade Concert season closes with an innovation - a patriotic medley for orchestra and chorus combining Henry Wood's *Fantasia on British Sea Songs*, Edward Elgar's *Land of Hope and Glory* and Hubert Parry's *Jerusalem*. It is so well received that the medley becomes an irreplaceable part of Proms tradition.

Freed in New York

15th July 1945 Alan Freed, the disc jockey who first attached the term 'rock'n'roll' to the black rhythm and blues music adored by white American teenagers, moves from station WJW in Cleveland to WINS in New York City. Nicknamed 'Moondog' because of the ecstatic way he howls and shouts between records, he is now free to give the music a national platform.

It's party time!

3rd December 1954 Winifred Atwell is a real rarity - a classically trained pianist from Trinidad and Tobago who plays medleys of old-time songs in a party-time style. She is the first artist of colour to have a No. 1 record in the UK, with the Christmas-timed *Let's Have a Party*, and is a big musical influence on a shy young piano-playing lad named Reg Dwight - the future Elton John.

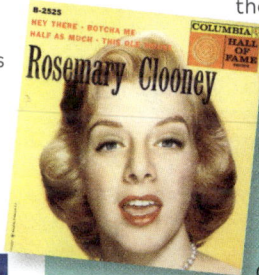

Rosemary Clooney

In the same year that she stars with Bing Crosby and Danny Kaye in the movie *White Christmas*, Oklahoma-born singer Rosemary Clooney enjoys the biggest hit of her career with *This Ole House*. Though her version is jolly and uplifting, the song has a much more sombre origin as a contemplation on the inevitability of death. Country singer Stuart Hamblen wrote it after finding a dead body in a broken-down shack while on a hunting trip with John Wayne.

Doo wop debut

Sh-Boom by the Crew Cuts marks the arrival of a new vocal group sound nicknamed 'doo wop' whose origins are on the street corners of the black neighbourhoods of US east coast cities. The Crew Cuts are smartly dressed white college boys but their record is a straight copy of the original by the Chords, a group of young black singers who learned to harmonise under the street lamps of New York City.

The late Johnny Ace

25th December 1954 Rhythm and blues singer Johnny Ace (real name John Alexander) dies when he shoots himself in the head playing with what he thinks is an unloaded revolver. A track he had only recently recorded, *Pledging My Love*, becomes a huge posthumous hit and an instant favourite with the young Elvis Presley.

Norman sings!

Just beginning a decade-long spell as Britain's top box-office movie star is cloth-capped knockabout comedy king Norman Wisdom, who reveals another side to his talents in the film *Trouble in Store* by singing *Don't Laugh at Me* to his co-star Moira Lister. Not only does he have a fine tenor voice, the song is his own composition and becomes his signature tune for the rest of his life.

Dino sways to solo fame

Dean Martin, best known as the straight man to madcap comedian Jerry Lewis, underlines his talents as a solo performer with *That's Amore*, a song in mock Neapolitan opera style, and the mambo tune *Sway*. An important influence on Elvis Presley's ballad style, 'Dino' will finish the decade with an impressive seventeen hits, a budding Hollywood career in westerns and crime capers, and a permanent place in the infamous Rat Pack as Frank Sinatra's whisky drinking sidekick.

MY FIRST 18 YEARS
TOP 10   1954

1. **This Ole House** *Rosemary Clooney*
2. **I See the Moon** *Stargazers*
3. **Ebb Tide** *Frank Chacksfield and his Orchestra*
4. **Don't Laugh at Me** *Norman Wisdom*
5. **The Happy Wanderer** *Obernkirchen Children's Choir*
6. **Young at Heart** *Frank Sinatra*
7. **Sway** *Dean Martin*
8. **Mr Sandman** *The Chordettes*
9. **Sh-Boom** *The Crew Cuts*
10. **Secret Love** *Doris Day*

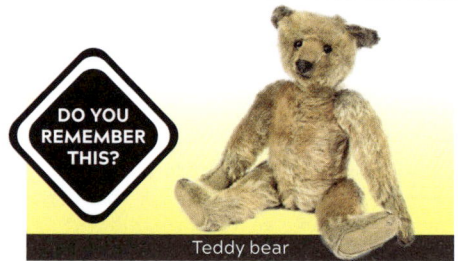

Open | Search | Scan

DO YOU REMEMBER THIS?

Teddy bear

Reeves by request

One of country music's all time superstars, Jim Reeves gets his first UK exposure from an unlikely quarter. Reeves is a Texan singer attached to the *Louisiana Hayride* radio show whose minor novelty hit *Bimbo* is somehow heard by the producer of BBC radio's *Children's Favourites* in London. *Bimbo* becomes one of the show's most requested songs right through to the late 1960s, long after Reeves exchanges his guitar and fiddles sound for the mellow balladry of *He'll Have to Go* and *I Love You Because*.

SPORT

Joe's 147 break
22nd January 1955 Britain's fifteen-times snooker world champion Joe Davis achieves the first officially recognised maximum 147 break in an exhibition match against Willie Smith at Leicester Square Hall.

Frankly fantastic
3rd March 1955 Another mighty Test match series sees England retain the Ashes. A major factor in England's 3-1 winning tour of Australia is the ferocious bowling of Northamptonshire's Frank 'Typhoon' Tyson, who takes a total of 28 wickets. His tally of seven wickets for just 27 runs in an innings in the third Test in Melbourne is the best by any England bowler in Australia for over 50 years.

End of the season
23rd April 1955 In a thrilling climax to the football league season, Chelsea secure the championship by four points from Wolverhampton Wanderers. Newcastle United go on to beat Manchester City 3-1 to win the FA Cup, with Jackie Milburn scoring after just 45 seconds - a new record. Luton Town win promotion to the First Division for the first time in their history. Don Revie (illustration) of Manchester City is voted player of the year.

Disaster at Le Mans
11th June 1955 The 24 Hours at Le Mans race sees the worst disaster in the history of motor racing. More than 80 spectators are killed and well over 100 injured when the car driven by Pierre Levegh launches into the crowd and bursts into flames after a collision. Levegh dies instantly. Astonishingly, the race is not stopped. The disaster results in an overhaul of crowd safety at international racetracks,

Moss wins at Aintree
16th July 1955 Stirling Moss is the first UK-born driver to win the British Grand Prix. He finishes his first Formula One race narrowly ahead of his fellow Mercedes driver Juan Manuel Fangio, the eventual world champion. The race is held at Aintree Motor Racing Circuit, built within the famous Aintree Racecourse, and opened only a year before. A notable Formula One debutant in the Grand Prix is Australian Jack Brabham, who will win the World Drivers' Championship on three future occasions.

16 JAN 1955
Freak weather causes London's sky to darken completely at 1.15pm.

13 FEB 1955
Israel acquires four of the seven Dead Sea scrolls.

11 MAR 1955
Death of Sir Alexander Fleming, discoverer of penicillin.

DOMESTIC NEWS

RAF aircraft disappear

11th January 1955 Two RAF Shackleton aircraft disappear without trace after leaving RAF St Eval on a routine patrol. Despite a three-day search the wreckage is not found and the nine men on board the two aircraft are presumed dead. The disappearance remains a mystery to this day.

February freeze

24th February 1955 Plummeting temperatures lead to widespread disruption as 70 roads across the country close due to heavy snow. Many rail services are cancelled, and in rural areas the RAF is enlisted to deliver emergency supplies. The year proves a strange one for weather, as a May gale strips topsoil from fields across Norfolk, and the summer brings a heatwave and drought.

Year of strikes

31st May 1955 A State of Emergency is declared as the Associated Society of Locomotive Engineers and Firemen go out on strike in a pay dispute that will last seventeen days. In April, national newspapers had gone unpublished for a month due to a strike of the printing press maintenance workers, meaning the country follows a month without news with three weeks without rail.

Polio vaccine success!

5th May 1955 Margaret Jenkins becomes the 500,000th person in London to receive the new polio vaccine. The vaccine, developed by American virologist Dr Jonas Salk, proves popular in England where post-war cases are averaging over 5,000 a year. Margaret is inspired to receive the vaccine after witnessing the terrible effects of the disease on two of her friends.

Last woman hanged

13th July 1955 Ruth Ellis becomes the last woman to be executed in the UK when she is hanged at HM Prison Holloway. Having shot her lover, David Blakely, outside a pub in Hampstead, Ellis admits to his murder and makes no attempt to defend herself. Despite this, there are widespread calls for clemency in the run-up to her death, and her case helps fuel the campaign for the abolition of the death penalty.

HMS *Sidon* explosion

16th June 1955 A faulty torpedo explodes aboard HMS *Sidon* in Portland Harbour, killing thirteen of the 56-strong crew. Thankfully, the remaining crew escape the vessel and are picked up by a rescue party from HMS *Maidstone*, moored alongside.

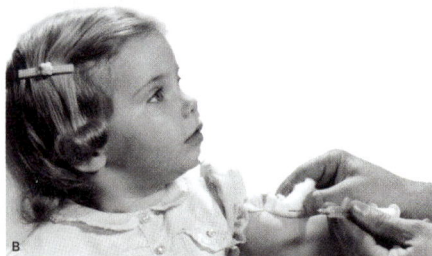

4 APR 1955
The British government signs 'pact of mutual cooperation' with Iraq.

14 MAY 1955
The Warsaw Pact is signed, forming Eastern bloc countries into a military alliance.

6 JUN 1955
American horror comics are banned in the UK.

Guinness Book of Records

27th August 1955 The *Guinness Book of Records* is born. The brainchild of Sir Hugh Beaver, the managing director of Guinness, it is published by twin brothers Norris and Ross McWhirter who become famous for their encyclopaedic knowledge of the book's contents. The publication becomes an instant success, topping the bestseller list by Christmas, and is still going strong today.

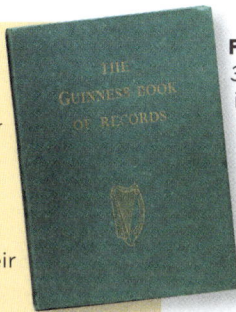

Formal 'green belts' Introduced

3rd August 1955 The Ministry of Housing and Local Government encourages local authorities to consider formally designating land around their communities as 'green belts', protected from urban development. Whilst the concept of green belts had existed since the 19th century, this is the first real push for their implementation.

Nazi nerve agents destroyed

25th-27th July 1955 'Operation Sandcastle' sees 16,000 Nazi bombs, captured during the war, shipped out into the Atlantic Ocean to be destroyed. The bombs contain the nerve agent Tabun and have been deteriorating in storage, posing a threat to the public. In July they are loaded aboard several vessels, which sail out into the ocean and are scuttled, taking the dangerous chemicals to the seafloor.

Philby named 'third man'

18th September 1955 The *People* newspaper reveals that British diplomats Burgess and Maclean, who had disappeared in 1951, are believed to be Soviet spies. This leads to the US press naming Kim Philby, a close associate of Burgess's, as the 'third man' in what would become known as the Cambridge Spy Ring. Philby is publicly cleared by then Foreign Secretary Harold Macmillan in November, and it will be another eight years before the truth of Philby's involvement is revealed.

Britain gets fish fingers!

26th September 1955 American company Birds Eye develop the fish finger in their factory in Grimsby. The easy-to-cook fish fingers quickly become the company's flagship product and remain a staple of British dinner times for decades to come.

Caerdydd Wales capital

20th December 1955 Caerdydd, or Cardiff, officially becomes the capital of Wales after competing with Caernarfon for the honour. Home Secretary Gwilym Lloyd George confirms the choice despite local authorities being divided on the issue.

Lego sold in Britain

In 1955 sets manufactured by the Danish Lego company become available in Britain for the first time. Sets feature the interlocking bricks synonymous with the brand, but later additions such as wheels and specialised parts are not invented until the 60s.

17 JUL 1955	5 AUG 1955	22 SEP 1955
Disneyland theme park opens in California.	Death of Brazilian singer-actress Carmen Miranda.	Independent Television launches in London.

1955

ROYALTY & POLITICS

Churchill retires
5th April 1955 After continuing ill health, Sir Winston Churchill finally steps down as Prime Minister at the age of 80. As expected, he names his successor as his long-time deputy and closest political ally, Sir Anthony Eden. Instead of taking a peerage, Sir Winston has chosen to carry on in the House of Commons as MP for the Woodford constituency.

Conservative victory
28th May 1955 Sir Anthony Eden calls a snap general election and is rewarded with an increased Conservative majority of 60 seats. Benefiting from a stable economy and a general feeling of national well-being, the Conservatives are the first party in 80 years to improve their majority after a term in office.

Margaret says no
31st October 1955 As expectation mounts of an announcement of the engagement between Princess Margaret and Group Captain Peter Townsend, a divorcee, the Queen's sister shocks the nation with a statement saying that she has taken the decision not to marry him. 'Mindful of the Church's teaching that Christian marriage is indissoluble, and conscious of my duty to the Commonwealth,' she writes, 'I have resolved to put these considerations before any others.' Although now 25 years old and free to wed with or without the Queen's approval, a decision to marry would have removed many of her royal privileges.

FOREIGN NEWS

Nuclear submarine
January 17th 1955 The US Navy's newest submarine sets sail. USS *Nautilus* is the world's first nuclear-powered sub and can stay underwater much longer than diesel-powered vessels.

Attlee resigns
7th November 1955 Clement Attlee announces his intention to resign as Leader of the Labour Party following the election defeat in May. Hugh Gaitskell wins the ensuing leadership election, comfortably beating Aneurin Bevan and Herbert Morrison in a ballot of Labour MPs.

25 OCT 1955 Last Allied forces leave Austria following independence agreement.

10 NOV 1955 Ownership of the minesweeper HMS *Pineham* is transferred to France.

20 DEC 1955 Cardiff is named capital of Wales.

Third world

18th April 1955 No longer under Dutch or British control, Indonesia's President Sukarno and India's Prime Minister Jawaharial Nehru convene a conference in Bandung with leaders of nations which have become independent or are fighting a colonial occupier. More than half of the world's population is represented. Sukarno calls it the first intercontinental conference of people of colour and introduces the term 'third world'. Bandung marks the beginning of a new world dynamic.

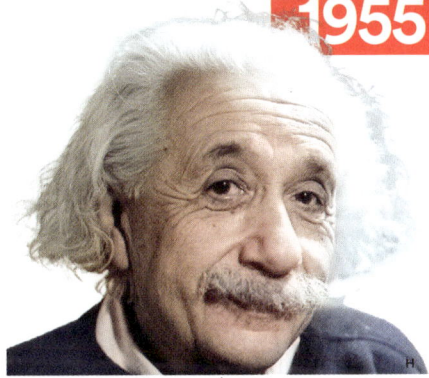

Einstein is dead

18th April 1955 Albert Einstein dies in hospital in Princeton aged 76. The most important physicist in history, his theory of relativity and his findings on quantum mechanics changed the way that people looked at the world and paved the way for nuclear energy and weapons.

I'm lovin' it

15th April 1955 Ray Kroc starts off selling milkshakes behind the counter but later buys the rights to the McDonald brothers' restaurants. Here hamburgers are prepared on an assembly line and orders are processed very quickly. In 1955, Kroc opens the first McDonald's franchise and launches a hamburger chain that will conquer the world.

US commits to Vietnam

1st November 1955 Now that France is turning its back on its former colonial stronghold of Vietnam, the US appoints the Military Assistance Advisory Group to support the government of Ngô Đình Diêm with military advice and equipment in combating the communist guerrillas in South Vietnam.

Castro and Che

12th June 1955 Cuban communist revolutionary Fidel Castro is released after a failed attempt to steal weapons with which to wage a guerrilla war against dictator Fulgencio Batista. Together with his brother Raúl and the Argentinian Che Guevara, he founds the '26th of July Movement', named after the day he was arrested in 1953 and started a revolution in Cuba.

Rosa Parks

1st December 1955 After a normal day at work in Montgomery, Alabama, seamstress Rosa Parks buys a ticket for the bus and takes a seat in an empty seat at the back, where black people must sit according to the law. When the bus is so full that there is no room left in the white section, the driver tells her to give up her seat. The law in Alabama requires that blacks must give up their place to whites if there is no other place available. Rosa refuses to do so and is arrested. A successful boycott of the bus company is quickly organised to which black travellers respond en masse for a total of 381 days. After a protracted legal case challenging the legality of Rosa's conviction, the US Supreme Court rules in favour of her, racial segregation on public buses is declared unconstitutional and the disobedient Parks becomes one of the pioneers of the civil rights movement.

Europe is one

6th November 1955 The Council of Europe chooses a European flag. The blue flag represents the blue sky of the western world, against which twelve golden stars in a circle radiate the unity of Europe. The twelve stars represent perfection according to the biblical book of Jonah.

Cash for questions

Double Your Money, presented by Hughie Green, where contestants can earn as much as £1,000 by answering questions while sweating it out in a sealed booth, is compelling viewing and becomes one of television's most popular shows.

Craft for kids

Picture Book, another programme in the *Watch with Mother* stable, is shown for the first time. Presented by Patricia Driscoll, it encourages children to get crafty and make things with the help of Bizzy Lizzie and Sossidge the Dachshund.

⬙ ENTERTAINMENT

The Man with the Red Book

Eamonn Andrews is the genial host of a new show, *This is Your Life*. Armed with a red book, Andrews famously surprises a celebrity guest each episode and then, back at the studio, takes them through a nostalgic celebration of their life and career, with numerous long-lost friends and acquaintances popping up. Kind of like a funeral, but where you're still alive to hear the nice stuff people say about you.

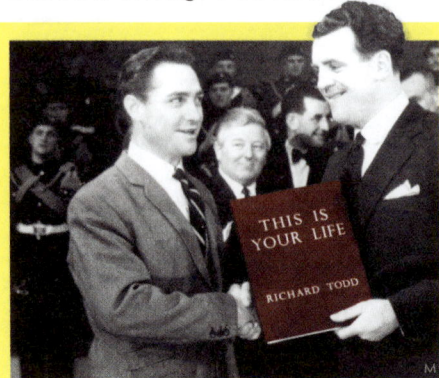

King David

Comedian, actor and singer, the multi-talented Dave King is one of Britain's most bankable stars in the 1950s and this year fronts his own television show, *The Dave King Show*.

All animals are equal

George Orwell's penetrating political fable *Animal Farm* is made into the first British feature-length animation, directed by husband-and-wife team John Halas and Joy Batchelor with all animal voices done by Maurice Denham.

Picture perfect

Pietro Annigoni's portrait of the Queen, painted for the Fishmongers' Company, is a major draw at the RA's summer exhibition, making it the most successful show since the First World War. One RA official tells *The Times* that it was not uncommon for people to pay the 2s. entrance fee even when the exhibition was about to close, just to see Annigoni's picture of Her Majesty in the dark blue robes of the Order of the Garter.

Scotch mist

Brigadoon, Vincente Minnelli's film adaptation of Lerner and Loewe's 1947 whimsical stage musical about two Americans who stumble upon a ghost Scottish village that appears for one day only every hundred years, is a charming enough tale. But audiences are most impressed by the dance routines carried out with aplomb by the dream pairing of Gene Kelly and Cyd Charisse.

The Benny Hill Show

Benny Hill (born Alfred Hawthorne Hill), one of television's early successes with his cheeky innocence and knack for a visual gag, is given his own BBC show. The show reflects his roots in variety and would notoriously feature hordes of scantily clad girls, who often end up chasing (or being chased by) Hill. Laced with a large dose of sexual innuendo.

Get busy with the fizzy

Soda Stream, founded in 1903, brings out the first machine for the home carbonisation of drinks. Now families can have pop at the press of a button.

Lady and the Tramp

In this charming Disney tale of a beautiful pedigree spaniel and a raffish but kind-hearted mongrel, Peggy Lee writes and performs a number of voices and songs including *He's a Tramp* and *The Siamese Cat Song*. In the same year, Disney's first theme park opens in California on 17th July.

1955

The Woodentops
On 9th September, The Woodentops appear for the first time in *Watch with Mother*'s Friday afternoon slot.

Izzy wizzy let's get busy
After several appearances in other shows, a mute teddy glove puppet (operated by Harry Corbett), who communicates via a magic wand, gets his own show. Initially called *Sooty,* before becoming *The Sooty Show,* the little yellow bear is joined by the disruptive and much noisier Sweep two years later.

Newly minted
Dovetailing with the launch of independent television, advertising history is also made on 22nd September when Unilever airs the very first advertisement on UK TV, for Gibbs SR toothpaste.

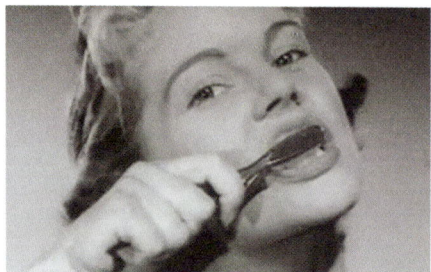

Sunday Night at the London Palladium
Broadcast on 25th September and presented by Tommy Trinder, *Sunday Night at the London Palladium* is dreamt up by Val Parnell. *Sunday Night at the Palladium* will to give ITV audiences a top-drawer galaxy of stars. Together with the glamorous Tiller Girls dance troupe and even a play-along game, *Beat the Clock, Sunday Night at the Palladium* is the jewel in ITV's crown.

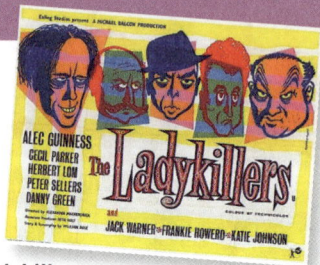

The Ladykillers
A deliciously dark comedy, *The Ladykillers* is a farcical, heist-gone-wrong movie in which Alec Guinness leads a band of crooks masquerading as a string quintet. When their diminutive but indefatigable elderly landlady, Mrs Wilberforce (Katie Johnson) discovers their latest robbery and insists they return the loot, they are too soft-hearted to finish her off and instead turn on each other.

The Dam Busters
One of Britain's most memorable war films, *The Dam Busters* recreates the daring RAF assault on the Ruhr Valley dams under the command of Guy Gibson (Richard Todd), using the bouncing bomb invention of Barnes Wallis, played by Michael Redgrave.

MUSIC

'Bird' is dead

12th March 1955 The unquestioned king of bebop, alto saxophonist Charlie Parker, is found dead in a hotel room in New York at the age of 34. His friend and collaborator Dizzy Gillespie pays for his funeral. Nicknamed 'Bird', Parker's sheer artistry and invention made him one of jazz music's prime innovators and influences, in spite of long struggles with heroin abuse and mental health issues. Summing up Parker's contribution to jazz, Miles Davis pays the ultimate tribute: 'You can tell the history of jazz in four words - Louis Armstrong, Charlie Parker'.

Ruby sets a record

19th March 1955 With five discs in the UK Top Twenty, shy Belfast-born singer Ruby Murray achieves a feat that has never been equalled by any female performer since. By the end of November, she also sets the record - still unbeaten 70 years later - for the most consecutive weeks (52) in the chart by any female artist. Her sudden success fades with dispiriting speed. The most curious legacy of her short time in the limelight is how quickly her name is adopted as cockney rhyming slang for curry.

Unchained and unforgettable

24th June 1955 Occasionally a song from a movie far outlives the movie itself. So it is with *Unchained Melody*, written for an undistinguished prison drama called *Unchained*. No fewer than fourteen versions are recorded in 1955, with that by Jimmy Young rising to No. 1. The song will reach No. 1 on two more occasions in the 1990s in versions by the Righteous Brothers and Robson and Jerome.

Alma in dreamland

15th July 1955 Reaching No. 1 for the first and only time is Alma Cogan from BBC radio's *Take It From Here*, with the jaunty *Dreamboat*. Alma is only the second English-born female singer (Lita Roza is the other) to top the chart during the whole of the 1950s.

Julie cries a river

Like a film noir movie in miniature, *Cry Me a River* tells of love gone wrong from the point of view of a woman who's too tired to care any more. Originally written for Ella Fitzgerald, the song receives its classic treatment courtesy of the sultry voice of Julie London and a smoky jazz accompaniment. Julie's disc fares modestly on first release but takes off when she reprises it in *The Girl Can't Help It*, a film packed wall to wall with rock'n'roll stars.

Slim yodels on

29th July 1955 The yodelling, rhinestone-wearing Slim Whitman tops the UK chart for eleven weeks with *Rose Marie*, the title song from the same Oscar Hammerstein operetta that gave him his first hit with *Indian Love Call* in 1952.

Elvis signs for RCA
25th November 1955 Elvis Presley joins RCA, one of the top two record companies in the US, in a deal that propels him into the major league of music stars. The Sun label that nurtured Elvis is paid an unprecedented $35,000 transfer fee and retains the right to re-release the tracks it made with him.

MY FIRST 18 YEARS
TOP 10 — 1955

1. **Mystery Train** *Elvis Presley*
2. **Mambo Italiano** *Rosemary Clooney*
3. **Cherry Pink & Apple Blossom White** *Pérez Prado*
4. **Stranger in Paradise** *Tony Bennett*
5. **Softly, Softly** *Ruby Murray*
6. **Earth Angel** *The Penguins*
7. **Close the Door** *Jim Lowe*
8. **Never Do a Tango with an Eskimo** *Alma Cogan*
9. **The Ballad of Davy Crockett** *Fess Parker*
10. **Cry Me a River** *Julie London*

Open | Search | Scan

Crockett mania hits the charts
Heard over the credits of a new Walt Disney TV series and film, the opening line of *The Ballad of Davy Crockett* - 'born on a mountaintop in Tennessee' - is on every child's lips. Fess Parker plays Davy and sings the ballad on screen, but his original version has to compete with covers by Tennessee Ernie Ford, Max Bygraves, Burl Ives and Broadway musical star Bill Hayes, who claims the highest UK chart placing early in 1956. Crockett-mania lasts a year and creates insatiable demand for Davy-style coonskin hats.

The worst record ever made?
In a year packed with musical oddities like *Close the Door (They're Coming Through the Window)* and *Never Do a Tango with an Eskimo*, BBC TV personality Eamonn Andrews outdoes them all with the strange *Shifting, Whispering Sands*. The record finds the *What's My Line?* chairman narrating a rather sinister story in his best Irish brogue, with strings and a heavenly choir rising behind him. Years later it will be voted the worst record ever made.

DO YOU REMEMBER THIS?

French knitting

SPORT

Rocky retires
27th April 1956 Having retained his world heavyweight boxing crown by beating Archie Moore in September 1955, Rocky Marciano announces his retirement from the ring. He is the only heavyweight champion to date to finish his career undefeated.

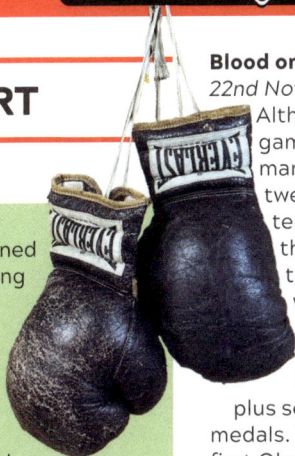

The mystery of Devon Loch
24th March 1956 In one of the great unresolved mysteries in British sport, the Queen Mother's horse Devon Loch falls on the final straight at the Grand National. Five lengths ahead and only 40 yards from the finish line, he buckles and collapses on his stomach, allowing ESB to steal through and win. The Queen Mother's reaction is a stoic 'Oh, that's racing!'.

Trautmann breaks his neck
5th May 1956 In Manchester City's 3-1 FA Cup Final victory over Birmingham, goalkeeper Bert Trautmann injures his neck but plays on. Only seven days later is the injury diagnosed as a fracture that could have killed him. A German prisoner of war who stayed in the UK after the Second World War, Trautmann has overcome the qualms of supporters who refused to accept a former enemy soldier in their ranks. His heroism at Wembley wins universal admiration.

Blood on the water
22nd November - 8th December 1956 Although known as 'the friendly games', the Melbourne Olympics is marred by a brutal grudge match between Hungary and the USSR in water polo. Nicknamed 'the blood on the water' match, Hungary defeat the Soviet team 4-0 and go on to win gold in the final. British success is limited to six gold medals including Christopher Brasher's win in the 3,000m steeplechase, plus seven silvers and eleven bronze medals. The Melbourne games are the first Olympics to be staged in the southern hemisphere.

Charlton debuts with two
6th October 1956 Bobby Charlton, one of the famous 'Busby babes' and future star of England's 1966 World Cup-winning team, makes his debut for Manchester United at the age of nineteen. He scores twice in a 4-2 defeat of Chalton Athletic.

Death of A. A. Milne, creator of Winnie the Pooh.

25 FEB 1956

Soviet leader Nikita Khrushchev makes secret speech revealing Stalin's crimes.

9 MAR 1956

Greek-Cypriot leader Archbishop Makarios deported from Cyprus.

DOMESTIC
NEWS

Corgi toy cars
9th July 1956 Mettoy release the first of their model cars to a delighted audience of British children. These die cast toys, manufactured in Swansea, would soon become firm favourites, with the first launch featuring models of popular family cars like the Ford Consul, Austin A50 and Morris Cowley.

London gets Routemaster buses
8th February 1956 The AEC Routemaster bus goes into service in London for the first time. Running initially on Route 2, the Routemaster becomes famous for its red paint, open rear 'step-on/step-off' platform, and light aluminium frame. It becomes one of London's most iconic features, only retiring from service in 2005.

Diplomats confirmed spies
11th February 1956 The missing diplomats Guy Burgess and Donald Maclean resurface in Moscow, having disappeared under mysterious circumstances in 1951. This confirms suspicions that they were spies who had been passing information to the Soviets throughout the 30s and 40s, and casts doubt on their friends and associates as rumours grow of a five-man spy ring.

First transatlantic telephone cable
25th September 1956 TAT-1, the first transatlantic telephone cable, opens between the UK and North America. In its first 24 hours of service it carries over 700 calls, finally allowing friends and families separated by the Atlantic to speak regularly.

Berni Inn opens in Bristol
27th July 1956 The first Berni Inn Steakhouse opens at 'the Rummer' pub in Bristol. The concept is loosely based on American steakhouse models and Berni Inns quickly become famous for their heavily stylised restaurants, featuring faux-Tudor oak beams, and value for money. The chain is taken over and later sold to Whitbread in the 90s when many become Beefeater restaurants.

23 APR 1956
C.S. Lewis and Joy Gresham marry in Oxford.

9 MAY 1956
Gower peninsula designated UK's first Area of Outstanding Natural Beauty.

3 JUN 1956
Third class travel is abolished by British Railways.

Goodbye to the Lancaster
15th October 1956 The RAF and a grateful nation say goodbye to the iconic Second World War Avro Lancaster bomber as the last is retired from service.

ROYALTY & POLITICS

Calder Hall opens
17th October 1956 Her Majesty the Queen opens the new nuclear power station at Calder Hall, the first commercial nuclear power station in the world. Just a month later, the DIDO nuclear reactor opens at Harwell, bringing the UK to the forefront of atomic energy.

Premium Bonds launched
1st November 1956 The government's first Premium Bonds are available to buy with the top prize of £1,000 awarded in June 1957. The first bond is purchased by the Lord Mayor of London, Sir Cuthbert Ackroyd, for £1.00.

PREMIUM SAVINGS BOND
Issued by the Lords Commissioners of H.M. Treasury under Section One of the National Loans Act, 1939.
NOT TRANSFERABLE
EK
£5
EK
SERIAL NUMBERS INCLUSIVE
FIVE UNITS

Duke of Edinburgh's Award
February 1956 Prince Philip launches his innovative 'Duke of Edinburgh's Award'. Initially only for boys aged fifteen to eighteen, the award is for completing projects in areas such as volunteering, developing personal skills, achieving physical goals, and going on expeditions. It is hoped that this will help motivate young people to become valuable members of society. In the first twelve months, 7,000 boys enroll on the scheme, which is later expanded to include girls, a greater age range, and other countries.

Cleaning up the smoke
5th July 1956 The Clean Air Act becomes law. Prompted by the deadly London smog of December 1952, the Act introduces controls on the burning of coal in urban areas including the setting up of smokeless zones.

IRA launches border campaign
12th December 1956 The Irish Republican Army launches a series of simultaneous attacks by around 150 members on targets around the border with Northern Ireland. These include attacks on courthouses, barracks and transmitters. In response, the Government of Northern Ireland uses the Special Powers Act to intern republican suspects without trial, leading to the arrest of hundreds of people. The border campaign would continue for five years.

Last days of Eden
22nd November 1956 Reeling from both a biliary tract illness and widespread condemnation of his actions over Suez, Sir Anthony Eden departs for Jamaica for a period of rest and recuperation. Back in Westminster by mid-December, he finds political support at an all-time low. His resignation as Prime Minister follows in January.

18 JUL 1956 The UK withdrawals all of its troops from the Suez Canal.

14 AUG 1956 Death of playwright Bertolt Brecht.

2 SEP 1956 Juan Manuel Fangio wins his third straight F1 World Drivers' Championship.

FOREIGN
NEWS

FOREIGN
NEWS

Alpha Bravo Charlie

1st March 1956 NATO introduces an international spelling alphabet, so that important words are spelt using a prede-termined telephonic alphabet and are not misunderstood.

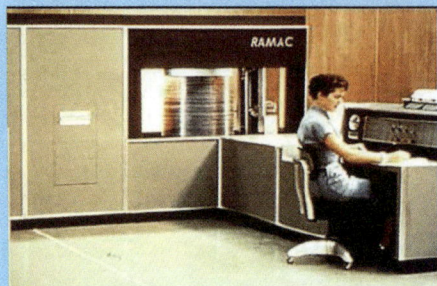

c

Birth of data storage

13th September 1956 Launched today, the IBM 305 RAMAC is the first computer to use a hard drive to store data - up to five megabytes at this point. It is man-sized, one and a half metres long and can be rented for $3,200 per month.

Doenitz released

1st October 1956 Karl Doenitz, who took over as Führer of Germany following Adolf Hitler's suicide, is released from Spandau Prison in West Berlin. Doenitz was a committed Nazi who over-saw Germany's naval oper-ations during the Second World War and managed his country's surrender in May 1945.

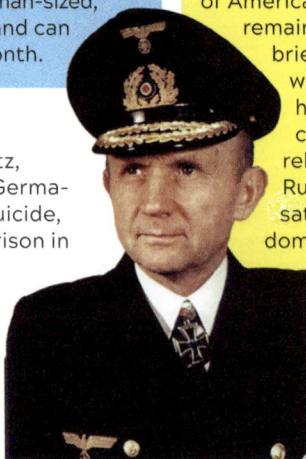

Hungarian uprising

23rd October 1956 Emboldened by protests in Poland against Soviet rule, demonstrators take to the streets in Budapest demanding economic and political reform and the removal of oc-cupation forces. When unarmed civilians are gunned down in Parliament Square, the rebellion descends into all-out war. Hungarian-language broadcasts on the US-run Radio Free Europe raise hopes of American intervention but the US remains on the sidelines. After a brief moment on 28th October when the uprising appears to have succeeded, Soviet troops counter attack and put down the rebellion with brutal force. The Russian position is that allowing a satellite state even small free-doms would fatally weaken Soviet control of Eastern Europe. By 10th November the fighting has ceased, Prime Minister Imre Nagy is under arrest and Janos Kador has been installed in his place.

17 OCT 1956	7 NOV 1956	3 DEC 1956
Calder Hall nuclear power station is opened by the Queen.	Dwight D. Eisenhower is re-elected as US President.	Tax on petrol rises 40% in wake of Suez crisis.

Suez crisis

29th October 1956 President Nasser of Egypt nationalises the Suez Canal, taking it out of British control. This follows growing closeness between Egypt and the Soviet Union, which is funding the building of the giant Aswan Dam. The UK and France respond with a plan for military intervention, without the knowledge or approval of the US. The secret scheme, formulated by UK premier Sir Anthony Eden in conjunction with France and Israel, is for Israel to attack Egypt and the UK and France to intervene on the pretext of separating the adversaries. Although British forces inflict massive damage on the Egyptian infrastructure, the US demands their withdrawal. For the first time ever, the US and the Soviet Union are on the same side at the United Nations. As the junior partner in the Anglo-American relationship, and with the US threatening the UK with severe economic consequences, Eden has no choice but to comply. Huge damage is done to Britain's reputation overseas and to the supposed 'special relationship' between the US and UK. Although damaged militarily, the crisis enhances Nasser's status at home and across the Middle East. The Soviets also gain from the crisis, as the events have distracted world attention from their brutal crackdown of the Hungarian uprising.

Buckling up

Ford is the first major car manufacturer to introduce a two-point seat belt as a safety feature, though it is only an optional extra that just two per cent of buyers take up. Volvo will introduce a three-point belt running over the shoulder and offering better protection in 1959.

⬙ ENTERTAINMENT

The lad 'imself on TV

Hancock's Half Hour, already a successful radio comedy programme, successfully migrates to BBC TV on 6th July.

Armchair Theatre

ITV introduces *The Outsider*, the first play in their long-running anthology *Armchair Theatre* on 8th July, filmed live at ABC's Manchester studios. *Armchair Theatre*, which is aired after the must-watch *Sunday Night at the Palladium,* is ITV's riposte to critics who suggest commercial television offers nothing intellectually nourishing and in time will bring works of social realism by younger British playwrights to a wider audience.

Rock'n'roll rebels

10th July 1956 Rock Around the Clock, a low-budget film featuring Bill Haley and the Comets, causes havoc in cinemas leading to widespread condemnation of the 'riots' in the press. At the Gaiety cinema in Manchester, about 50 youths are ejected from the build-ing after causing a distur-bance and ripping up some of the fittings. They continue to mill around outside, where they dance in the streets and hold up traffic before the police are called. Similar problems are reported around the country and some cinemas decide to ban the film.

Val Parnell's Saturday Spectacular

Following the success of *Sunday Night at the London Palladium,* impresario Val Parnell is determined to dominate week-end programming and lends his name to this light entertainment show which each week hosts stars from teen heartthrob Johnnie Ray to performing porcine pup-pets Pinky and Perky.

Whack-O!

Frank Muir and Dennis Norden are the writers behind this BBC comedy which pits Jimmy Edwards' drunken, conniving school master, Professor James Edwards, against the plum-voiced pupils at Chis-elbury School, where regular caning is the order of the day. Its obsession with beating small children may be distasteful today but *Whack-O!* will run for a total of 60 episodes, from 1956 to 1960, then in colour from 1971 to 1972.

Pop Art genesis

Artist Richard Hamilton prefigures the Pop Art movement when he exhibits his collage, *Just What Is It That Makes Today's Home So Modern, So Desirable?* at the Whitechapel Art Gallery's exhibition *This Is Tomorrow.*

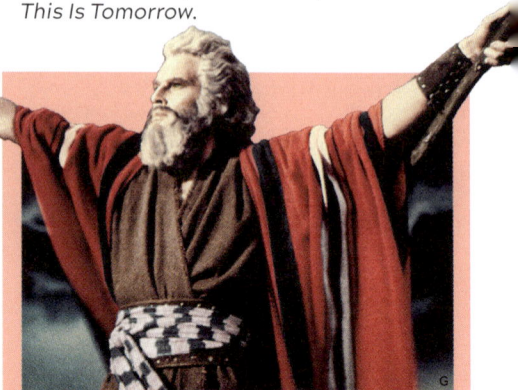

The Ten Commandments

Part of the cinema industry's arsenal against the encroaching dominance of television is the biblical epic - big-budget movie blockbusters telling some of the oldest stories of all. *The Ten Command-ments,* directed by Cecil B. de Mille in his final film, shot in widescreen, lasting al-most four hours, and at the time the most expensive film ever made, is perhaps the biggest blockbuster of all. Charlton Hes-ton is a chiselled Moses who invokes his God to help perform some spectacular miracles (including parting the Red Sea) right before audiences' eyes.

Monkey tea

25th December 1956 The first TV com-mercial for PG Tips tea airs this year, featuring five chimpanzees enjoying a brew. The adverts are a sensation, leading customers to ask for 'monkey tea' in shops and generating a huge boost in sales for PG Tips who now enjoy a large share of the British tea market. The simian stars - Louis, Sam, Gill, Chopper and Noddy - are all young rescue chimps and their earnings are used by owners Molly Badham and Nathalie Evans to start Twycross Zoo in 1963.

Forbidden Planet

A science-fiction riff on Shakespeare's *The Tempest*, *Forbidden Planet* feeds the frenzy for outer space stories in a most imaginative way as Leslie Nielsen's Commander John J. Adams leads a mission to the planet Altair 4 where he encounters survivors of a previous expedition; scientist Doctor Edward Morbius, his daughter Altaira and Robbie the Robot, a character that was to inspire countless fancy dress costumes.

Zoo-time

Desmond Morris, an artist and academic specialising in animal behaviour, broadcasts live from London Zoo and is regularly joined by Congo, a young chimpanzee who enjoys painting and drawing. Picasso is reportedly a fan of Congo's abstract impressionism.

The King and I

Yul Brynner gives what *The Sketch* calls 'a breathtaking performance' in the film adaptation of *The King and I*, adding, 'It's hard to take one's eyes off this astonishing artist.' Brynner won an Academy Award for best leading actor.

Showgirl

Marilyn Monroe and her husband Arthur Miller fly into London on 14th July where they are met by hundreds of press photographers and Sir Laurence and Lady Olivier. Monroe is in England to star opposite Olivier in *The Prince and the Showgirl*, adapted from the play *The Sleeping Prince* by Terence Rattigan.

Reach for the Sky

Kenneth More is the third choice to play Douglas Bader, the courageous double amputee who became a Second World War flying hero, after the role is turned down by Richard Burton and Laurence Olivier. More meets the real-life Bader for a round of golf prior to filming (Bader beat him) and feels some connection, portraying him as a stubborn charmer, although without Bader's famously salty language. This story of courage over adversity, teamed with some quite spectacular flying scenes, makes *Reach for the Sky* the highest-grossing film in the UK this year.

Mr Teasie Weasie comes to Birmingham

On 10th January, hundreds of onlookers gather in New Street, Birmingham to witness Diana Dors officially open a new salon in the growing empire of TV and celebrity hairdresser Raymond, aka Mr Teasie Weasie. After Ms Dors smashes a bottle of champagne against the plate glass door, the salon welcomes its first customer, Miss Edwards, a headmistress. Later that year, the famously extravagant Dors flies Raymond over to Hollywood to attend to her hair at a cost of £3,123 (around £75,000 today). In his syndicated tell-all memoirs he claims the cheque bounced.

KENNETH MORE
REACH FOR THE SKY
The Story of DOUGLAS BADER
MURIEL PAVLOW · LYNDON BROOK
LEE PATTERSON · ALEXANDER KNOX

Six-Five Special

Six-Five Special is one of the first BBC programmes to tempt a teenage audience with a hip and happening line-up of musical acts that tap into the growing appetite for skiffle, jazz and rock'n'roll. The first episode goes out at 6:05pm on 16th February, in the 6pm-7pm slot previously known as the Toddler's Truce when no programming took place so that parents could get children ready for bed. Broadcast live with a studio full of youthful audience members, it is presented by Pete Murray whose catchphrase is, 'Time to jive on the old six-five.' Six-Five Special features early performances from Lonnie Donegan, Marty Wilde and Cliff Richard.

Look Back in Anger

Look Back in Anger by John Osborne, one of the 'angry young men' group of writers, opens at the Royal Court Theatre on 8th May. Rather appropriately, The Stage in its review thought John Osborne, 'a young man in a tearing temper'.

DO YOU REMEMBER THIS?

Vacuum cleaner

MUSIC

Elvis goes global

27th January 1956 The year belongs to Elvis Presley, beginning with the release of his debut RCA single Heartbreak Hotel. It's the first of five US No. 1s in 1956 and a record packed with the clanking guitar chords, thumping rhythm and slurred words that millions will either adore or deplore. Most of all, America is unprepared for how Elvis looks and moves during an Ed Sullivan Show TV appearance that attracts a mind boggling 60 million viewers. The UK remains oblivious to the Presley phenomenon until Heartbreak Hotel is released on the rather posh HMV label - home of Rubinstein and Barbirolli - in mid-May. A single play on Family Favourites on a Sunday lunchtime changes the lives of the nation's teenagers, including a mesmerised John Lennon sitting down to a roast dinner at his Liverpool home. The world will never be quite the same again.

Chuck at Chess

16th April 1956 An immortal rock'n'roll anthem is committed to disc in Chicago's Chess Records studios. The song is Roll Over Beethoven, written and recorded by blues guitarist Chuck Berry in protest at the lack of rock on US radio. While Berry isn't yet the icon of rock that future generations would recognise, it will become one of the most recorded rock'n'roll songs of all time, with versions by Presley, the Beatles, Electric Light Orchestra and many others.

Robin's song

18th February 1956 Now that over half of British households own a television set, its growing influence on the record charts is obvious. A case in point is the many hit versions of the theme song from ITV's *The Adventures of Robin Hood*, which is performed on screen and on record by Dick James and children from his son Stephen's school in Cricklewood. A No. 14 UK hit, the record's royalties help him set up as a music publisher and, in 1963, to take a chance on publishing the songs of a pair of unknowns named Lennon and McCartney.

Satchmo blows in

3rd May 1956 The wait is over! As the long-standing Musicians Union ban on American musicians performing in the UK is replaced by an exchange scheme, British jazz fans can enjoy something they have been dreaming about for years - a visit by the legendary Louis Armstrong and his hand-picked team of All Stars.

Love forever true

17th July 1956 The release of the movie musical *High Society* is timed to coincide with the fairy tale wedding of the decade - actress Grace Kelly to Prince Rainier III of Monaco. It is Kelly's last film before her retirement from the screen and includes in its Cole Porter score her sublime duet with Bing Crosby, *True Love*.

Jazzing the charts

23rd June 1956 Who says jazz has no place in the pop chart? Humphrey Lyttleton shows it can be done with *Bad Penny Blues*, whose breathless piano riff inspires the Beatles' *Lady Madonna* in 1968. Another leading UK jazzman, Johnny Dankworth, offers *Experiments With Mice*, an affectionate spoof of the big band styles of Stan Kenton and the late Glenn Miller set to *Three Blind Mice*.

Sinatra swings

22nd July 1956 Frank Sinatra's *Songs for Swinging Lovers*, is the first No. 1 in the UK's newly launched LP chart. It is one of the first proper 'concept' albums, featuring songs linked thematically that tell the story of a love affair.

No love song finer

27th July 1956 Making its first appearance on the US LP chart is *Ella Fitzgerald Sings the Cole Porter Songbook*, one of a series of Fitzgerald albums honouring the work of America's finest songwriters. It includes one of the decade's most touching vocal performances - *Ev'ry Time We Say Goodbye*, an obscurity by Cole Porter standards now given a whole new life. With its theme of long separations and short reunions, the track resonates deeply with servicemen and their sweethearts and becomes one of the top five most requested items on BBC radio's *Family Favourites*.

Crombie goes rock

10th September 1956 Britain's very first home-grown professional rock'n'roll outfit make their performing debut in Portsmouth. Tony Crombie and his Rockets have named themselves in homage to Bill Haley and his Comets.

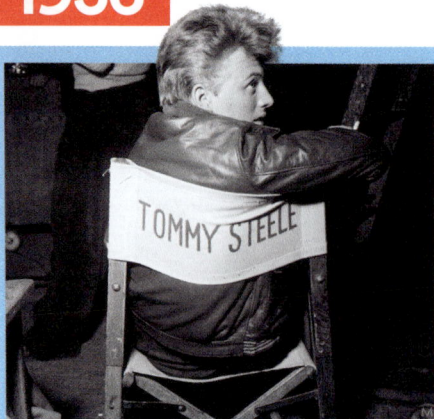

Tommy on top

27th October 1956 Ever since Elvis's explosive arrival, the hunt has been on for a British equivalent. Now Decca Records has the answer: a Bermondsey-born merchant seaman called Tommy Hicks now renamed Tommy Steele to add a touch of muscularity. Tommy has a grin as wide as a mile, a Hank Williams-type twang and lots of teen appeal. Meanwhile, the coffee bar where he was discovered, the 2i's in London's Soho, becomes a mecca for would-be rockers from all over the nation.

Swann songs from Flanders

31st December 1956 Premiering at a Notting Hill theatre is a two-man show with no scenery, dancing girls or pit band, just wheel-chair-using Michael Flanders and pianist Donald Swann casting a wry musical eye over everything from relations with Europe to the terrible British weather. *At the Drop of a Hat* becomes a word-of-mouth hit, transfers to the West End and begets a best-selling live album.

MY FIRST 18 YEARS

TOP10 — 1956

1. **Blue Moon** *Elvis Presley*
2. **Blue Suede Shoes** *Carl Perkins*
3. **Whatever Will Be, Will Be** *Doris Day*
4. **I Walk the Line** *Johnny Cash*
5. **The Great Pretender** *The Platters*
6. **Lost John** *Lonnie Donegan*
7. **Elevator Rock** *Tommy Steele*
8. **The Gnu Song** *Flanders and Swann*
9. **Why Do Fools Fall in Love** *Frankie Lymon*
10. **I've Got You Under My Skin** *Frank Sinatra*

Open | Search | Scan

Rock'n'roll is here to stay

More proof emerges that rock'n'roll really is the sound of the age. From New Orleans comes the piano and saxophone sound of Fats Domino and *Blueberry Hill*, while Sun Records in Memphis make up for losing Elvis to RCA by signing a whole host of young singers who turn up at their door - Johnny Cash, Jerry Lee Lewis and Roy Orbison included. One Sun discovery, Carl Perkins, even gives Elvis a run for his money with a snarling version of his own song, *Blue Suede Shoes*. In Nashville, Gene Vincent brings a tortured gasp to the anguished *Be Bop-a-Lula* in the same month that Georgia's outrageous piano thumper Little Richard kicks up a storm with *Rip it Up*.

SPORT

England's clean sweep
16th March 1957 England dominate the Five Nations rugby championship, clinching the Grand Slam, the Triple Crown and the Calcutta Cup in the final 16-3 win over Scotland.

Althea wins Wimbledon
6th July 1957 Althea Gibson becomes the first black woman to win the Wimbledon singles title, beating fellow American Darlene Hard 6-3, 6-2. It is her second Grand Slam title, following her success at the French Open a year earlier.

J. GREAVES

Goodbye and hello
15th May 1957 Stanley Matthews dons an England shirt for the last time, in a 4-1 victory over Denmark in Copenhagen. It is his 54th appearance in an international career interrupted by the war. As one footballing hero departs, another enters at the start of the 1957-58 season. Seventeen-year-old Jimmy Greaves scores for Chelsea on his First Division debut against Tottenham Hotspur and plays his first match for England Under 23s a month later. The full England debut of this legendary goal scorer is only eighteen months away.

Giant steps for John Charles
1st August 1957 Nicknamed 'the Gentle Giant', Welsh international striker John Charles leaves Leeds United to join Italian club Juventus for a British record £65,000 transfer fee. He helps his new side win three championships and two Italian cups before returning to Leeds in 1962.

A rare Ryder Cup win
5th October 1957 Momentarily breaking the American stranglehold on the competition, Great Britain win golf's Ryder Cup for the first time since 1924. Competing at Lindrick Golf Club near Worksop, a strong home side including Peter Alliss and Max Faulkner beats the US by a score of 7½ to 4½ points. Welshman Dai Rees becomes only the third captain of the Great Britain side to lift the Cup.

200 wickets in a season
10th September 1957 Tony Lock of Surrey becomes the last bowler to take 200 wickets in a County Championship season. The advent of covered pitches and limited-over matches makes the feat unrepeatable.

13 JAN 1957	1 FEB 1957	25 MAR 1957
Death of Hollywood actor Humphrey Bogart.	The world's first electric portable typewriter goes on sale in US.	The Treaty of Rome establishes the six-member European Economic Community.

1957

Midlands earthquake

11th February 1957 An earthquake scoring 5.3 on the Richter scale strikes the East Midlands. Centred on Derby, this proves to be the worst British post-war quake until 1984 and is felt across central England and as far away as Norwich and Topsham. Buildings and infrastructure are heavily damaged close to the epicentre.

Toddler's Truce ends

16th February 1957 The break in television programming between 6 and 7pm known as the 'Toddler's Truce' is abolished after campaigning from the Independent Television Authority. The Truce had been introduced to provide a respite from television for one hour between 6 and 7pm to allow families to put their toddlers to bed, but the ITA claimed this led to a loss of advertising revenue during the shutdown, giving the BBC an unfair advantage.

Asian Flu

June 1957 The so-called Asian flu pandemic sweeping through the world reaches the UK. Caused by the H2N2 strain, a vaccine is made available in October, but the pandemic lasts well into 1958 and leads to an estimated 20,000 - 33,000 deaths in Britain. Worldwide deaths are estimated at between 1 and 4 million.

April Fool!

1st April 1957 The BBC broadcasts a report on the 'Spaghetti Harvest' in its most famous April Fool's Day prank. Shown as part of its serious Panorama programme, the three-minute report follows a Swiss family apparently harvesting spaghetti from trees. It is given authenticity by respected presenter Richard Dimbleby's voiceover, and as pasta is relatively rare in Britain, hundreds call in to ask how they can grow their own at home.

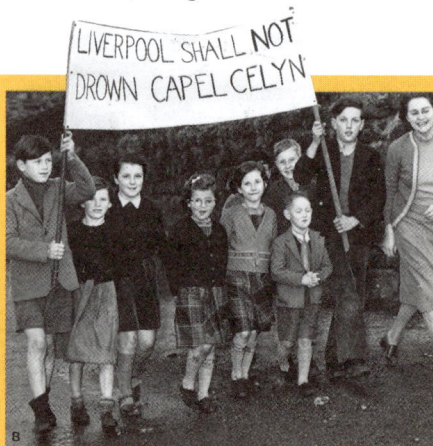

Tryweryn Bill controversy

31st July 1957 The Tryweryn Bill causes controversy, as Liverpool City Council is permitted to build a reservoir that will drown the Welsh village of Capel Celyn. Almost every single Welsh MP votes against it, as the village is one of a handful of entirely Welsh-speaking communities left in Wales. Despite protest the bill is passed, and the village is flooded in 1965.

Malayan independence

31st August 1957 The Federation of Malaya gains formal independence from Britain, with Tunku Abdul Rahman becoming the first prime minister.

9 APR 1957

The Suez Canal is reopened to all shipping.

2 MAY 1957

US political demagogue Senator Joseph McCarthy dies.

27 JUN 1957

The British MRC publishes a report sugesting a link between smoking and lung cancer.

Isle of Wight crash

15th November 1957 An Aquila Airways Short Solent 3 flying boat crashes into a chalk pit on Salcombe Down on the Isle of Wight. The flight had left Southampton Water en route to Madeira, before experiencing difficulties and turning back. Of the 58 people on board 45 are killed, with the remainder rescued by three soldiers on a night exercise who happen to be nearby.

Which? magazine

1st October 1957 The Consumers' Association launches the magazine *Which?*, hoping to improve the standard of goods and services in the UK by comparing the products on the market. The first edition features reports on, among other things, electric kettles, no-iron cottons, and British cars.

Nuclear reactor fire

10th October 1957 The worst nuclear accident in British history is caused by a fire in the graphite core of the nuclear reactor at Windscale in Cumbria. On the morning of the 10th, one of the core's fuel cartridges overheats and catches fire; by the following day eleven tons of uranium are burning. The flames are eventually subdued by shutting off air to the reactor, but not before a large amount of radioactive material is released into the atmosphere. Following the disaster, milk produced in the 200-square-mile area around the reactor is found to have dangerously high levels of iodine and is destroyed.

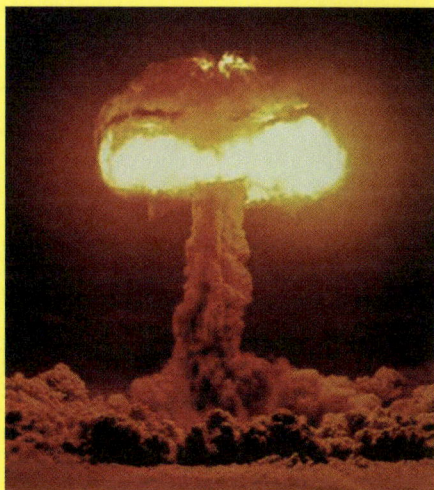

Hydrogen bomb tested

8th November 1957 Britain conducts its first fully successful test of a hydrogen bomb as part of Operation Grapple. A previous test in May had been only partially successful, with the explosion reaching only a fraction of its expected power. The November test, at Kiritimati, or 'Christmas Island', meets all expectations. The UK becomes the third recognised thermonuclear power.

Lewisham rail crash

4th December 1957 Two trains collide in intense fog near Lewisham station in London, killing 90 and injuring 173 people. A steam train to Ramsgate collides with an electric train to Hayes which had stopped at a red signal, leading to the destruction of a carriage and the collapse of a bridge above the crash site. Thankfully, a train that was due to pass over the bridge is able to stop just in time, avoiding further casualties.

19 JUL 1957
First rocket with nuclear warhead fired in Nevada.

3 AUG 1957
USSR announces successful test of an intercontinental ballistic missile.

19 SEP 1957
Sterling crisis forces bank rate rise and two-year freeze on public sector investment.

1957

ROYALTY & POLITICS

Charles starts school
28th January 1957 In a break with tradition, the Queen and the Duke of Edinburgh decide to send Prince Charles, now eight years old, to an all-boys day school. Having been educated at Buckingham Palace by private tutors from five years old, Prince Charles is welcomed by Hill House School in nearby Knightsbridge.

'Never had it so good'
20th July 1957 In a speech at Bedford football ground, Prime Minister Harold Macmillan makes the remark that defines his premiership and in some ways defines the era. 'Most of our people have never had it so good,' he tells Conservative party workers - a phrase that echoes the Democrat slogan during the 1952 US presidential campaign.

A TV royal first
25th December 1957 The Queen delivers her Christmas Day message to the Commonwealth from the Long Library at Sandringham. It is the first of her annual messages to be televised with pictures as well as sound.

Wolfenden reports
5th September 1957 The Wolfenden Committee report is published, with recommendations to change the existing legislation regarding homosexuality. After two years of deliberation, the Commission proposes that homosexual relations between consenting adults should be decriminalised. The law will remain unchanged until 1967.

FOREIGN NEWS

King's first national address
17th May 1957 Over 30,000 people gather to demonstrate at Washington DC's Lincoln Memorial for a Prayer Pilgrimage for Freedom. The main speaker is Dr Martin Luther King Jr, who founded the Southern Christian Leadership Conference earlier this year to campaign for full civil rights for all African-Americans. It is King's first address before a national audience. The demonstration marks the third anniversary of the US Supreme Court's decision to end segregation in public education. It is the largest ever demonstration for civil rights to date and lays the groundwork for future marches on Washington.

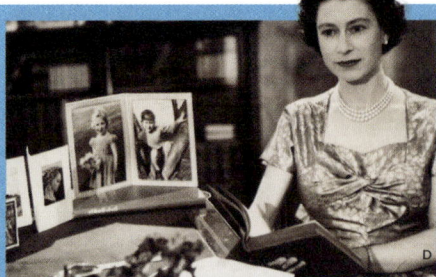

17 OCT 1957
Asian flu pandemic peaks in UK, claiming 600 lives in a week.

15 NOV 1957
Flying boat crashes in the Isle of Wight killing 45.

5 DEC 1957
Three days of London smog causes up to a thousand deaths.

66

Gromyko appointed

15th February 1957 Andrei Gromyko is made foreign minister of the Soviet Union. Soviet ambassador to the US during the war and ambassador to the UK in 1952-53, Gromyko has been handed one of the most important diplomatic roles of the Cold War. From now until the Gorbachev era in the mid-1980s, the much travelled Gromyko's impassive stone face comes to personify the Soviet Union at its most unbending. Not for nothing is his nickname 'Mr Nyet'.

Sputnik in space

4th October 1957 While most eyes look to the US for the next step in space travel, the Soviet Union steals a march with its own space programme. Sputnik becomes the first artificial object to orbit the Earth. A month later, the Soviets launch a second Sputnik with the dog Laika on board. Laika becomes the first living creature in space but does not survive the flight.

Anne Frank House

3rd May 1957 The publication of *The Diary of Anne Frank* in 1947 created great interest in the Amsterdam house where the Frank family was hidden during the Second World War. The Anne Frank Foundation, launched today, aims to prevent its demolition, and restore the house. The campaign succeeds and the Anne Frank House opens as a museum in 1960.

Bubble wrap is born

Is it possible to create washable wallpaper? Two engineers in New Jersey come up with what they think may be a solution - an air-filled plastic exterior, created by sewing two shower curtains together.
The material turns out to be unsuitable as wallpaper, but miraculously it does make the perfect packaging material.

Independence for Ghana

6th March 1957 At midnight, the British colonies of Gold Coast, Ashanti, Northern Territories and Togoland are merged to form Ghana, an independent nation that is now part of the British Commonwealth. Ghana is the first sub-Saharan African colony to gain independence.

1957

◉ ENTERTAINMENT

Medical emergency
British TV's first medical soap opera, *Emergency Ward 10* broadcasts its first episode on 19th February. Following the lives and loves of the staff at Oxbridge Hospital, casualties are blessedly low. In fact, a maximum of five deaths are allowed a year in the interests of viewer morale. The show makes stars of the cast, including John Alderton who plays Dr Moone (his co-star Jill Browne becomes his first wife in 1964) and among those filling the beds on the ward are Albert Finney and Joanna Lumley.

The Bridge on the River Kwai
David Lean's gripping war drama sweeps the board at the Oscars and earns Alec Guinness the best actor award for his performance as the stuffy, obsessive but upstanding Colonel Nicholson. While *The Bridge on the River Kwai* is one of the greatest of all epic war films, it is also a more subtle rumination on the complexities of honour, integrity, and human will.

The towering triumph of adventure from the makers of "Lawrence of Arabia."

WILLIAM HOLDEN
ALEC GUINNESS · JACK HAWKINS

THE BRIDGE ON THE RIVER KWAI

Star gazing
The Sky at Night is aired for the first time on 24th April, presented by the enthusiastic Patrick Moore. Despite its late-night slot around midnight, the programme, which covers every aspect of astronomy, is very popular largely due to the rapid eloquence and endearing eccentricity of Moore, who continues to present the programme until his death in December 2012, the longest-serving presenter in television history.

Spinning plate
The Frisbee, originally called the Pluto Platter, is launched on 23rd January by Wham-O. The invention of an LA building inspector called Fred Morrison, the Frisbee was developed after Morrison and his girlfriend started throwing a popcorn tub lid around at the beach. The Frisbee, which took its name from the American Frisbie Pies, makes Morrison a millionaire.

I'd love a Babycham
Babycham is the first alcoholic drink to be advertised on UK TV. Described as a 'champagne perry', it is made in the West Country and comes in cute little bottles. Marketed squarely at women with the slogan, 'I'd love a Babycham', glasses, ice buckets and drinks mats featuring Babycham's playful, Bambi-like fawn contribute towards the complete, glamorous Babycham experience.

I'd love a BABYCHAM

Televised teaching

At 2pm on 24th September, the first programme from BBC Television for Schools is watched by children from participating schools. The advent of educational programmes designed specifically to be watched as part of the learning curriculum is a new and inspiring way to get pupils to engage with subjects and involves children gathering around a large television on a stand.

New life on screen

Panorama courts controversy when it includes a 30-second film showing the final stages of the birth of a baby on 4th February. It's a short sequence from a film about Dr Grantley Dick Read's natural birth by relaxation system, intended to link with the news that the Natural Childbirth Association had been inaugurated the previous week. Parents are warned beforehand so they can choose whether to allow their children to watch.

I'm too sexy for this film

Roger Vadim's film *And God Created Woman* starring his wife, Brigitte Bardot as a nubile, over-sexed teenager is released in UK cinemas in March. *Picturegoer* magazine's opinion reflects those of French critics who think audiences have seen enough of the 'pert, gifted curvaceous' French actress and that she is simply, 'too sexy, too often'! The box office tells a different story however, and *Kinematograph Weekly* challenges anyone to 'try and get a seat at the Cameo-Royal, Charing Cross Road where Brigitte Bardot's latest is playing'.

Doyen of DIY

Which TV personality received the most mail in the late 1950s? You might be surprised to learn it was Barry Bucknell, presenter of *Do-It-Yourself*, who, after a slot offering advice on fixing and making in *About the Home*, was offered his own show in 1957. In *Do-It-Yourself*, the reassuring Barry, dressed in shirt and tie (and a cardigan for outdoor work) showed the nation how to put up shelves, lay linoleum, hang a door or make a Christmas tree stand. Ten secretaries were required to handle the 35,000 letters a week he received.

Quantifiable style

Mary Quant opens her second Bazaar shop in the King's Road in London. Quant's wearable, youthful designs, made in small quantities and with an ever-changing selection of stock, revolutionise fashion for young women. Her clothes become one of the defining looks of the next decade.

The mark of Zorro
Don Diego de la Vega by day, masked crusader Zorro by night: this 1957 Disney TV series spawned a number of swash-buckling toys including masks, Spanish guitars and duelling swords with chalk tips, allowing budding swordsmen to leave a warning for their enemies with the mark of Zorro. Parents are less thrilled when chalk 'Z's start appearing on their soft furnishings!

Haley's here!
5th February 1957 Arriving on the *Queen Mary* are Bill Haley and the Comets, the first US rock'n'roll act to tour the UK. *The Daily Mirror* hires a train to bring the band straight to London but it's soon apparent that the slightly tubby Haley is not quite the stuff of which teenage dreams are made.

All for Britain
Patricia Bredin is the United Kingdom's very first entrant into the Eurovision Song Contest with the song *All* which lasts just 1 minute and 52 seconds. She comes seventh out of ten contestants.

Saturday sounds
1st June 1957 BBC radio bosses make an important concession to young music fans by launching *Saturday Skiffle Club* in a 10am spot previously reserved for cinema organ music. By November, the show has well over two million listeners. After the skiffle boom fades, the show is renamed *Saturday Club* but continues as a two-hour mix of records, live sessions and pop news presented by the ever-affable Brian Matthew.

MUSIC

Shirley makes her entrance
Young, fiery and from the mixed race community of Cardiff's Tiger Bay, Shirley Bassey is an explosive talent, but why does her record company stereotype her as a calypso singer? Her first chart entry is a cover of Harry Belafonte's *Banana Boat Song*, while *Kiss Me Honey Honey Kiss Me* is a piece of silliness that does no justice to her smouldering vocal power. As the rave notices for her appearances at London's Café de Paris, El Rancho Vegas and Ciro's in Hollywood show, Shirley is much more at home with classy ballads and a caba-ret clientele.

Calypso king
1st March 1957 Making his first appear-ance on the UK record chart is Harry Belafonte with *The Banana Boat Song*, a song first heard sung by the dock workers of Kingston, Jamaica. Such is the husky beauty of his voice that it's hard to believe he was dubbed by another singer in the 1954 film *Carmen Jones*.

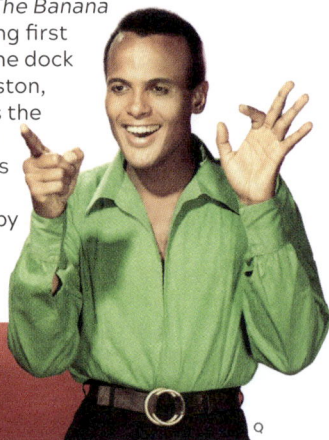

Teenage idols

The Presley phenomenon has left every record company in the US desperate to sign its own rock'n'roll-singing teen idol. Ricky Nelson, adolescent star of the TV comedy *The Ozzie and Harriet Show,* learns the guitar and cuts a stream of pleasing country-style hits. Paul Anka, a precocious fourteen-year-old from Canada, sets a love poem to his babysitter to a cha-cha beat and sells a million with *Diana.*

Skiffle rolls on

Skiffle's grip on Britain's youth continues as Nancy Whiskey and Chas McDevitt revive the railroad murder ballad *Freight Train* and the four-man Vipers offer *Don't You Rock Me, Daddy-O.* Sticking with the railroad theme, US bluegrass guitarist Johnny Duncan - the singer who replaced Lonnie Donegan in Chris Barber band - seizes the moment with *Last Train to San Fernando.* Lonnie himself widens his repertoire slightly with a comic song that is nearly 80 years old - *Puttin' On the Style.* It's his first No. 1.

Holly days

19th August 1957 Topping the US chart are a group from Lubbock, Texas, whose influence on the developing rock music scene will be colossal. Led by 21-year-old Buddy Holly, the Crickets have a tight, unembellished sound that will be a blueprint for the British beat group style in the early 1960s.

Lennon meets McCartney

6th July 1957 History is made at a church fete in Woolton, Liverpool, where sixteen year old John Lennon and his skiffle group the Quarrymen perform on the back of a truck. Afterwards a mutual friend introduces John to Paul McCartney who impresses by showing him the chords to Eddie Cochran's *Twenty Flight Rock.* After some demurring, John invites Paul - who is two years younger - to join the fledgling group.

Jackie packs a punch

10th September 1957 Released today in the US is a breakthrough track in the careers of singer Jackie Wilson and songwriter Berry Gordy. *Reet Petite* is a scorching dance track with a punch appropriate to a singer who was once a professional boxer. Gordy puts the proceeds towards setting up the Tamla label in Detroit - the first of several labels he will bring together under the Motown banner.

Little Richard goes gospel

15th November 1957 The most flamboyant and exciting rock'n'roller of all, the big-haired and fabulously bejewelled Little Richard, stuns his fans by renouncing the devil's music and devoting himself to gospel. The hits keep coming nevertheless - *Long Tall Sally, Tutti Frutti, Lucille* and *The Girl Can't Help It* in this year alone - and he keeps his promise until the offer of a tour of the UK in 1962 entices him back.

Weedon shows the way

25th December 1957 The most prized gift in any would-be guitar player's Christmas stocking this year is Bert Weedon's newly published guitar tutor, *Play in a Day*. An Essex-born session guitarist, Bert has created a 'how to' manual that virtually every UK guitar player of note learns from, including John Lennon, Pete Townshend and Eric Clapton.

Brothers in harmony

Proof that rock'n'roll can have a softer side is provided by two brothers from Brownie, Kentucky. Schooled in country music and harmony singing, Don and Phil Everly make an instant impact with the lovelorn *Bye Bye Love* and swiftly follow it with *Wake Up Little Susie*, the comical story of a movie date gone wrong. UK fans will have to wait until 1960 for their first nationwide tour.

MY FIRST 18 YEARS
TOP 10 — 1957

1. **All Shook Up** *Elvis Presley*
2. **Bye Bye Love** *The Everly Brothers*
3. **Diana** *Paul Anka*
4. **That'll Be the Day** *The Crickets*
5. **Reet Petite** *Jackie Wilson*
6. **A White Sport Coat** *Marty Robbins*
7. **Long Tall Sally** *Little Richard*
8. **Puttin' on the Style** *Lonnie Donegan*
9. **Last Train to San Fernando** *Johnny Duncan*
10. **Freight Train** *Nancy Whiskey*

Open | Search | Scan

Death of Sibelius

20th September 1957 Finnish composer Jean Sibelius dies at the age of 91. His *Karelia Suite* and *Finlandia* were among the crowning works of the Romantic period that saw the flowering of distinct national styles in classical music.

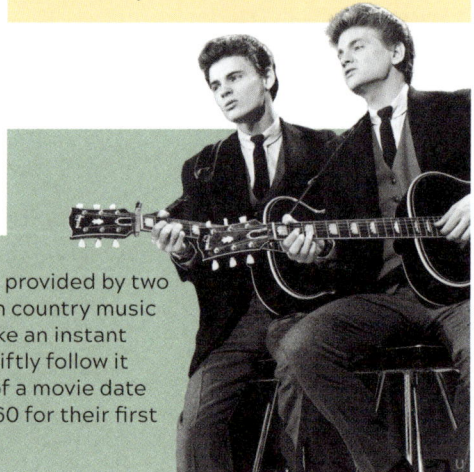

SPORT

Disaster at Munich

6th February 1958 One of the worst tragedies in the history of English football unfolds at a snow-hit Munich airport, where a plane carrying the Manchester United team back from a European Cup tie in Belgrade crashes on its third attempt to take off. Six of the players are killed, with a seventh - England international Duncan Edwards - dying fifteen days later in hospital. The death toll of 23 also includes backroom staff, several journalists and most of the air crew. United manager Matt Busby is twice given the last rites. Bobby Charlton and Dennis Viollet also survive after being pulled clear of the wreckage by goalkeeper Harry Gregg. In the aftermath, assistant manager Jimmy Murphy pulls together a scratch team for the rest of the season from youth players and those loaned by other clubs. The team finishes ninth in the league and battles through to the FA Cup Final, where Bolton Wanderers are the victors in a game most memorable for a goal by Nat Lofthouse that even he admits should never have stood after his shoulder charge on Harry Gregg. The scars of Munich run deep but out of the disaster Matt Busby begins to fashion a new team of 'Busby babes' that will finally bring European glory to Manchester United ten years later.

Pele shoots Brazil to first World Cup

8th - 29th June 1958 The sixth FIFA World Cup takes place in Sweden, with all four of the home nations participating. England and Scotland make early exits, but Northern Ireland and Wales prove surprise packages by reaching the quarter finals. The Wales display against Brazil in the quarters is particularly outstanding, limiting Brazil - and the seventeen-year-old Pele, shining in his first World Cup. In the final in Stockholm, Brazil defeat Sweden 5-2, Pele scoring twice. It is the first time that Brazil have won the World Cup.

Seven in a row for Surrey

29th August 1958 Surrey win cricket's County Championship for a record-breaking seventh season in succession. Surrey's dominance in the decade has much to do with the captaincy of Stuart Surridge in 1952-57 and his successor Peter May.

DO YOU REMEMBER THIS?

Plastic soldiers

1 JAN 1958	13 FEB 1958	14 MAR 1958
BOAC 102 Britannia flies from London to New York in a record 7 hours and 57 minutes.	Death of suffragette leader Christabel Pankhurst.	The South African government prohibits the African National Congress (ANC).

1958

Grandstand begins

11th October 1958 A new Saturday after-noon programme ushers in a new era of television sporting coverage. *Grandstand* is a miscellany of live events and sports news devised by BBC TV's head of outside broadcasts, Peter Dimmock, who also acts as anchor man for the first three weeks before David Coleman takes over. Coleman's ability to reel off statistics while reading football scores from a tele-printer becomes one of the show's most iconic features. Over the years, major sporting occasions such as the Grand National, the FA Cup Final and the Five Nations rugby are incorporated into the programme alongside ice skating and ski-ing in the winter and Test match coverage in the summer. The programme endures with many format changes until 2007.

Hawthorn is champion

19th January - 19th October 1958
Two British drivers dominate the 1958 Formula One World Championship. Stirling Moss wins four Grands Prix while Mike Hawthorn wins only one in his Ferrari F1 246, but the latter's overall performance secures the Championship by a single point.

DOMESTIC NEWS

Brits cross Antarctica!

2nd March 1958 Sir Vivian Fuchs leads a British team to complete the very first land crossing of the Antarctic. The Commonwealth Trans-Antarctic Expedi-tion team utilise dog sleds and Sno-Cat caterpillar tractors to cover the distance from the Weddell Sea to the Ross Sea via the South Pole in just 100 days.

Arrival of the motorways

24th March 1958 Britain begins to develop its first full-length motorway, the M1, which will eventually link London and Leeds. In December, the country's first stretch of motorway, the Preston Bypass, opens, ushering in a new era for Britain's roads.

First female peers

30th April 1958 Changes to the House of Lords allow for the creation of 'Life Peers', people who will enter the Lords for the duration of their lifetimes and not pass a title on to their children. This includes women, and Bar-bara Wootton, Baroness Woot-ton of Abinger becomes the first to enter the Lords in August.

16 APR 1958

Death of Rosalind Franklin, unsung contributor to the discovery of DNA.

15 MAY 1958

Soviet satellite Sputnik III launched.

16 JUN 1958

Imre Nagy is executed in Soviet Union for his role in the Hungarian uprising.

Iconic black cabs

The Austin FX 4 London taxi appears on the capital's streets for the first time and becomes as iconic as the red telephone box or double-decker bus. Produced until 1997, the sight of its sleek black chassis and warm orange light spells relief for millions of visitors to the capital.

Subscriber Trunk Dialling

5th December 1958 Subscriber Trunk Dialling, direct telephone calls without an operator, are introduced for the first time in Bristol. The Queen puts in the very first call using the new system to the Lord Provost in Edinburgh.

Clothes on Carnaby Street

Clothing boutique 'His Clothes' is opened by John Stephen on Carnaby Street in London. It is the first such shop to open there and begins the street's meteoric rise to fame. Carnaby becomes the go-to place for exciting fashion in the 1960s and is referenced in music and pop culture for decades to come.

Parking meters appear!

10th July 1958 Parking meters appear on British streets for the first time, with the very first installed in Mayfair, London. Westminster City Council charges 6d. for one hour's parking.

Little Chef

The very first Little Chef opens in Reading in Berkshire in 1958, introducing visitors to its famous 'Olympic' breakfast for the very first time. The American-style diner, created by Sam Alper, soon becomes a feature of service stations and rest stops across the country.

Race riots in London

30th August 1958 Disgraceful scenes are witnessed in London as around 400 white individuals descend on the multi-ethnic area of Notting Hill and begin attacking the houses of West Indian residents. The riots demonstrate rising race tensions in parts of London, and lead to five nights of violence and 108 arrests.

---

18 JUL 1958

The British Empire Games and Commonwealth Games open in Cardiff. England wins with a total of 80 medals.

14 AUG 1958

KLM pasenger plane crashes west of Ireland, killing 99 people.

5 SEP 1958

Fierce storm sweeping from Isle of Wight to London brings record-breaking hailstones and at least two tornados.

1958

ROYALTY & POLITICS

A little local difficulty
6th January 1958 Chancellor of the Exchequer Peter Thorneycroft and Treasury ministers Enoch Powell and Nigel Birch resign from Harold Macmillan's Cabinet over his refusal to go further with public expenditure cuts. In a typical Macmillan put-down, he dismisses the resignations as 'a little local difficulty'.

CND launched
17th February 1958 The Campaign for Nuclear Disarmament is launched by philosopher Bertrand Russell at Westminster's Central Hall with the aim of persuading governments in east and west to get rid of their nuclear weapons.

Day to remember
23rd February 1958 Independent Television News journalist Robin Day grills Harold Macmillan for thirteen minutes in the first ever one-to-one TV interview of a British Prime Minister. Day's lack of deference is something new and combative in political broadcasting.

On the 'never never'
27th October 1958 The ending of hire purchase restrictions fuels a new consumer boom. A wealth of goods from washing machines to electric guitars can now be bought on the so-called 'never never'.

Charles named Prince of Wales
26th July 1958 Prince Charles, who is nine years old and first in line to the throne, has the title of Prince of Wales conferred on him by his mother Queen Elizabeth II.

FOREIGN NEWS

Treaty of Rome
1st January 1958 Signed a year ago and now in place, the Treaty of Rome establishes the European Economic Community, the forerunner of the European Union. Its signatories are Italy, France, West Germany, the Netherlands, Belgium and Luxembourg. A common market is now being established between the treaty nations as mutual import tariffs disappear and common customs tariffs are imposed on imports from outside the EEC.

---

28 OCT 1958
Pope John XIII succeeds Pope Pius XII.

24 NOV 1958
Mali and on the next day Senegal become autonomous states within French Community.

19 DEC 1958
First radio broadcast from space: US President Dwight D. Eisenhower sends a Christmas message.

Great Leap Forward

12th January 1958 Chinese leader Mao Zedong announces plans for what he calls 'the Great Leap Forward' - a five-year plan to boost food production by relocating farmers into people's communes. It is a fiasco that has a catastrophic impact on food supplies and results in several years of famine and a death toll of more than 45 million.

Pasternak says no

29th October 1958 Russian novelist Boris Pasternak rejects the Nobel Prize for Literature. Under pressure in the Soviet Union for the anti-communist slant in his books and fearing for his family, he makes what he calls 'a voluntary refusal' to make the trip to Stockholm to accept the award.

General Charles de Gaulle

13th May 1958 General Charles de Gaulle becomes Prime Minister of France. One of the many challenges facing him is the rebellion of Algerian nationalists. Although prepared to grant independence, he must halt the slide towards civil war.

Khrushchev ups the ante

27th May 1958 Nikita Khrushchev issues an ultimatum to the western powers: vacate the US, British and French sectors of West Berlin by 27th May 1959 or the Soviet-controlled East German administration will move in.

The cassette is born

1st June 1958 US radio and recording corporation RCA reveal a portable cartridge-style tape recording system housed in plastic casing. It is the forerunner of the much smaller compact cassette that will become the industry standard in the 1970s.

Chip off the blocks

12th September 1958 US physicist Jack Kilby succeeds in combining electronic components with different functions on a slab of germanium to form the first integrated circuit. The microchip becomes an indispensable part of almost all modern technology.

NASA has lift-off

1st October 1958 The National Aeronautics and Space Administration (NASA) is inaugurated, replacing the National Advisory Committee for Aeronautics (NACA) as the agency overseeing space exploration in the US.

ENTERTAINMENT

Talk of the Town
The Talk of the Town opens in what was formerly the London Hippodrome in central London. A joint venture between impresario Bernard Delfont, producer Robert Nesbitt and hotelier Charles Forte, the Talk of the Town is a glamorous theatre-restaurant offering fine dining, three house bands, a spectacular floor show and a performance by an international star, of whom Eartha Kitt is the first.

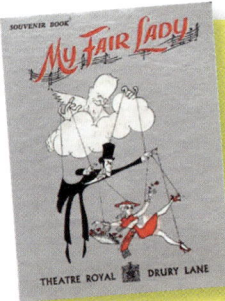

Loopy for hula hoops
American toy company Wham-O are really cashing in on circular-based toys. First the Frisbee in 1957 and in this year, it launches the hula hoop, named after the hip-swivelling Hawaiian dance. Britain goes crazy for the hula hoop with demonstrations, competitions and special hula hoop dance evenings.

My Fair Lady
Anticipation is high on the evening of 30th April as stars gather for the premiere of the Lerner & Loewe musical *My Fair Lady* at the Theatre Royal. Reprising their Broadway roles, Julie Andrews and Rex Harrison star as Eliza Doolittle and Professor Henry Higgins while Stanley Holloway is Eliza's grifting father, Alfred P. Doolittle. Reviews of the first night are unanimous in declaring *My Fair Lady* a triumph.

Chop suey and chips
Butlin's introduces exotic cuisine to its campers when it puts chop suey - with chips - on the menu at all of their holiday camps. Meaning 'bits and pieces', chop suey is a dish unknown in China, but it becomes a staple of Chinese takeaway menus in Britain.

Blue Peter
The very first edition of *Blue Peter* is broadcast on 16th October. Presented by former Miss Great Britain Leila Williams with Christopher Trace, it lasts just fifteen minutes and is only intended to run for six weeks but it will go on to become a British institution and the long-est-running children's programme in the world.

Sinking ship
A Night to Remember, a believable and sympathetic portrayal of the tragic sinking of RMS *Titanic*, based on the 1955 book by Walter Lord, is released on 3rd July starring Kenneth More, playing it calm as First Officer Lightoller. The film strives to be an authentic re-telling of the disaster. No expense is spared to achieve this, and the £600,000 budget makes it the most expensive British film ever made at the time.

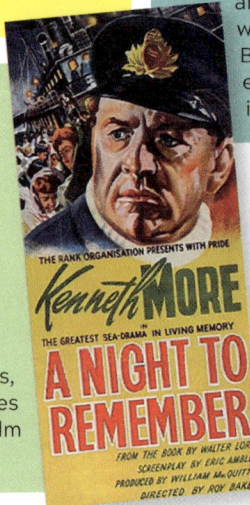

Good impression
Seven Impressionist paintings; two Cézannes, three Manets, a Van Gogh and a Renoir, from the collection of the late Jakob Goldschmidt, go on sale at Sotheby's in London on 15th October. The paintings sell in just 21 minutes for a total of £781,000, drawing applause from those present in the crowded saleroom.

The last curtsey

In a year when the very last debutantes go to Buckingham Palace for their court presentations, William Douglas-Home's play *The Reluctant Debutante* opens at the Cambridge Theatre in May. Starring Anna Massey who has herself been presented at court, it gently satirises the clichés of debutante life from pushy mothers to put-upon fathers. Vincente Minnelli also makes a film of *The Reluctant Debutante* this year, starring Rex Harrison and Kay Kendall.

Woman's Realm

The first issue of *Woman's Realm* magazine hits the shelves on 22nd February 1958. Among the articles in this debut issue is a knitting pattern for a teddy bear's scarf, ideas for decorating an austere bathroom, and potato printing to brighten up a book collection.

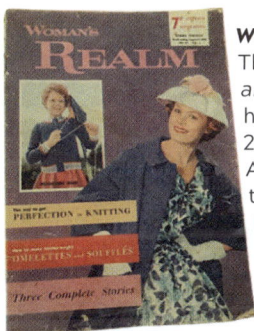

Dinky Toys

Dinky Toys made by Meccano of Binns Road, Liverpool are at the height of their popularity, with the range ever-expanding and including models of American and luxury British cars such as the Chrysler New Yorker Convertible and Aston Martin DB3S racer. In November this year, the company launch Dublo Dinky toys which are smaller in size and intended to integrate with its Hornby train sets.

Jets vs. Sharks

The entire Broadway cast of *West Side Story* is flown over for the UK staging of this ground-breaking new musical, which replaces the warring families of *Romeo and Juliet* with rival teenage gangs in New York's slums. *West Side Story* opens in Manchester on 14th November before moving to Her Majesty's Theatre in London on 12th December. The show is like no other musical, and thrills with its themes of violence and passion, staccato dialogue, a stunning score by Leonard Bernstein and its dramatic, rhythmic choreography by Jerome Robbins.

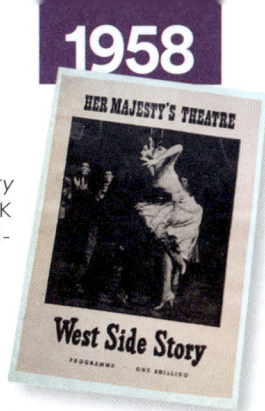

Coffee culture

The rising popularity of skiffle and jazz music during the 1950s coincides with the emergence of the teenager. New destinations open where this new demographic can meet, talk, hear music and dance. It leads to the growth of coffee bar culture in cities, with venues such as the Casbah Coffee Club in Liverpool, Cy Laurie's Jazz Club in Windmill Street, London or the tiny 2i's coffee bar in Soho's Old Compton Street where musical acts like Tommy Steele and Cliff Richard start out. At the 2i's there is no room to dance so teenagers instead hand-jive, as seen on the teenage TV show *Six-Five Special*.

Bell, Book and Candle

Witchcraft becomes cool in this sparkling film starring Kim Novak as Gillian, a bored, modern-day witch and owner of a primitive art shop, who deploys enchantment in order to seduce her nice, handsome neighbour played by James Stewart. With wonderfully witchy support from Elsa Lanchester and Hermione Gingold, *Bell, Book and Candle* is the inspiration for the 1960s hit comedy series, *Bewitched*. The Novak-Stewart partnership is on-screen again this year in Alfred Hitchcock's *Vertigo*.

HER MAJESTY'S THEATRE

West Side Story

PROGRAMME ONE SHILLING

What a Carry On

The first in what would become 31 *Carry On* films, *Carry on Sergeant* is released, with William Hartnell, Bob Monkhouse and Shirley Eaton in this comic caper about National Service. The film is the third most successful this year and when another film using the same prefix, *Carry On Nurse*, enjoys similar success in 1959, the classic, cheeky British comedy series is born.

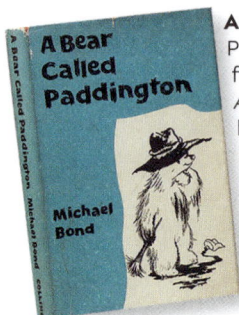

A Bear from Darkest Peru

Paddington Bear appears for the first time when *A Bear Called Paddington* by Michael Bond is published on 13th October. Bond was inspired to write the story after finding a lone bear on a shelf in a shop on Christmas Eve, 1956. He bought the bear for his wife. The label worn by Paddington and his small suitcase referenced the refugees and evacuees Bond remembered from the war.

Back in the USSR

The Associated Rediffusion documentary *USSR Now*, a non-political survey of the people and culture around the USSR, directed and presented by Michael Ingrams and produced by Caryl Doncaster, is shown on 28th January, and takes British television cameras further into Russia than the Kremlin has ever previously allowed.

A perfect read!

The Darling Buds of May, a novella by H. E. Bates, is published by Penguin Books in July. Bates's joyful tale of the boisterous Larkin family, living hand-to-mouth in the most extravagant way in rural Kent charms readers and makes a literary hero out of the flirtatious, wheeling-dealing, tax-evading champion of free enterprise, Pop Larkin.

MUSIC

Last days of the 78

Slowly but surely, those big and very breakable 78rpm records are being phased out by Britain's record companies. The medium of choice is now the much more user-friendly 45 rpm vinyl disc, first piloted by RCA in the US in 1951. This year, for the first time, many UK-made records are being released only as 45s, though it will be 1960 before 78s are abandoned altogether.

Domenico at the double

1st February 1958 There are two major song contests in Europe - the Sanremo Festival in Italy and the Eurovision Song Contest. Now singer-composer Domenico Modugno has achieved a remarkable double by winning both contests with the same song, *Nel blu, dipintu di blu* - or, as it is soon becomes much better known, *Volare*. It's a real chest-beater of a song, a surprise US No. 1 and is soon adopted as an international football chant.

Elvis joins the Army

24th March 1957 Elvis Presley is inducted into the US Army and is immediately subjected to a military-style haircut. After weeks of army training, Elvis is shipped off to Germany on the USS *General George M. Randall*. Elvis proves an exemplary soldier but his spell in the Army is troubled by homesickness and grief following the death of his mother in August.

Connie calls the tune

16th May 1958 The biggest new American star of the year is Connie Francis - Concetta Rosa Maria Franconero to give her full name - who now sits at No. 1 in the UK with a revival of 1920s tune *Who's Sorry Now*, her father's favourite song. Another discovery from Arthur Godfrey's talent-spotting TV show.

Buddy in Britain

20th March 1958 Halfway through a UK tour are Buddy Holly and the Crickets, with a young comedian named Des O'Connor compering. Tonight they're in Liverpool, playing two shows at the Philharmonic Hall. This is Buddy's first and only visit to Britain, culminating in a spot on *Sunday Night at the London Palladium*.

Jerry Lee faces the press

22nd May 1958 With red-hot piano stompers like *A Whole Lotta Shakin' Goin' On* and *Great Balls of Fire* to his name, Jerry Lee Lewis is another huge talent from Sun Records and without doubt rock'n'roll's hottest property after Elvis. But today, on the first day of his tour of the UK, his career suddenly falls apart as he introduces Myra, his new bride, to the British press. The trouble is that Myra is just thirteen and is his cousin. Instant scandal erupts, MPs call for his deportation, and the tour ends in chaos.

A first for John, Paul and George

12th July 1958 Still known as the Quarrymen, John Lennon, Paul McCartney and George Harrison pool their money and make their first record together in a tiny studio in Liverpool. With acquaintances Colin Hanton and John Lowe, they record a 78rpm disc of Buddy Holly's *That'll Be The Day* and a song that Paul and George have composed together, *In Spite of All the Danger*.

Too sexy for television?

24th July 1958 Entering the EMI recording studios for the first time is eighteen year-old Harry Webb, who works for Atlas Bulbs in Enfield but has designs on a rock'n'roll career. Having put together a backing band called the Drifters with two guitarists, Hank Marvin and Bruce Welch, he is now working under the stage name of Cliff Richard. Six weeks later he makes his television debut on *Oh Boy!*, where the show's producer Jack Good instructs him to shave his sideburns and adopt a sultry sneer. Good has told Columbia, Cliff's record label, that he can't come on the show unless he sings the flipside *Move It* rather than the rather drippy top side, *Schoolboy Crush*. *Move It* is indeed the best rock'n'roll record yet made in Britain and climbs to No. 2 in the chart. A few days after the broadcast, the *Daily Mirror* asks 'Is this boy too sexy for television?'

Boone's book

3rd November 1958 Starring in the Royal Variety Performance is Pat Boone, who has just published a guide to clean living for teenagers called *Twixt Twelve and Twenty*. Boone started his career making limp cover versions of Fats Domino and Little Richard rock songs but is now settling into a ballad-singing groove with which he is much more comfortable.

Ralph Vaughan Williams dies

26th August 1958 Ralph Vaughan Williams dies at the age of 85. Composer of choral and orchestral works and many of our best-known hymns, he was also a pioneer collector of English folk songs.

Who's Rockingham?

28th November 1958 Fast-paced, colourful, funny and filmed with a raucous live audience, ITV's new rock'n'roll show *Oh Boy!* is a show that understands rock'n'roll. The show's house band, Lord Rockingham's X1, even have a No. 1 hit of their own with *Hoots Mon* - a rocked-up version of the traditional Scottish tune *A Hundred Pipers*.

SPORT

Hawthorn killed
22nd January 1959 Just three months after retiring from motor racing, reigning Formula One world champion Mike Hawthorn dies in a car crash near Guildford.

The Truman show
5th May 1959 Just months after sensationally beating Althea Gibson of the US in the Wightman Cup, eighteen-year-old British tennis star Christine Truman wins her first and only Grand Slam at the French Open. She defeats defending champion Zsuzsa Kormockzy of Hungary in straight sets and achieves the highest ranking of her career as world No. 2. Weeks later she reaches the Wimbledon final but is defeated by Maria Bueno. Admired for her relentless attacking play, Christine remains a top player for the next decade.

The magnificent Beryl
26th July 1959 The greatest female athlete in cycling history, Leeds-born Beryl Burton wins the first of five world championships in the individual pursuit in Liege, Belgium. Having overcome severe paralysis in her early teens, Beryl's story is inspirational, encompassing an eventual 96 national championships in time trialling, track pursuit and road racing, the breaking of both the men's and women's twelve-hour time record, and winning the Britain's Best All-Rounder competition for 25 consecutive years.

Elton at Wembley
2nd May 1959 The FA Cup Final pairs two hard-working but unfashionable clubs making their first appearances at Wembley. Nottingham Forest defeat Luton Town 2-1 despite the scorer of their opening goal, Roy Dwight, breaking a leg. Watching the BBC's coverage at home is Roy's piano-playing cousin Reg, ten years before his name change to Elton John.

Billy Wright retires
25th April 1959 England captain Billy Wright retires from football after guiding Wolverhampton Wanderers to a third league championship in six years. Since debuting for Wolves in 1946, he has made 500 appearances for his club and has amassed a record-breaking 105 England caps.

3 JAN 1959

Alaska joins the US as its 49th state.

1 FEB 1959

Swiss men vote against voting rights for women.

2 MAR 1959

A ceremony marks the start of the construction of the Sydney Opera House.

DOMESTIC
NEWS

Fog chaos!
29th January 1959 Dense fog causes chaos across the country as roads, train lines and airports are closed. Focused on London, the problem extends across the Midlands, East Anglia, the South of England and parts of Wales, with visibility reduced to only a few metres in places.

CND March!
30th March 1959 The Campaign for Nuclear Disarmament organise their first major march from the Atomic Weapons Establishment in Aldermaston to London. Setting off on the 27th, the march culminates in a rally in Trafalgar Square, and is attended by approximately 60,000 people.

Iceland fires on Brits
30th April 1959 The First Cod War between Britain and Iceland heats up as an Icelandic vessel, *Thor*, fires what appear to be warning shots at a British trawler entering disputed waters. The trawler is pursued by *Thor*, before HMS *Conquest* is deployed to the area and drives the Icelandic vessel off. The disputes will continue well into the 1970s.

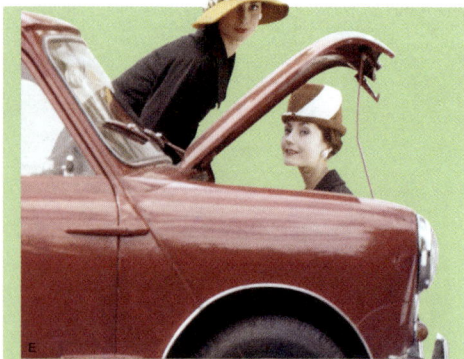

Make it Mini
8th May 1959 The very first Mini Cooper rolls off the production line ahead of its official launch in August. The British Motor Corporation's iconic vehicle is ten feet long, with two doors, and a top speed of 70 miles per hour. It is designed to carry a driver and three passengers, although the leg room available is famously extremely limited!

Places get postcodes
28th July 1959 An experiment is launched in the City of Norwich to introduce modern postcodes. In use in some areas, such as London, since the 19th century, the new postcodes stick to a simple formula, and are soon rolled out nationwide.

Auchengeich mining disaster
18th September 1959 47 men are killed at Auchengeich near the village of Moodiesburn when an electrical fault in a colliery fan catches fire. The colliery is flooded with toxic smoke, and later with water to extinguish the fire, leaving only one survivor.

2 APR 1959
Seven US astronauts are selected for Mercury space programme.

24 MAY 1959
Death of US Secretary of State John Foster Dulles.

11 JUN 1959
D. H. Lawrence novel *Lady Chatterley's Lover* is banned in US.

Southend pier fire
7th October 1959 Hundreds of people are trapped as a pavilion on Southend's pier catches fire. The 1.5-mile pier is home to its own railway, which stops due to the blaze, forcing tourists trapped by the fire to climb down into boats which bring them ashore.

Airports go duty-free
17th November 1959 Duty-free shopping is introduced for the first time at Prestwick and Renfrew Airports in the UK after the concept was introduced at Shannon Airport in Ireland in 1947 by Brendan O'Regan. Shoppers can now purchase items free of local taxes and duties if they are bringing them home from their travels.

Bush TR82 Radio
Bush launch their iconic TR82 Transistor Radio featuring Ogle Design. The portability of these radios, and their edgy design, sees them become enormously popular in the 1960s as the rise of popular music sees more and more time spent huddled around the radio.

ROYALTY & POLITICS

A television first
8th September 1959 Prior to visiting France and West Germany, President Eisenhower visits the UK for talks with Harold Macmillan. During the trip, he and Macmillan share a remarkable first when they give a joint live television broadcast in which they exchange pleasantries, reminisce, and discuss the problems currently facing the world.

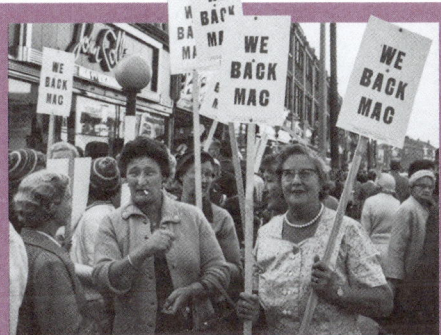

Conservatives retain power
8th October 1959 The Conservatives win the general election for a third successive time and increase their majority to 100 seats. It is a personal triumph for Harold Macmillan and, because of the size of the defeat, an unexpected threat to Hugh Gaitskell's leadership of the Labour Party. Among the new MPs entering the House of Commons are future Prime Minister Margaret Thatcher and future Liberal Party leader Jeremy Thorpe.

8 JUL 1959
First deaths of US military personnel in Vietnam,

7 AUG 1959
The Explorer 6 transmits the first photo of Earth from space.

16 SEP 1959
French President Charles de Gaulle announces proposals for Algerian independence.

The Queen expects

8th August 1959 Buckingham Palace announces that 'the Queen will undertake no further public engagements', which is royal code for saying that she is pregnant with her third child. Royal etiquette dictates that the monarch should not be seen to be carrying a child. The Queen will give birth to Prince Andrew on 19th February 1960.

Princess Margaret is engaged

11th October 1959 Although it will not be announced officially until February, Princess Margaret accepts a proposal of marriage from the society photographer Antony Armstrong-Jones.

FOREIGN NEWS

Revolution in Cuba

1st January 1959 Having defeated the 10,000-strong force of Cuban dictator Fulgencio Batista in May 1958, guerrilla forces under Fidel Castro, Che Guevara and Camilo Cienfuegos head for the capital Havana. Batista flees the country and surrenders. The next day, Guevara and Cienfuegos enter Havana, followed by Fidel Castro six days later. Castro, who becomes President a month later, advocates friendship with the US in his first speeches. Rebuffed by the Eisenhower administration, he will begin transforming Cuba into a communist state.

Leopoldville riots

4th January 1959 The campaign for independence in the Belgian Congo takes a new turn as riots break out in Leopoldville (latter-day Kinshasa) leaving at least 49 dead. The rioting triggers a rush for independence, which Belgium grants in June 1960.

Race for space

The space race between the superpowers is now in full swing. Early in 1959, the Soviets launch Luna 1, the first object to fly past the Moon while the US trains astronauts for its first manned space mission. During May, a US Jupiter rocket launches two primates into space who become the first living creatures to return safely to Earth.

12-14 СЕНТЯБРЯ 1959 СССР

14 OCT 1959
Death of swashbuckling actor Errol Flynn, aged 50.

2 NOV 1959
First section of the M1, the first British motorway, is opened to traffic.

1 DEC 1959
USSR and western nations sign treaty to leave Antarctica as a wilderness.

Barbie's world
9th March 1959 The first Barbie dolls, a blonde and a brunette, are exhibited at the International Toy Fair in New York City. Ruth Handler, co-founder of toy manufacturer Mattel, adapts an existing German design to create an adult dress-up doll inspired by her daughter Barbara's pleasure in dressing up cardboard dolls. Named after her, Barbie is one of the most successful toys of the century. Two years later, a male doll is launched as Barbie's companion and named after Ruth's son Kenneth.

An independent Cyprus
14th December 1959 After Cyprus is granted independence from the UK in August, Greek Cypriot leader Archbishop Makarios is elected President.

Parkas on sale
Originating in Inuit culture, the parka is introduced as part of US Army wear during the Korean war in a version made of nylon with a quilted lining and a fur-trimmed hood. Known as the fishtail parka, it is popularised through sales in army surplus outlets.

Lycra is launched
The enduring search for a replacement for rubber is partly resolved with the invention of spandex by a scientist named Joseph Shivers at US chemical company DuPont. A tough, elastic and heat-resistant synthetic fibre, it is launched as Lycra in Europe in 1959.

ENTERTAINMENT

Ho Chi Minh Trail
26th September 1959 The Viet Cong, as the US calls the National Front for the Liberation of South Vietnam, begins military action as the government of Ho Chi Minh (photo) is building roads through North Vietnam, Laos and Cambodia to South Vietnam - the so-called Ho Chi Minh Trail - to supply the army and the Viet Cong.

Dalai Lama
18th April 1959 The Dalai Lama flees to India when the invading Chinese bomb his palace in Tibet. In India, the refugee Tibetans are allowed to build houses, schools, hospitals and monasteries and so retain Tibetan traditions. From his hiding place the Dalai Lama grows into a spiritual leader of global importance.

Jukebox Jury
Jukebox Jury, hosted by David Jacobs, airs on the BBC on 1st June. Each episode, Jacobs plays a short excerpt from a selection of 7-inch singles to a panel of four celebrities who discuss and ultimately decide if a song is hit or miss. The first show's panel includes DJ Pete Murray and singing star Alma Cogan; later, panellists such as the Beatles and the Rolling Stones help *Jukebox Jury*'s viewing figures hit more than twelve million.

Swashbuckling blunders

ITV's Crusades-era adventure series, *Ivanhoe*, starring Roger Moore with a fabulously bouffant quiff, comes to an end when Moore returns to Hollywood, although ITV continues to repeat the 39 episodes. Moore had insisted on carrying out many of the stunts himself and suffered several injuries during filming; three cracked ribs as a result of a fight scene, and he was knocked out when a battleaxe fell on his head (fortunately he was wearing a helmet at the time).

Roger Moore "Ivanhoe"

Avon calling

Pioneering beauty company launch in the UK. Their door-to-door saleswomen are known for visitations where on ringing the doorbell 'Ding-dong' they would call out, 'Avon calling'.

Carry on Teacher

Just six months after *Carry On Nurse* is in cinemas, the Carry On franchise wastes no time in bringing out a third film, *Carry on Teacher*, with Kenneth Connor, Hattie Jacques, Leslie Phillips and Joan Sims among the 'expert gagsters' in what the *Daily Mirror* describes as a 'load of golden, corny laughter'!

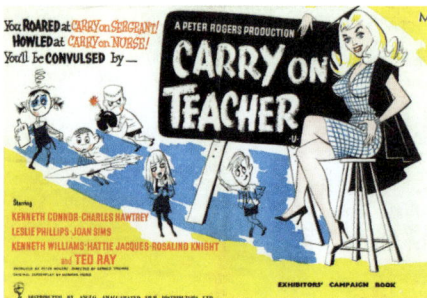

BIRDS EYE ®

Arctic rollout

Ernest Velden, a Jewish lawyer from Czechoslovakia, sets up the Birds Eye factory in Eastbourne which produces the Arctic roll - a swiss roll-style dessert with an ice cream centre. Capable of producing a staggering 17 million Arctic rolls a year, it is estimated that by the 1980s, twenty-five miles of this nostalgic dessert is being consumed by the British public every month.

Colour *Bonanza*

Bonanza, the TV series about the Cartwright ranching family, and their sprawling Ponderosa ranch in Nevada, airs its first episode on NBC on 12th September, runs for fourteen seasons and is credited with encouraging Americans to invest in colour television sets. The show is first broadcast in Britain on 8th April 1961 and at its peak enjoys a global audience of 400 million. It makes stars of its cast, particularly Michael Landon who plays Joseph 'Little Joe' Cartwright.

Bread ahead

Low-calorie food range Slimcea is introduced by Procea Products with a light-as-air bread as its flagship product. Advertised with the line, 'Show them you're a Slimcea girl' the bread becomes a rival to Hovis's lo-cal loaf Nimble (launched 1955). Nimble uses the metaphorically apt hot-air balloon in its commercials, but both brands do well as women battle to squeeze into the wasp-waisted fashions of the late fifties.

Hot Summer Night

The *Armchair Theatre* play, *Hot Summer Night*, features the first interracial kiss on television, between Andree Melly and Jamaican-born actor Lloyd Reckord. Reckord forms the New Day Theatre Company, which performs at the Royal Court theatre the following year but in one interview insists it must be 'a company for actors of all races.'

Journey to the Centre of the Earth

For true authenticity, the 1959 movie adaptation of Jules Verne's science fiction adventure story is filmed in the stunning Carlsbad Caverns of New Mexico, thought to be the lowest point beneath the surface of the Earth. Working 1,100 feet under-ground and at night so that the caverns' tourism business would be uninterrupted, James Mason heads the cast as Edinburgh professor, Oliver Lindenbrook, who leads an expedition to the Earth's core via a vol-cano after finding a message in a piece of volcanic rock. Among the extraordinary wonders Lindenbrook and his party encounter on their adventure are a mushroom forest, the city of Atlantis and gargantuan chameleons with twenty-foot tongues! Pop singer and heartthrob Pat Boone co-stars and is the obvious choice to sing the film's soundtrack.

Sing Something Simple

'Songs simply sung for song-lovers' is how the *Radio Times* describes this half-hour show which is broadcast on the BBC Light Programme for the first time on 3rd July. Listeners can enjoy Cliff Adams and the Adams Singers, accompanied by Jack Emblow on the accordion, with numbers such as *Drifting and Dreaming* and *Sweet Rosie O'Grady*. The show runs for 42 years until 2001, making it the longest-running continuous music programme in the world.

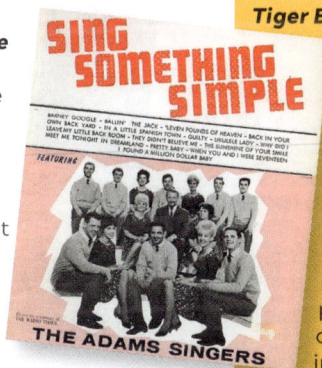

Tiger Bay

Twelve-year-old Hayley Mills makes her screen debut in this beautifully shot thriller set against the decaying industrial backdrop of Cardiff's Tiger Bay. Mills' character, an orphaned young girl, witnesses a murder and befriends the Polish sailor who commits the act; her father, John Mills, plays the police inspector in pursuit. With its glimpses of street culture and multi-racial community in Cardiff, the film paves the way for the social realism adopted by many British film makers in the early 1960s.

DO YOU REMEMBER THIS?

Dip pen

Lenny the Lion

Lenny's Den, the latest programme featuring the lion with a lisp, Lenny, worked by ventriloquist Terry Hall, starts on Sunday 18th October. Lenny, whose catchphrase is 'Aw, don't embawass me', is one of the first non-'human' ventriloquists' dummies, and he's fashioned out of fox fur and papier-mâché. Even though Lenny is one of the hardest-working stars in showbusiness, the puppet only has to be remade once.

Ben-Hur

MGM is in serious financial difficulties when it embarks on making the William Wyler-directed Roman epic, *Ben-Hur* and they have to speculate before they can accumulate; the famous chariot race scene alone costs a staggering one million pounds. The gamble pays off and when *Ben-Hur* is released in cinemas, the public flock to see this action-packed, no-expense-spared Roman epic. *Ben-Hur* wins a record-breaking eleven Academy Awards at the Oscars the following year.

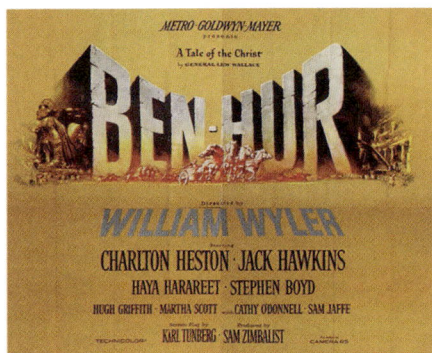

What a drag

Some Like it Hot, Tony Curtis and Jack Lemmon give brilliant turns as jazz musicians on the run from the Mob who drag up to join an all-girl band. But they are just one aspect of Billy Wilder's joyous comedy, which goes on to be voted American Film Institute Best Comedy of All Time. Marilyn Monroe, as singer Sugar Kane, is at her vulnerable, enchanting best.

MUSIC

The day the music died

3rd February 1959 On the day commemorated in Don McLean's *American Pie* as 'the day the music died', tragedy strikes just outside Mason City, Iowa. Buddy Holly, Ritchie Valens and J. P. Richardson (known as the Big Bopper) are killed when their light aircraft crashes after take-off in the middle of a winter tour of America's mid-west states.

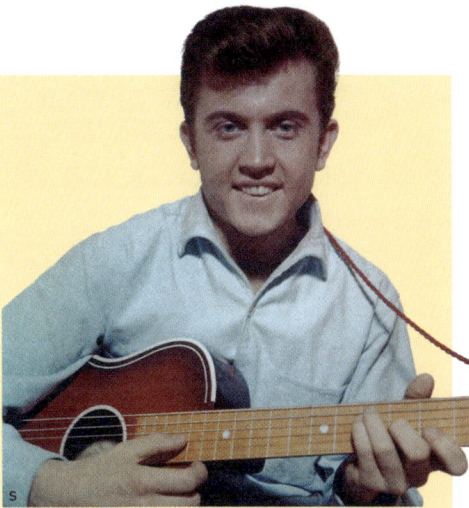

Terry in trouble

3rd March 1959 Although one of the better British rock'n'roll singers, Terry Dene has had a troubled time dealing with stardom. Arrests for vandalism and marriage problems have given him a bad-boy image. Called up for National Service in a blaze of publicity, he has now been discharged from the Army as 'mentally unfit', provoking questions in Parliament and an avalanche of hatred from the press. Within a few years Terry disappears completely, his story a salutary lesson in how not to handle fame.

Lady Day departs

17th July 1959 The greatest jazz voice of them all, Billie Holiday, is found dead in New York at the age of 44. She had cirrhosis of the liver complicated by her long-term drug addiction. Nicknamed 'Lady Day', Billie struggled with abuse.

Mourning Mario

7th October 1959 Having entered a Rome clinic for tests just days before, Mario Lanza dies suddenly from a heart attack aged 38. Rumours will persist for years regarding possible Mafia involvement in his death. His grief-stricken wife Betty dies from a drug overdose just five months later.

Kind of Blue

17th August 1959 Jazz takes a giant leap forward with the release of *Kind of Blue* by Miles Davis, which sells over five million albums without making any compromises towards a more commercial sound. Opening with the mesmeric *So What*, it has a tang of sophistication and danger that is the essence of contemporary New York.

A solid second

11th March 1959 The fourth Eurovision Song Contest takes place in Cannes. Having declined to take part in 1958, the BBC is pinning its hopes on *Sing Little Birdie* sung by husband and wife duo Teddy Johnson and Pearl Carr. Their song comes a solid second to the Netherlands' entry *Een beetje*, sung by Teddy Scholten.

Frankie goes to Hollywood

America is the holy grail for UK performers. The latest to try making it there is the high-kicking Frankie Vaughan, whose visit starts well with rave reviews for shows in Las Vegas and New York. He even stars in *Let's Make Love*, a musical with Marilyn Monroe, but the Hollywood experience leaves him rattled and yearning for home. Evading Marilyn's advances and forsaking the American dream, he switches his focus back to the UK.

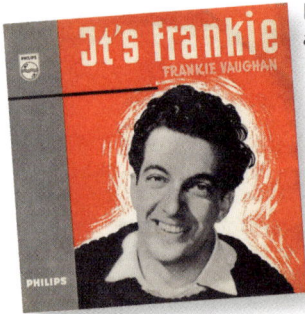

MY FIRST 18 YEARS

TOP10 1959

1. **A Fool Such as I** *Elvis Presley*
2. **It Doesn't Matter Anymore** *Buddy Holly*
3. **Til I Kissed You** *Everly Brothers*
4. **Only Sixteen** *Sam Cooke*
5. **The Three Bells** *The Browns*
6. **Sea of Love** *Marty Wilde*
7. **Petite Fleur** *Chris Barber Band*
8. **Chantilly Lace** *The Big Bopper*
9. **What'd I say** *Ray Charles*
10. **Mack the Knife** *Bobby Darin*

Open | Search | Scan

Tommy and Cliff move on

The first two superstars of British rock'n'roll are starting to leave the rock sound behind. Having played himself in the movie *The Tommy Steele Story*, Tommy Steele is focusing more on family-friendly songs like Lionel Bart's *A Handful of Songs* and *Little White Bull*. Cliff Richard is edging towards a softer, more countrified sound with *Living Doll*, which Bart wrote for *Serious Charge* (Cliff's debut film) but Cliff has now re-recorded in a gentler style. The shift in tone works: the record is his first No. 1, a global million seller and provides the template for such mid-tempo fare as *Travellin' Light* and *Please Don't Tease*.

Sellers takes aim

Offering the last word on popular music in 1959, Peter Sellers makes one of the funniest comedy albums ever. Sellers takes aim at Frank Sinatra, Lonnie Donegan, *My Fair Lady* and much more with brilliant impersonations and merciless parody. Produced by George Martin, *Songs for Swingin' Sellers* also has the most macabre cover of the year - a waist-down view of a body hanging from a tree.

What'd he say?

Blind singer-pianist Ray Charles shows what happens when you mix the sensuality of the blues with the ecstatic energy of gospel music. His freewheeling *What'd I Say* is an epic blend of vocals, piano and big-band blast that takes up two sides of a 45 and sends black music to a whole new level.

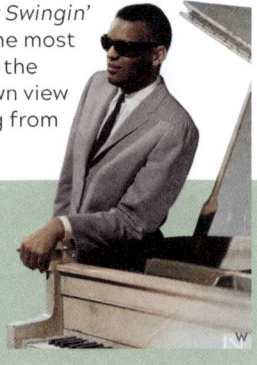

SPORT

Burnley are champions

30th April 1960 In one of the tightest finishes to the First Division ever, Burnley snatch the championship from Wolverhampton Wanderers by one point on the last day of the season, so spoiling the latter's dreams of winning the elusive league and FA Cup 'double'.

A troubled tour

9th June - 23rd August 1960 South Africa's impending cricket tour of England has been in doubt due to growing feeling against the country's apartheid policy, especially after the Sharpeville massacre in March. Should England be playing against a side that excludes black players? There are demonstrations at the grounds but the tour goes ahead and results in a 3-0 series win for England with two matches drawn.

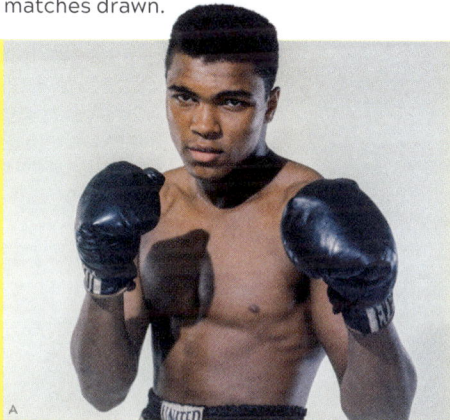

Arnold at the Open

6th - 9th July 1960 Having won both the US Masters and US Open titles earlier in the year, the charismatic and modest-mannered American golfer Arnold Palmer competes in the British Open for the first time, finishing as runner-up to Australian Kel Nagle by a single shot. He will make a winning return to the Open in 1961 and 1962.

A ten-goal spectacular

18th May 1960 Hampden Park in Glasgow is the venue for one of the most memorable football matches of all time. Real Madrid defeat Eintracht Frankfurt 7-3 in the final of the European Cup in front of a crowd of 127,000.

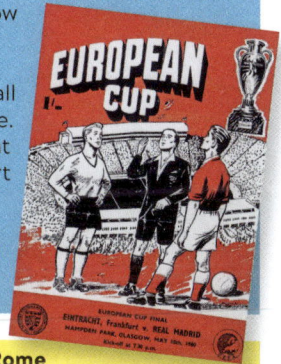

All roads lead to Rome

25th August - 11th September 1960 In the seventeenth Olympic Games of the modern era, held in Rome, the Great Britain team again achieves only a modest tally of medals - two gold, six silver and twelve bronze. Among the most indelible memories of the Games are Herb Elliott of Australia annihilating the field in the 1500 metres; the young Cassius Clay (later Muhammad Ali) almost dancing to gold for the US in the light heavyweight division of the boxing; and gold medallist Abebe Bikila of Ethiopia running the marathon barefoot and becoming the first black African champion in Olympic history.

29 JAN 1960	1 FEB 1960	22 MAR 1960
French settlers in Algeria begin rebellion against independence.	Civil rights sit-in begins at a lunch counter in Greensboro, North Carolina.	First patent for lasers is granted.

DOMESTIC NEWS

Dr. Martens hit the street

1st April 1960 The iconic Dr. Martens 'AirWair' style 1460 boots are marketed for the first time in the UK. Having bought the patent, the R Griggs Group in Northamptonshire begins producing a smooth cherry-red boot with distinctive yellow stitching. The boots soon become synonymous with counter-culture movements like punk, new wave, and grunge, and remain popular to this day.

European free trade

4th January 1960 The Stockholm Convention is signed to create the European Free Trade Association, with Britain as a founder member. The Association involves seven countries; Austria, Denmark, Norway, Portugal, Sweden, Switzerland, and the UK, all of whom are unable or unwilling to join the European Economic Community, the forerunner of the European Union.

Independence for many

Several countries gain independence from the British in 1960, including British Somaliland on 26th June, Cyprus on 16th August, and Nigeria on 1st October.

Miners killed at Six Bells

28th June 1960 An explosion of firedamp at the Six Bells Colliery in Monmouthshire kills 45 of the 48 men on duty. Maintenance work taking place within the colliery meant that less than half of the 125 usual employees were on duty, avoiding a far greater death toll.

Whisky fire kills 19

28th March 1960 A fire breaks out at a warehouse in Glasgow's Cheapside Street. The warehouse holds over a million gallons of whisky and 30,000 gallons of rum, and as brave firemen and salvage corps personnel battle the flames, an explosion destroys the building. The fire claims the lives of 19 men, making this Britain's fire services' worst peacetime disaster.

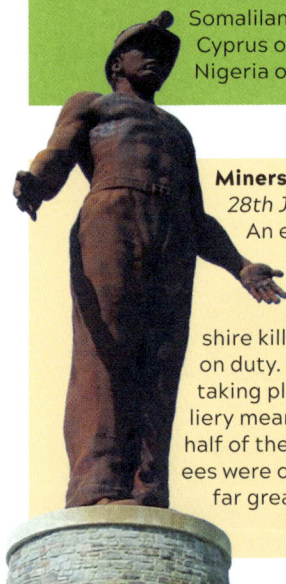

Sheerness Dockyard closes

31st March 1960 The closing ceremony at the Sheerness Dockyard takes place, ending almost 300 years of naval history on the Isle of Sheppey and the loss of 2,500 jobs associated with the dockyards.

1 APR 1960

World's first weather satellite launched from Cape Canaveral.

7 MAY 1960

Brezhnev replaces Voroshilov as President of USSR.

8 JUN 1960

Argentine government demands that Israel release Adolf Eichmann.

Britain gets binbags

1st November 1960 Black plastic binbags for the disposal of household waste are introduced for the first time in Hitchin, Hertfordshire. This new product, developed by Imperial Chemical Industries, soon becomes a standard household item across the country.

Last man conscripted

31st December 1960 National Service, in place since 1949, finally comes to an end, with the last call ups taking place in November. The last young men to enter National Service will remain in the programme until 1963.

The Lady Chatterley trial

2nd November 1960 Penguin Books is found not guilty under the Obscene Publications Act, after publishing the full, uncensored version of *Lady Chatterley's Lover* by D. H. Lawrence. During the trial, Penguin Books successfully argues that despite the book containing obscene passages, the literary value of the novel is such that censorship is not in the public's best interest.

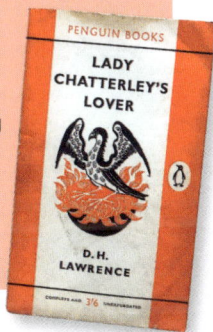

Traffic wardens deployed

15th September 1960 Two years after getting its first parking meters, the capital welcomes its first traffic wardens. The wardens are the brainchild of Athelstan Popkiss, Chief Constable of Nottingham City Police.

ROYALTY & POLITICS

Goodbye to the farthing

31st December 1960 The farthing, a feature of British purses since 1707 and English purses since the 13th century, finally ceases to be legal tender. Whilst still usable in the Falklands and British Antarctica, this familiar coin leaves British pockets for good from 1961 onwards.

Place your bets

1st September 1960 The Betting and Gaming Act is passed by Parliament, enabling betting shops and bingo venues to operate under licence from local councils. It also aims to stamp out illegal gambling by banning the use of 'runners' by bookmakers to collect money from punters. The measures help change the face of the average British high street and accelerate the conversion of loss-making cinemas into revenue-earning bingo halls.

1 JUL 1960

Granting of Belgian Congo independence sparks civil war.

1 AUG 1960

Aretha Franklin's first recording for Columbia Records.

30 SEP 1960

The Flintstones created by Hanna-Barbera premieres in the US.

Wind of change

3rd February 1960 Prime Minister Harold Macmillan makes a speech in the South African parliament calling on the country to recognise what he calls 'a wind of change' sweeping through Africa. Macmillan and his Colonial Secretary Iain Macleod have adopted a policy of preparing British colonies for independence while South Africa has been tightening apartheid and the machinery of white rule. His speech contributes to the South African decision to declare itself a republic and leave the Commonwealth in 1961.

Prince Andrew is born

19th February 1960 The Queen gives birth to her third child, Andrew Albert Christian Edward, at Buckingham Palace. This is the first time in 103 years that a child has been born to a reigning monarch.

Margaret and Tony wed

6th May 1960 After a six-week official engagement that surprises even the most seasoned royal watchers, Princess Margaret marries Antony Armstrong-Jones at Westminster Abbey.

Nye Bevan dies

6th July 1960 Aneurin 'Nye' Bevan dies of stomach cancer at the age of 62. Elected to Parliament for Ebbw Vale in 1928, Bevan was a key player in Clement Attlee's post-war Labour government, where as Minister of Health he oversaw the launch of the National Health Service.

Gaitskell retains leadership

3rd November 1960 After a fractious Labour Party conference, Labour's Hugh Gaitskell sees off a leadership challenge from Harold Wilson. He wins the ballot of Labour MPs by 166 votes to 81.

17 OCT 1960	14 NOV 1960	31 DEC 1960
News Chronicle newspaper closes after 30 years.	Belgium threatens to leave the UN due to criticism of its policy in Congo.	Compulsory National Service (conscription) ends in UK.

Kenyan emergency ends

12th January 1960 The seven-year state of emergency in Kenya is finally ended as the British colony prepares for independence. Those years have seen vicious fighting between UK forces and the Mau Mau or Kenya Land and Freedom Army, with war crimes committed on both sides.

El Guerrillero Heroico

5th March 1960 At a memorial service for the victims of an explosion on the cargo ship *La Coubre*, Alberto Korda takes the iconic photo of revolutionary leader Che Guevara. *El Guerrillero Heroico* becomes one of the most famous symbols of the 1960s, the portrait appearing on posters and T-shirts across the world.

Under the sea

23rd January 1960 Oceanographers Jacques Piccard and Don Walsh make a deep dive into the Mariana Trench in the Pacific Ocean. After almost five hours, during which a porthole cracks and their bathyscaphe almost collapses under the high pressure, they reach a depth of 10,916 metres, the deepest point ever reached by man.

Sharpeville massacre

21st March 1960 South African police fire indiscriminately into a crowd of unarmed black protesters in the Sharpeville township. Within a week the South African government declares a state of emergency and arrests 18,000 people including the young Nelson Mandela. The scale of the massacre sends shock waves across Africa and moves the anti-apartheid movement in the country towards armed resistance.

Eichmann is captured

11th May 1960 The Israeli secret service Mossad carries out an undercover operation in the Argentine capital Buenos Aires, where they kidnap the high ranking Nazi official Adolf Eichmann and smuggle him to Israel. Eichmann was responsible for the deportation of millions of Jews to concentration camps during the Second World War. A trial for his crimes awaits Eichmann in Israel in 1962.

Congo crisis begins
30th June 1960 The Belgian Congo receives its independence and is from now known as the Republic of the Congo. The country is unprepared for the huge political and social changes and an army mutiny and a bitter, prolonged civil war follow.

Spy plane shot down
1st May 1960 US pilot Gary Powers is flying over the Soviet Union to secretly photograph military installations when his U-2 plane is shot down by a Russian missile. Powers ejects but is captured and given a ten-year sentence for espionage during July.

Kennedy is President
8th November 1960 Democratic presidential candidate John Fitzgerald Kennedy defeats Republican Vice President Richard Nixon by a tiny margin. At 43 years old, Kennedy is the youngest US President in history and the first Roman Catholic.

Three billion people
The world population exceeds three billion, having almost doubled since 1900. In the coming years the population will grow much faster, especially in Asia and Africa.

ENTERTAINMENT

Quick on the Draw
Etch-a-Sketch, a drawing toy which allows children to doodle, erase and doodle again, is launched in the US. Requiring no ink, no mess and no batteries, knobs are used to move a stylus which pushes aluminium powder behind a screen, forming lines to make pictures.

Millions watch Cliff 'Move It'
Hosted by Bruce Forsyth, *Sunday Night at the Palladium* is already essential family viewing each weekend, but in January 1960, when Cliff Richard & the Shadows are on the bill, the programme attracts an incredible twenty million viewers.

New BBC HQ

The BBC opens its big, shiny, brand new Television Centre at White City in west London on 29th June 1960, the third such purpose-built television headquarters in the world. It was designed by Graham Dawbarn with a distinctive, circular main block (known as the 'doughnut'). For those who spend time watching BBC children's television over the next forty years, the building's postcode - W12 8QT - will become imprinted on their memory.

Nan reads the news

Nan Winton (right), a journalist and continuity announcer, is put in front of the camera and becomes the first female newsreader to present the national news for the BBC. She is not actually the first in television; Barbara Mandall had read the news for ITN in 1955, and unfortunately Winton's new role is short-lived. An audience survey apparently reveals that viewers feel a woman reading the news is 'not acceptable'.

And they're off

Aintree's Grand National is televised for the first time on 26th March and is won by the favourite Merryman II. Sixteen cameras are used and commentators Peter O'Sullevan and Peter Bromley survey the race from a somewhat rickety tower constructed in the middle of the course.

Welcome to Weatherfield

On 9th December, ITV viewers are first introduced to the residents of *Coronation Street*, including barmaid Annie Walker, who works at the Rovers Return, and Elsie Tanner at no. 11, who is dealing with her ne'er do well ex-convict son. And at no. 3, university student Ken Barlow is arguing with his parents who think he's embarrassed about his working-class roots. The creation of Tony Warren, *Coronation Street* initially is commissioned for thirteen pilot episodes, but it will go on to become the longest-running TV soap in the world, airing its 10,000th episode in 2020. The legendary cobbles of 'Corrie' have been the scene of marital strife, neighbourly feuds, murder, betrayal as well as regular doses of inimitable Northern humour. As for aspirational university student Ken Barlow, he never leaves the Street, making William Roache the longest-serving actor ever in a soap.

The Angry Silence

Richard Attenborough co-produces and takes the lead role in this gritty drama about a factory worker whose refusal to take part in an unofficial strike leads to violent repercussions. In the face of criticism that the film was anti-strike and anti-trade union, Attenborough attends several private showings of the film to trade union members and has the opportunity to explain his side.

Psycho Killer

Alfred Hitchcock serves up a frankly petrifying cocktail of sex, madness, and murder in *Psycho*. This classic and hugely influential horror is set in a creepy motel run by the strange but apparently harmless Norman Bates, a character played with pitch perfect awkwardness by Anthony Perkins. As if Janet Leigh's horrifying end in the shower isn't bad enough, audiences are stunned when she's killed off only halfway through the film.

Return of the King

Elvis completes two years of military service and on the flight home from West Germany, his plane stops to refuel at Prestwick in Scotland, the one and only time, the King 'visits' the United Kingdom. Keen to capitalise on the success of his pre-service film career, he makes the very topical *GI Blues* this year, as well as the Western, *Flaming Star*.

MUSIC

I am Spartacus!

Kirk Douglas ripples his oiled muscles as the rebellious slave in Spartacus, in this Roman epic in which 30-year-old director Stanley Kubrick directed a cast of 10,500 and juggled a budget of $12 million prompting the US entertainment magazine *Variety* to suggest, 'he has out-DeMilled the old master in spectacle'. The famous scene in which the army of defeated slaves refuse to identify their leader, bears parallels with the real-life experiences of Howard Fast, author of the original book, who had written it while imprisoned for refusing to name communist sympathisers to investigators from the House for Un-American Activities Committee.

Eddie Cochran killed in crash

17th April 1960 Little more than a year after Buddy Holly's death, another rock'n'roll innovator meets a tragic end - Eddie Cochran, the creator of that great anthem of teenage discontent, *Summertime Blues*. En route for London Airport after completing a UK tour, his taxi hits a tree in Chippenham.

Lonnie's comic cut

31st March 1960 With the skiffle boom in fast decline, Lonnie Donegan is turning away from American folk songs to comedy material. His shift in style is vindicated by *My Old Man's a Dustman*, a relatively clean version of a ditty popular with British soldiers for over half a century. Recorded live during a gig at the Gaumont Cinema in Doncaster, it puts Lonnie back at No. 1 for the first time in three years. Not only that, it sets a new record: it's the first single in UK chart history to hit the top in its first week of sales.

Pig of the Pops

Pinky and Perky's Pop Parade is the latest TV vehicle for the porcine puppet twins, whose high-pitched, sped-up warbling of popular songs has inexplicably turned them into stars. The pair are the creation of Jan and Vlasta Dalibor, refugees from Czechoslovakia where pigs are a symbol of good luck. In order to identify which was which, Perky is given a 'pork pie' hat!

PINKY and PERKY
ANNUAL

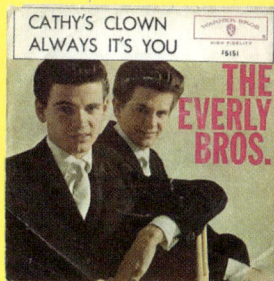

Don and Phil switch labels

17th February 1960 The Everly Brothers leave the small Cadence record label that nurtured them to join Warner Brothers, a new power in the industry. The fee is a record-breaking one million dollars. Their first record for their new home is a 24 carat classic written by Don himself - *Cathy's Clown*.

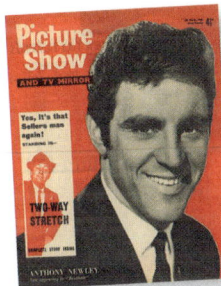

Newley son parade

28th April 1960 A year ago, former child actor Anthony Newley made the film *Idol on Parade*, playing a rock singer conscripted Elvis-style into the Army. By playing a pop idol he has become one, as he now sits proudly at No. 1 with the Lionel Bart song *Do You Mind*. Newley is unusual in that he sings rock'n'roll with an English accent.

New Kidd in town

4th August 1960 In a year of teen idols and Elvis imitators, the chart topping *Shakin' All Over* by Johnny Kidd and the Pirates is a welcome slice of British-made rock'n'roll grit. Johhny's real name is Fred Heath and his band, originally called the Nutters, haven't looked back since changing their name and adopting pirate garb. They wrote and recorded *Shakin' All Over* in less than an hour, intending it as a flipside. Contrary to their publicity, Johnny wears an eye-patch for effect, not because he lost his eye on the Spanish Main.

So long, farewell

23rd August 1960 Oscar Hammerstein, lyricist partner of composer Richard Rodgers, dies at his home in Pennsylvania. He completed work on their final musical, *The Sound of Music*, while fighting cancer. All the lights on Broadway are darkened in tribute.

Beatles in Hamburg

17th August 1960 The Beatles begin six months of performing at nightclubs on the notorious Reeperbahn in Hamburg. When they return to Liverpool they will shock audiences with their vastly improved musicianship and showmanship.

The backing steps forward

25th August 1960 Hitherto known as Cliff Richard's backing group, the Shadows launch their own hit-making career with *Apache*, an instrumental spotlighting the crystal-clear lead guitar work of Hank Marvin and the tom-tom drumming of Tony Meehan. Hank's Newcastle pal Bruce Welch on rhythm guitar and charismatic bassist Jet Harris complete the line-up.

THE TWIST
CHUBBY CHECKER
THE RECORD THAT STARTED EVERYBODY TWISTIN'
PARKWAY

Chubby does the Twist

19th September 1960 When Hank Ballard fails to turn up to promote a record called *The Twist* on the television show *American Bandstand*, resident dance teacher Chubby Checker improvises some steps on the spot. Twist your body from side to side, he instructs, while stubbing out an imaginary cigarette with your toe. The dance takes off, Chubby makes his own record of *The Twist* and has an unexpected No. 1.

MY FIRST 18 YEARS
TOP 10 — 1960

1. **Save the Last Dance for Me** *The Drifters*
2. **Are You Lonesome Tonight** *Elvis Presley*
3. **Cathy's Clown** *The Everly Brothers*
4. **Wonderful World** *Sam Cooke*
5. **Poor Me** *Adam Faith*
6. **El Paso** *Marty Robbins*
7. **Itsy Bitsy Teenie Weenie ...** *Brian Hyland*
8. **Shakin' All Over** *Johnny Kidd and the Pirates*
9. **Baby Sittin' Boogie** *Buzz Clifford*
10. **Georgia on My Mind** *Ray Charles*

Open | Search | Scan

DO YOU REMEMBER THIS?

Roller skates

A deathly No. 1

29th September 1960 The controversial fad for 'death discs' in the US spreads to Britain as Welsh singer Ricky Valance's *Tell Laura I Love Her* reaches No. 1. In the same vein as Mark Dinning's *Teen Angel* (girl dies trying to retrieve her boy's high school ring from a car stalled on a level crossing) and Jody Reynolds' *Endless Sleep* (girlfriend attempts suicide), *Laura* is the tale of a boy who dies in a stock car race trying to win enough money for a wedding ring.

Death of Johnny Horton

5th November 1960 Country singer Johnny Horton is killed in a car accident in Texas aged 35. He is best known for story songs with historical flavour, notably the chart-topping *Battle of New Orleans* and the movie theme *North to Alaska*.

Adam keeps Faith

12th November 1960 Adam Faith (left) has come a long way since performing in Soho's coffee bars as plain Terry Nelhams. Now the UK's favourite pop star after Cliff Richard, Adam has a little boy lost image and an ingratiating way of pronouncing 'baby' as 'by-bee' on hits like *Poor Me* and *What Do You Want*.

SPORT

All-British final at Wimbledon
7th July 1961 Wimbledon sees an absorbing all-UK ladies singles final with a ruthless Angela Mortimer beating an injury-hit Christine Truman in three sets to claim her third Grand Slam.

Wage cap abolished
18th January 1961 English professional footballers celebrate the abolition of the maximum wage (currently £20) six decades after the Football Association imposed it. The Professional Footballers Association's campaign for reform has been led by Fulham player Jimmy Hill whose teammate Johnny Haynes is among the first to benefit by becoming English football's first £100-a-week player.

Spurs at the double
6th May 1961 Tottenham Hotspur become the first club this century to secure the elusive league champion-ship and FA Cup 'double'.

Six goals - and none of them count
26th January 1961 Denis Law scores all six goals for Manchester City in an FA Cup game at Luton. As the game is abandoned twenty minutes from time due to a waterlogged pitch, none of the goals stand. When the game is replayed, Luton win 3-1.

Team tragedy at Brussels
15th February 1961 The entire US team of skaters, officials and chaperones travelling to the World Figure Skating Championships in Prague are among 73 people killed as their plane crashes close to Brussels Airport.

Australia retain the Ashes
1st August 1961 The cricketing summer peaks with a decisive fourth Test between England and Australia at Old Trafford. Richie Benaud's bowling proves crucial on the last day as he takes six wickets for 70 runs. Australia win by 54 runs and so retain the Ashes.

DOMESTIC NEWS

Farewell 'white' fivers
13th March 1961 The old 'white' £5 note, in circulation since 1793, is withdrawn and is no longer legal tender. The note featuring black print on white paper has been slowly replaced since 1957 with the 'Series B' note, a multicoloured version featuring Britannia.

1961 Tottenham Hotspur League Champions
1882 W31 1921

SPURS COMPLETE THE FIRST HALF OF THE DOUBLE

25 JAN 1961	5 FEB 1961	29 MAR 1961
Military coup in El Salvador.	First edition of *The Sunday Telegraph* goes on sale.	After a 4½ year trial Nelson Mandela is acquitted of treason.

Jaguar E-Type
15th March 1961 The brand-new Jaguar E-Type is launched, capable of reaching speeds of 150 miles per hour and doing 0 to 60mph in under seven seconds. Available in a two-seater coupé or roadster model, the car soon becomes famous for its speed and elegance.

Fire safety
1st May 1961 A fire breaks out at the Top Storey Club in Bolton blocking the venue's exit and 19 people lose their lives. An inquiry shows that an exit that could have saved the victims was prevented from opening by a false dance floor, and public outcry leads to a change in the Licensing Act.

Middlesborough race riots
19th August 1961 Cannon Street in Middlesborough becomes the latest part of the UK to see terrible race riots, which break out following the murder of a young white man, Jeffrey Hunt. The chief suspect in the murder is Asian, and the attack precipitates three nights of violence centred around the Taj Mahal Club.

Mothercare
September High Street staple Mothercare opens its first store as the 'Mother and Child Centre' in Kingston-upon-Thames. For 58 years Mothercare provides childhood necessities to expectant mothers across the country, until the brand comes under administration in 2019.

Portrait stolen
21st August 1961 Bus driver Kempton Bunton steals Goya's *Portrait of the Duke of Wellington* from the National Gallery. Bunton writes to Reuters News Agency demanding £140,000 be donated to a charity providing free television licences to the poor, but his ransom is ignored. Four years later the painting is returned, but whilst Bunton is prosecuted for the theft, he is found guilty only of stealing the frame.

Wales licensing hours
8th November 1961 Welsh counties vote in a referendum on opening hours for public houses. The counties of Anglesey, Cardiganshire, Caernarfonshire, Carmarthenshire, Denbighshire, Merionethshire, Montgomeryshire, and Pembrokeshire all vote to oppose the sale of alcohol on a Sunday.

---

6 APR 1961
New York Governor Nelson Rockefeller authorises building of World Trade Center.

5 MAY 1961
Alan Shepard becomes first American in space.

27 JUN 1961
Michael Ramsey appointed Archbishop of Canterbury.

More states independent

Sierra Leone, Tanganyika and Kuwait all gain independence from Britain in 1961, though Kuwait requests British military assistance in June to establish its independence from Iraq.

Islands evacuated

10th October 1961 The islands of Tristan da Cunha, a British Overseas Territory, are evacuated thanks to a large volcanic eruption. All 264 inhabitants of the islands are brought to an old RAF base in Hampshire, where they live until able to return in 1963.

Birth control

4th December 1961 Birth control pills become available on the National Health Service for the very first time, causing a revolution in family planning.

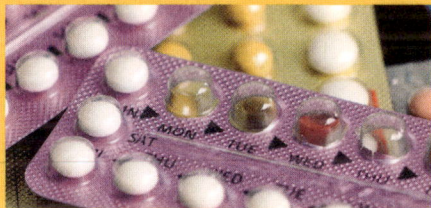

Mass arrests at ban-the-bomb demo

18th September 1961 The biggest CND demonstration yet sees multiple arrests for civil disobedience in and around Trafalgar Square. Up to a thousand people are charged after making sit-down protests on the day on which the USSR has mounted a twelfth nuclear test.

Duke of Kent marries

8th June 1961 Prince Edward, Duke of Kent, marries Katharine Worsley, daughter of baronet Sir William Worsley, at York Minster. The Duke is the son of King George VI's brother Prince George, who was killed in a wartime air crash.

ROYALTY & POLITICS

UK applies for EEC membership

31st July 1961 Although many in his own Conservative Party regard it as a surrender of sovereignty, Harold Macmillan announces that the UK will make a formal application to join the European Economic Community. The Labour Party remains officially opposed.

14 JUL 1961
Huge crowds in London greet Soviet astronaut Yuri Gagarin.

6 AUG 1961
Stirling Moss wins his 16th and final Formula 1 race at the the Nürburgring.

8 SEP 1961
President Charles de Gaulle escapes assassination attempt.

1961

Immigration curbs announced
1st November 1961 The Macmillan government outlines its intention to introduce a Commonwealth Immigration Bill to limit numbers taking up residence in the UK. The new restrictions will become law in July 1962.

FOREIGN NEWS

First man in space
12th April 1961 Soviet space rocket Vostok 1 takes off from Kazakhstan with the first human to reach space on board. Cosmonaut Yuri Gagarin flies 327 kilometers above the planet's surface in an orbit around the Earth at 27,400 km/h. The flight lasts 108 minutes. An engaging personality and unquestionably heroic, Gagarin becomes a poster boy for the Soviet space program and is feted across the world during the following months.

Bay of Pigs
16th April 1961 Having cut all ties with Fidel Casto's regime in Cuba, the newly installed President Kennedy accepts a CIA plan to overthrow Fidel Castro's government using Cuban exiles trained in the US. Some 1,500 exiles led by CIA officers begin the invasion at the Bay of Pigs but encounter the much larger force of the Cuban National Army. Kennedy refuses to use US warships to turn the tide and the invasion is abandoned after three days. The US is humiliated while Castro looks to the Soviet Union for protection.

WWF founded
29th April 1961 One of the world's largest conservation organisations, the World Wildlife Fund (WWF) is founded with an office in Morges, Switzerland. Conceived as an international fundraising organisation in support of existing conservation groups, the WWF becomes a major campaigner on issues relating to the protection of nature, with the backing of many notable figures including Prince Philip, naturalist Peter Scott, biologist Julia Huxley and environmentalist Max Nicholson.

24 OCT 1961
Island of Malta is granted independence by UK.

15 NOV 1961
London landmark the Euston Arch is ordered to be demolished.

21 DEC 1961
John F. Kennedy and Harold Macmillan meet in Bermuda to talk about nuclear policy.

South Africa leaves the Commonwealth
31st May 1961 South Africa votes to leave the British Commonwealth in a whites-only referendum. Elizabeth II is no longer Queen of South Africa and the country becomes a republic.

Destination Moon
25th May 1961 The US may have lost the battle to put the first man in space but President Kennedy sets his sights on the next milestone in space travel. He commits his country to landing a man on the Moon 'and returning him safely to Earth before the end of this decade'. With this, the president gives the green light to the Apollo program.

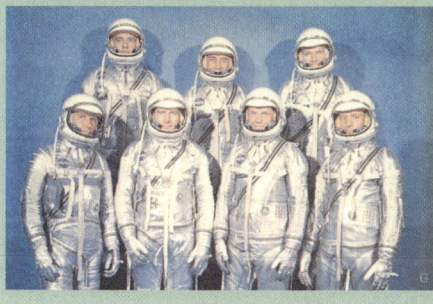

King of all bombs
30th October 1961 Three days after the stand-off at Checkpoint Charlie, the Soviets flex their muscles once again by testing the 'Tsar Bomba' or 'king of all bombs'. The 50 megaton hydrogen bomb is the largest man-made explosion ever and breaks windows as far away as Finland.

First hatchback
1st July 1961 Renault launches the small family car that will compete with the popular Citroën 2CV and the Volkswagen Beetle: the Renault 4.

Berlin Wall is built
13th August 1961 East Germany begins construction of the Berlin Wall to stop its citizens escaping to the city's western sectors. Since the 1950s, hundreds of thousands have sought refuge in West Germany and the damage to the East German economy and its political credibility is enormous. A 156-kilometer-long barrier of concrete blocks and barbed wire is built around the whole of West Berlin, interrupted by border posts manned by East German troops with orders to shoot anyone who tries to cross. In October, the crisis is heightened when Soviet tanks attempt to take control of Checkpoint Charlie, the Allied crossing point. US and Soviet tanks stand directly opposite each other for sixteen hours until the latter withdraw. One mistake and a third world war could be triggered.

ENTERTAINMENT

Curry in a hurry
Batchelors launch the Vesta Curry, the ultimate in exotic convenience food (actually, the only type of exotic convenience food). Press advertisements stress how a Vesta curry can save on drudgery and reassure cautious Brits that it isn't 'too spicy'. Despite its questionable authenticity, Vesta paves the way for the ready meal revolution.

The Milky Bars are on me!
The Milky Bar Kid, a skinny blond lad in round glasses and Western gear, makes an unconvincing cowboy but his largesse with bars of white chocolate is legendary. The first Milky Bar Kid is played by Terry Brooks who is paid the generous sum of £10 every time an advert is shown. Terry eventually outgrows his costume and leaves the heady world of TV commercials to become an air conditioning engineer in Basildon.

Eyes down
The Betting and Gaming Act leads to a craze for bingo across the country as players can now win big cash prizes. Seaside businesses complain that holidaymakers are addicted to bingo which is diverting money away from their seasonal trade, and landladies insist on cash up front in case guests are spent-up by the end of their stay. Eric Morley, chairman of Mecca dance halls, at the forefront of the bingo movement, tells the *Daily Mirror* that the suggestion that mothers are abandoning their children four or five times a week to indulge their bingo habit is 'nonsense'.

Portraits before a scandal
Numerous portraits of well-known figures and members of the royal family drawn by society osteopath and artist Stephen Ward are published as a series in the respected weekly paper, *The Illustrated London News*. A portrait of the Duke of Edinburgh even appears on the cover. Two years later, Ward is implicated as a key player in the scandalous Profumo Affair.

Yabadabadoooo!
The 'modern Stone Age family', *The Flintstones* are first introduced to British viewers on 5th January when the Hanna-Barbera cartoon airs on ITV. The pure genius of the Flintstones concept, where a typical twentieth-century family sitcom format is transposed to the animated prehistoric town of Bedrock, gives endless scope for storylines featuring Fred and Wilma Flintstone and friends, Barney and Betty Rubble plus the family pet an exuberant, bouncy dinosaur called Dino. It's a vintage year for cartoon debuts as *Yogi Bear* and *Top Cat* also both first appear.

Praise be

The BBC broadcasts the very first episode of *Songs of Praise* from the Tabernacle Baptist Chapel in Cardiff on 1st October, with soprano Heather Harper as guest vocalist.

AT 5.0 ON **RADIO 1**
AND ON RADIO 2
Alan Freeman
with
PICK OF THE POPS

He worked on the *Teenagers'* station in Melbourne (where he was born), and then in the U.S., and then in Europe. He settled in England in 1958, and has helped as to 'stay bright' ever since

Dimbleby and the Duke

On 29th May, Prince Philip is the first member of the royal family ever to be interviewed on television when he appears in a pre-recorded twelve-minute slot on Panorama. A respectful but visibly nervous Richard Dimbleby questions the Duke about the Commonwealth Technical Training Week, of which he is patron. The royal interviewee seems visibly at ease leading the *Daily Mirror* to comment how he, 'appeared more relaxed than his interviewer'.

Pick of the Pops

Alan 'Fluff' Freeman joins the radio show *Pick of the Pops* on 30th September and every Sunday night takes viewers through the music chart's top tunes. With his free-flowing presentation style, peppered with catchphrases ('Not 'arf!') Freeman becomes the occasionally parodied but much-loved archetypal radio DJ.

Spot the difference

Dodie Smith's 1956 children's novel *One Hundred and One Dalmatians*, is brought to the screen by Disney with Pongo and Missus on a mission to rescue their adorable clutch of puppies from the mad monochromist, Cruella de Vil.

DO YOU REMEMBER THIS?

Tobacco pipe

The Dulux Dog

During the filming of a TV commercial for Dulux paints, the director's Old English Sheepdog, Dash, keeps running into shot to play with the child actors. It is decided that Dash is so photogenic he can appear in the advert and the Dulux Dog is born. He's the first of fourteen different Old English Sheepdogs to be the 'face' of Dulux over the years.

Bedside manner

Richard Chamberlain as young Dr. James Kildare set hearts a-flutter when he begins his internship at Blair General Hospital on 20th October 1961. Chamberlain was by no means the first choice to play the role, which was originally meant for William Shatner, but he is unknown no longer and the medical drama *Dr. Kildare* catapults him to stardom.

Pingwings

The Pingwings, the latest creation from Smallfilms, is shown on ITV through August and September. In the handmade tradition of the company, the bird like puppets, which approximate to penguins, have been expertly knitted by Peter Firmin's sister, Gloria.

Breakfast at Tiffany's
Audrey Hepburn stars in one of her best roles, as the Midwest girl who reinvents herself as the fun-loving New York socialite, who flirts her way around Manhattan while falling for a struggling writer.

The Rag Trade
Nobody messes with the workers at Fenner's Fashions who will drop everything whenever the familiar order 'Everybody out!' is uttered by shop steward Paddy Fleming. The show, starring Miriam Karlin and Barbara Windsor (photo), is positioned as a comedy but has plenty to say about gender rights and workplace politics.

The Hustler
Paul Newman brings a magnetic swagger to the screen as 'Fast' Eddie Felson, a talented, small-time pool shark whose self-destructive compulsion to win is played out in the small hours and smoky shadows of America's billiard halls. British audiences are unfamiliar with the game of pool but it matters little when we watch Newman and Jack Gleason play a marathon match with balletic elegance. And when Newman smirks and says, 'You know, all of a sudden, you feel you can't miss?', it's hard not to believe him.

MUSIC

Dylan's in town
24th January 1961 A young singer-guitarist from Minnesota named Robert Zimmerman arrives in New York to play the folk clubs of Greenwich Village. He changes his name to Bob Dylan in tribute to the Welsh poet Dylan Thomas.

save the last dance for me

THE DRIFTERS

High school hitmakers
30th January 1961 As recent hits prove, New York is the engine room of early 1960s pop. Working for Atlantic Records, producers Jerry Lieber and Mike Stoller have transformed the Drifters' flagging fortunes with Latin-laced hits like *Save the Last Dance for Me* and have launched the group's lead singer Ben E. King on his own career with *Spanish Harlem* and *Stand By Me*. Now they're nurturing a wave of young musical talent from the Brooklyn high schools. When soon-to-be-married school leavers Gerry Goffin and Carole King write the No. 1 *Will You Love Me Tomorrow* for black singing trio the Shirelles, it's just the start of a new era of honest, beautifully crafted and intelligent pop songs about teenage life and love.

MOTOWN

Motown on the march

11th March 1961 Less than a year after it was launched by record producer Berry Gordy, Detroit's Motown label has its first million seller - *Shop Around* by the Miracles, led by William 'Smokey' Robinson. Over in Liverpool, the Beatles are adding Motown songs like the Miracles' *You Really Got a Hold on Me* and the Marvelettes' *Please Mr Postman* to their repertoire and making the label's trademark backbeat part of their sound.

Second place again

18th March 1961 The UK's Eurovision Song Contest entry is *Are You Sure* written and sung by a young Everlys-like duo from Wiltshire called the Allisons. It comes a strong second to Luxembourg's *Nous Les Amoureaux*, sung by Jean-Claude Pascal.

Elvis quits live performing

25th March 1961 Elvis Presley proves his pulling power once again with a movie, *GI Blues*, which capitalises on his return from Army service. Its hit song *Wooden Heart* is his seventh UK No. 1. But there is bad news for fans as he performs what manager 'Colonel' Tom Parker insists will be his last live show, in Hawaii. From now on, it will be movies and records only.

Meek and wild

31st August 1960 Biggles actor John Leyton reaches No. 1 in the UK with *Johnny Remember Me* after singing it in in the television soap opera *Harpers West* One, in which he plays wild pop idol Johnny St Cyr.

Happiness for Helen

28th September 1961 Reaching the grand old age of fifteen and free to leave school is Helen Shapiro - and this on the very day that her biggest hit to date, *Walkin' Back To Happiness*, enters the UK chart.

Out of the Shadows

30th September 1961 Just as *Kon-Tiki* is sailing up the charts to No. 1, the Shadows are shaken by the departure of drummer Tony Meehan. Brian Bennett from Marty Wilde's Wildcats takes his place. Meehan's future lies at Decca Records as a producer and talent scout. One of his early tasks at Decca is to turn down the Beatles.

Platform blues

17th October 1961 A fateful meeting happens on a platform at Dartford railway station. Mick Jagger and Keith Richards are both eighteen and last met in primary school. They bond over the Chuck Berry and Muddy Waters albums that Keith is carrying and realise they have a shared love of American blues.

Brian meets the Beatles

9th November 1961 Now regulars at the Cavern Club in Liverpool, the Beatles' lunchtime set attracts Brian Epstein from the nearby NEMS department store. Intrigued, he meets them backstage and within days becomes their manager.

MY FIRST 18 YEARS

TOP10 **1961**

1. **Please Mr Postman** *The Marvelettes*
2. **Take Five** *Dave Brubeck*
3. **Stand By Me** *Ben E. King*
4. **Midnight in Moscow** *Kenny Ball and his Jazzmen*
5. **Walkin' Back to Happiness** *Helen Shapiro*
6. **Goodness Gracious Me** *Peter Sellers, Sophia Loren*
7. **Will You Love Me Tomorrow** *The Shirelles*
8. **My Kind of Girl** *Matt Monro*
9. **On the Rebound** *Floyd Cramer*
10. **Blue Moon** *The Marcels*

Open Spotify | Search Scan

A shore thing

2nd December 1961 Entering the UK chart for a record-breaking 52 weeks without reaching No. 1 is Acker Bilk's *Stranger on the Shore*, the theme tune of a BBC TV serial about a French teenager in Brighton. Best known as a bowler-hatted clarinet-playing jazz man, Acker originally called the melody *Jenny* after his daughter. It fares even better in the US, where it tops the chart and sells a million.

Cliff's new movie

13th December 1961 *The Young Ones* starring Cliff Richard receives a glittering world premiere at the Warner Theatre, Leicester Square. It is Cliff's third film and the first in which he has headline billing.

That Joyous, Jumping, Jubilant Musical!
CLIFF RICHARD · ROBERT MORLEY
CAROLE GRAY and
THE SHADOWS

The young ones

14 Hit Tunes including "THE GIRL IN YOUR ARMS" and "THE SAVAGE"

NOW ON RELEASE!

The sound of Fury

The current king of pop impresario Larry Parnes's stable of acts is Billy Fury, a Liverpool boy who as plain Ronald Wycherley once made his living on the Mersey tugboats. As a live performer he's the closest the UK has to Elvis but on disc he's more subdued, preferring ballads rather than rockers. From the hot songwriting team of Gerry Goffin and Carole King *Halfway to Paradise* is his biggest hit yet.

SPORT

Stanley go out of business
6th March 1962 Financial pressures force the closure of Accrington Stanley, a football club ever-present since 1921. Three months later, Oxford United are elected to take Stanley's place in the fourth division. A re-constituted Accrington Stanley will reclaim a league place in 2006.

ACCRINGTON STANLEY F.C.
PEEL PARK, ACCRINGTON
Official Programme 4d

A toxic World Cup
10th June 1962 England exit the FIFA World Cup in Chile at the quarter final stage, losing 3-1 to Brazil, the defending champions. Brazil go on to beat Czechoslovakia 3-1 in the final. The tournament is marred by on-field violence, notably in Italy's 2-0 defeat of Chile which earns the epithet of 'the battle of Santiago'. Walter Winterbottom stands down as England manager. He is replaced by Alf Ramsey, who has just guided Ipswich Town to their first ever league championship.

Golden moments at the Games
September - December 1962 Yorkshire-based sprinter Dorothy Hyman is the UK's top performer in the two major international athletics meetings of the year, the European Games in Belgrade and the Commonwealth Games in Perth, Australia. In Belgrade she wins the 100 metres gold and the 200 metres silver before securing bronze in the 4 x 100 metres relay final. Running for England in Perth she takes gold in both the 100 and 200 yard events. There is also European joy for 400 metres winner Robbie Brightwell, 5,000 metres winner Bruce Tulloh, marathon winner Brian Kilby and 20 kilometres walk winner Ken Thompson, putting Great Britain second in the final medal table behind the Soviet Union.

Bangor's European adventure
5th September 1962 British football's unlikely European heroes are tiny Bangor City, who enter the European Cup Winners' Cup as holders of the Welsh Cup and astonish the football world by beating Napoli 2-0 in the first leg of the first round. Napoli win the second leg 3-1 in front of an 80,000 crowd. With the scores level, Napoli win the playoff 2-1 at Arsenal's Highbury ground.

Hill tops in F1
29th December 1962 The last race of the F1 season, the South African Grand Prix, sees an enthralling all-British challenge for the Formula One drivers' championship. When Jim Clark is forced to retire twenty laps from the end, Graham Hill seizes the moment and beats him to the title by twelve points.

16 JAN 1962
Filming begins on 'Dr No' the first James Bond film.

20 FEB 1962
John Glenn is first US astronaut to orbit the Earth.

29 MAR 1962
Education Act creates system of locally funded tuition fees and grants for undergraduates.

DOMESTIC
NEWS

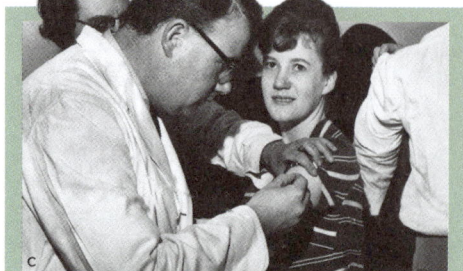

Smallpox outbreak
January 1962 Smallpox strikes Britain as five people with the virus arrive in the UK from an affected area in Pakistan. Two travel to Birmingham, one to Bradford, one to Cardiff and one to London. The outbreak results in six deaths in Bradford, whilst South Wales suffers nineteen. Across the country over a million people receive emergency vaccinations.

Goodbye trolleybuses!
8th May 1962 The last of London's trolley-bus or 'Diddler' routes is replaced with a diesel bus service. The new AEC Route-masters now cover all of the 68 trolley-bus routes, a network that was once the largest in the world.

Panda crossings
2nd April 1962 The first of the country's new 'panda' crossings opens outside Waterloo station in London, with Guild-ford and Lincoln receiving them shortly afterwards. The new crossings have triangular patterns rather than stripes, feature red and amber lights for traffic and the command 'cross' for pedestrians.

Britain's first casinos!
2nd June 1962 Britain gets its first legal casinos following the introduction of the Betting and Gaming Act 1960. One of the first opens in Brighton, Sussex, with another, the Clermont Club, opening in London's Mayfair.

Fascist Mosley attacked
31st July 1962 Racial violence once more hits the headlines in July 1962 as race riots break out in Dudley. In contrast, Oswald Mosley, fascist leader of the Union Movement, is attacked and knocked down by protestors intent on stopping him from marching through Manchester on the 29th. Whilst he is rescued by the police, he is pelted with fruit, eggs, coins, and stones, and just two days later, on the 31st, appears at a rally in Dalston, London. Thousands gather, and Mosley and his 'blackshirts' are attacked again, with 54 arrests made.

14 APR 1962
Georges Pompidou becomes Prime Minister of France.

25 MAY 1962
Coventry's new cathedral is consecrated.

29 JUN 1962
The Vickers VC-10 long-range airliner makes its first flight.

Space and satellites

14th June 1962 The European Space Research Organisation is formed with Britain joining eleven other countries to create the predecessor to the European Space Agency. Space is beginning to affect the public consciousness, as the Telstar satellite provides the first live transmissions of full-length television shows across the Atlantic.

Iconic cars launched

12th August 1962 The Austin and Morris 1100s launch (photo). Known simply as the "1100" they will go on to become the best-selling cars of the 1960s, selling more than a million vehicles in the UK. The Ford Cortina is also launched in September. but has to wait until the 70s for its heyday, becoming the best-selling car of that decade.

Flavoured crisps!

Flavoured crisps appear on British shelves for the first time as Golden Wonder launch a cheese and onion variety. Previously, crisps have only been available with a small sachet of salt for seasoning, and the launch of flavoured crisps in the UK is a sensation. Other flavours, such as salt and vinegar, follow later in the 60s.

Independence movements gain ground

1962 sees Jamaica, Trinidad and Tobago, and Uganda all gain their independence from Britain.

More motorways

The first phases of the M5 and M6 motorways open, with the M5 connecting Birmingham and north Gloucestershire, and the M6 bypassing Stafford.

DO YOU REMEMBER THIS?

Cigarette case

ROYALTY & POLITICS

Charles at Gordonstoun

1st May 1962 Fourteen-year-old Prince Charles starts at Gordonstoun School near Elgin in Scotland. There has been much discussion in the press about its suitability for the heir to the throne given the austerity of its regime and the school's emphasis on physical education.

Golden Wonder 5p
CARS GO-KARTS BICYCLES to be won
£40000 FAMILY PRIZE DRIVE
CHEESE & ONION FLAVOUR CRISPS

12 JUL 1962	4 AUG 1962	25 SEP 1962
Rolling Stones 1st performance (Marquee Club, London).	The Welsh Language Society, is founded as a pressure group campaigning for the protection and promotion of the Welsh language.	Boxer Sonny Liston wins the world heavyweight championship by defeating Floyd Patterson.

1962

No inquiry into thalidomide

17th May 1962 Following harrowing reports of mothers across Britain giving birth to babies with physical deformities, the UK government issues a warning concerning the morning sickness drug Thalidomide. Minister of Health Enoch Powell subsequently refuses to establish a public inquiry into the drug.

Night of the long knives

13th July 1962 In a breathtakingly savage reshuffle of his Cabinet that is widely seen as an attempt to save his own skin as Prime Minister, Harold Macmillan sacks seven of his senior ministers.

Losing an empire, looking for a role?

12th December 1962 In a speech at West Point Military Academy that is directly critical of the Macmillan government, former US Secretary of State Dean Acheson makes his famous statement that 'Great Britain has lost an empire but has not yet found a role'. The speech intensifies a feeling of drift in the 'special relationship' between the UK and US.

DO YOU REMEMBER THIS?

Transistor radio

FOREIGN NEWS

First limb reattachment

23rd May 1962 The world's first successful reattachment of a severed limb is carried out at a hospital in Boston, Masschusetts, by Dr. Ronald A. Malt. The patient is twelve-year-old Everett Knowles, whose right arm was sliced off at the shoulder by a train.

Eichmann executed

1st June 1962 Nazi henchman Adolf Eichmann is refused clemency and executed in Ramla, Israel, following his conviction on fifteen counts of crimes against humanity, war crimes, crimes against the Jewish people, and membership of a criminal organisation.

Escape from Alcatraz

11th June 1962 Three men escape from the maximum security prison on Alcatraz Island near San Francisco. They place papier-mâché masks in their beds to deceive the guards and flee on a boat made of life jackets stuck together. The men are never seen again.

---

1 OCT 1962
Brian Epstein signs a contract to manage The Beatles.

23 NOV 1962
World's first successful hip replacement operation at Wigan hospital.

22 DEC 1962
Big freeze begins in UK, lasting until March 1963.

Algeria independent

3rd July 1962 The granting of independence to Algeria by France sees the last gasp of the terror campaign. Three weeks after independence, civil war breaks out between the Provisional Government and the National Liberation Front (FLN). Independence is officially proclaimed on 31st July, with Ahmed Ben Bella as President.

Pop art

9th July 1962 Andy Warhol presents 32 paintings of Campbell's soup cans at the Ferus Gallery in Los Angeles. It is the essence of pop art: mass produced banality on the walls of a gallery. After the sudden death of Marilyn Monroe, Warhol releases a diptych with 50 portraits of the star, based on publicity pictures for the film *Niagara* (1953). The left canvas shows the glamorous movie star while the right canvas depicts her private side and the downside of fame.

Goodbye Norma Jean

5th August 1962 Norma Jean Mortenson - alias Marilyn Monroe - is found dead in her bed at her Los Angeles home, aged 36. An autopsy shows that Monroe died of an overdose of barbiturates, probably intentional. Conspiracy theories surround her death while rumours of entanglement with both John and Robert Kennedy will persist for years.

Mandela in jail

5th August 1962 Nelson Mandela is arrested by the South African authorities. He now leads the military wing of the African National Congress - called Umkhonto we Sizwe (Spear of the Nation) - which carries out acts of sabotage against the apartheid regime. He is jailed for five years, during which time he will be convicted on other charges and sentenced to life imprisonment on Robben Island.

Cuban missile crisis

28th October 1962 The Cold War reaches its most dangerous point during the thirteen days of the Cuban Missile Crisis. After the failed US-backed Bay of Pigs invasion in 1961, Cuban leader Fidel Castro appeals for military assistance from the Soviet Union. Soviet leader Nikita Khrushchev agrees and secretly places nuclear missiles in Cuba, aimed at the US mainland. In September, the missile installations are photographed from US spy planes. President Kennedy demands the immediate removal of the missiles and announces a blockade of Cuba, with US ships ready to stop Soviet ships reaching the island. As the world holds its breath, Kennedy and Khrushchev negotiate in secret. Kennedy offers a compromise - a promise not to attack Cuba and to withdraw US missiles from Turkey if the Soviets dismantle their nuclear base in Cuba. Khrushchev agrees. A devastating nuclear war is narrowly averted.

📺 ENTERTAINMENT

West Side Story in West End cinemas

West Side Story is chosen for the Royal Film Performance on 26th February after which it is shown at the Astoria cinema. In response to rave reviews in America, the cinema has been receiving a deluge of letters and money from film fans hoping to secure a seat in advance and be among the first to see the film version of the electrifying stage musical.

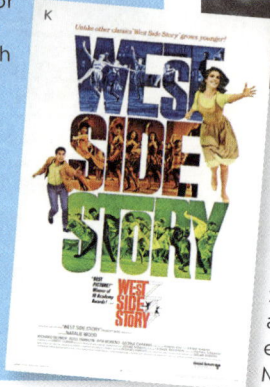

Animal Magic

The first episode of *Animal Magic*, produced by the five-year-old BBC Natural History Unit in Bristol and presented by Johnny Morris, is shown on 13th April. Morris, a natural mimic, would often act as a zookeeper at Bristol Zoo Gardens and give the various animals he encountered their own voices. More scientific intervals of the programme were presented by naturalists such as Tony Soper and Gerald Durrell. *Animal Magic* runs until 1983.

Look and Learn magazine

Fleetway publications launch a new juvenile magazine, *Look and Learn*, on 20th January in which editor David Stone promises readers, 'a treasure house of exciting articles, stories and pictures'.

At 26x35cm and with half of the magazine in colour, it stands out against its rivals on the newsstands. *Look and Learn* runs for 1,049 issues until its closure in 1982.

Fab Four Fan Club

Freda Kelly, assistant to Beatles manager Brian Epstein, takes over as secretary of the Fab Four's official fan club and rather naively gives her home address for fan club mail. Inevitably the family home is inundated with letters until she changes it to Epstein's office address.

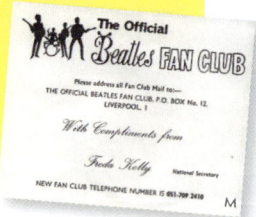

Just add water

Tang instant orange drink is used during John Glenn's Mercury space flight in February and remains on NASA crews' menus for future space expeditions. Tang, along with the UK powdered orange drink Bird's Apeel or Kellogg's Rise & Shine concentrated juice in a can, enjoy quite a vogue during the 1960s and '70s.

Fundraising frenzy

The first *Blue Peter* fundraising appeal urges viewers to collect used stamps to raise money for homes for homeless people.

Brains of Britain

School swots and student eggheads assemble this year for a classic quiz show on TV. *Top of the Form* successfully migrates from radio (where it's been since 1948) to television on 12th November with a quiz series for school teams.

It's a fair cop

The first episode of *Z-Cars* is broadcast on 2nd January and introduces a new kind of hard-hitting police drama. Rather than the familiar bobby on the beat in the *Dixon of Dock Green* vein, the show follows the officers of a modern police unit in the fictional town of Newtown, whose fight against crime is expedited by their Ford Zephyr police cars. The show hits just the right note and quickly gains 14 million viewers.

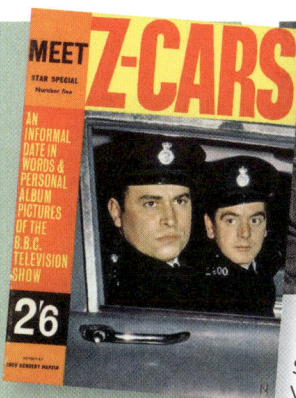

Steptoe and Son

On 7th June, the first episode of *Steptoe and Son* is broadcast, with Wilfrid Brambell as the wily, grubby-minded, snaggle-toothed Albert and Harry H. Corbett as Harold, his hapless and downtrodden son, always hoping for better things despite the cynical sneering of his father who he regularly refers to as 'you dirty old man'. Audiences love their bickering partnership and at the height of its popularity, *Steptoe and Son* attracts 28 million viewers.

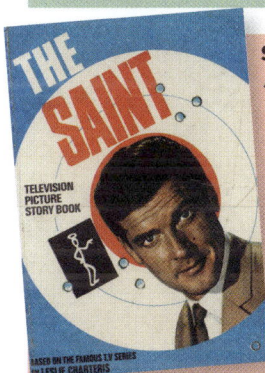

A nation of DIY-ers

Barry Bucknell's mission to teach the country how to 'do-it-yourself' gets more ambitious when he presents *Bucknell's House* and take viewers through a step-by-step renovation of a dilapidated house in Ealing, west London. Bucknell contributes to a huge DIY boom during which magazines like *Do-It-Yourself* and *Practical Householder* also provide instruction on how to renovate and modernise.

Saint Roger

As the suave and unruffled Simon Templar, who is a kind of mid-century Robin Hood, using unconventional means and over-stepping law to bring about justice, Roger Moore's stint as *The Saint* is something of a dry run for the role of James Bond. He part-purchases the rights to *The Saint* which is a canny business moves as it switches to colour in 1966 and is syndicated around the world.

The Jet(son) Set

With the Space Race well and truly under-way, Hanna-Barbera capitalises on the success of *The Flintstones* but instead of the Stone Age, catapult their next cartoon family into the Space Age. *The Jetsons* is a tongue-in-cheek look at the future as the Jetsons of Orbit City drive around in bubble-topped spaceships and get help at home from a robot called Rosey.

Satire on screen

Satire is to be a defining feature of the 1960s comedy scene, and *That Was The Week That Was*, broadcast first on 24th November, leads the way. Never afraid to court controversy, *TWTWTW* lampoons politicians, mocks public figures and even has a go at the royal family, drawing complaints regularly but doing no damage whatsoever to viewing figures. Hosted by David Frost, the show opens each week with a new song based on the week's news sung by Millicent Martin, and a rolling roster of cast members include Willie Rushton, Roy Kinnear, Lance Percival and cartoonist Timothy Birdsall.

Lawrence of Arabia

10th December 1962 Peter O'Toole was director David Lean's choice to play T. E. Lawrence in this retelling of *Lawrence of Arabia*, even though Montgomery Clift, Albert Finney and Marlon Brando were all considered. Filmed on a huge scale with a cast of thousands, Lean's masterpiece wins six Academy Awards including Best Picture and Best Director. It is the benchmark by which future directors will measure their own work.

To Kill a Mockingbird

Gregory Peck is cast as morally upstanding lawyer Atticus Finch in this faithful film version of Harper Lee's bestselling, Pulitzer-Prize-winning novel about the small-town bigotry in Depression-era Alabama, exposed by Finch's defence of a black man falsely accused of raping a white woman. Peck wins an Oscar for his role as does the playwright Horton Foote, for his sensitive and authentic adapted screenplay.

MUSIC

Make or break for the Beatles

1st January 1962 A make or break year for the Beatles begins with an audition for Decca Records, where ex-Shadows drummer turned Decca producer Tony Meehan opts to sign another group auditioning that day, Brian Poole and the Tremeloes. Manager Brian Epstein's last throw of the dice is to call on George Martin at Parlophone, who finally gives the boys a contract. Insisting that they record one of their own songs rather than the plodding *How Do You Do It,* their first release is *Love Me Do*. By this time Ringo Starr has replaced Cavern club favourite Pete Best on drums and John Lennon has married Cynthia Powell.

Cribbins on class

February - July 1962 The great British comedy song is alive and well and living at Parlophone Records. Label boss George Martin has already recorded Peter Sellers, the *Beyond the Fringe* team and Flanders and Swann. Now he has brought comic actor Bernard Cribbins to Abbey Road to make two hilarious if macabre commentaries on class differences - *Hole in the Ground* and *Right Said Fred.*

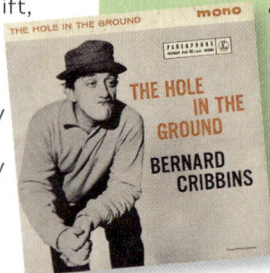

Another record for Cliff

11th January 1962 Cliff Richard's success story hits another level. In another 'first' for the singer, *The Young Ones* receives pre-release orders of 524,000 - a British record for advance sales. It is only the fourth record ever to reach No. 1 during its first week of release.

Seeger is free

19th May 1962 After a protracted legal process, folk singer and activist Pete Seeger has his 1955 conviction for contempt of Congress overturned. He had refused to answer questions about his political affiliations during anti-communist hearings.

American idols on tour

Among the US teen idols touring the UK this year is Neil Sedaka, who gave up a concert career for pop music. Neil is a former classmate of Carole King and writes with high-school pal Howie Greenfield. Sedaka hits like *Happy Birthday Sweet Sixteen* and *Breaking Up Is Hard To Do* are notable for their multi-tracking, as Neil harmonises with himself on cascades of 'doobydowns' and 'tra-la-las'. Also on tour is Bobby Vee, who has come a long way since filling in for Buddy Holly following the air crash that claimed Buddy's life.

NEIL SEDAKA
Exclusive RCA Recording Artist

Steaming to No. 1

21st July 1963 Songs by Carole King and Gerry Goffin are everywhere this year. *The Locomotion* is a No. 1 in the US for Little Eva, who babysits their daughter, while *Up on the Roof* is a charming, evocative hit for the Drifters. To cap it all, Carole is now releasing a record of her own - *It Might As Well Rain Until September*, a song of summer separation that treads similar ground to that other seasonal hit of 1962, Brian Hyland's *Sealed with a Kiss*.

Jersey boys' joy

15th September 1962 Two successive US chart toppers - *Sherry* and *Big Girls Don't Cry* - herald the arrival of a New Jersey vocal group whose music will still be celebrated in the 21st century by a much loved Broadway show. The Four Seasons are four streetwise Italian-American boys who draw on the writing and production talent of Bob Crewe and Bob Gaudio. Theirs is a black-influenced vocal sound built around one of the wonders of the early 1960s music scene, the phenomenal falsetto of Frankie Valli.

The name is Bond

Just as *Dr No* kicks off one of the most lucrative franchises in movie history, so its soundtrack sets a fantastic new precedent in movie music making. *The James Bond Theme* is composed by Monty Norman, orchestrated by John Barry and features an unforgettable guitar solo from Vic Flick - and it proves so iconic that it is incorporated into every subsequent Bond film.

Ray goes country

12th July 1962 Musically speaking, Ray Charles is a law unto himself. Following his stunning, genre-busting combinations of gospel, jazz and blues rhythms, he is now bringing his touch to the unfashionable world of country music with the album *Modern Sounds in Country and Western Music*. Contradicting predictions that it might damage his career, it's a huge seller, with its standout track - Ray's soulful version of the Don Gibson ballad *I Can't Stop Loving You* - topping the US and UK chart.

Soul brother No. 1

24th October 1962 Starring at the legendary Apollo Theatre in Harlem, New York City, is the self-styled 'soul brother number one', James Brown. A truly historic night of incredible physical and vocal gymnastics is recorded for posterity, and the subsequent album *Live at the Apollo* will remain on the US rhythm and blues chart for an unprecedented 66 weeks. Brown's breakthrough to the mainstream follows in June 1963 with a pleading revival of a 1940s Perry Como number - *Prisoner of Love.*

MY FIRST 18 YEARS
TOP 10 — 1962

1. **Come Outside** *Mike Sarne*
2. **Can't Help Falling in Love** *Elvis Presley*
3. **Telstar** *The Tornados*
4. **Dream Baby** *Roy Orbison*
5. **Hey Baby** *Bruce Channel*
6. **Run to Him** *Bobby Vee*
7. **He's a Rebel** *The Crystals*
8. **A Picture of You** *Joe Brown*
9. **The Young Ones** *Cliff Richard and the Shadows*
10. **Up on the Roof** *The Drifters*

Open | Search | Scan

Telstar spans the globe

4th October 1962 Taking its title from the telecommunications satellite launched in July, *Telstar* by the Tornados begins a five-week stay at the top of the British chart before repeating the feat across the world, including the US.

DO YOU REMEMBER THIS?

View-Master

Perfectly Frank

8th November 1962 Voice of the year is Frank Ifield, a UK-born Australian who adds a country twang, a yodel and a fetching harmonica to vintage songs like *I Remember You* and *Lovesick Blues*, both of them No. 1s.

Dusty goes solo

Playing their own brand of country-folk music on hits like *Island of Dreams*, the Springfields have made a big impression. Tom Springfield writes the songs and his sister Dusty is the focal point - until she goes solo in October and changes her whole look and style. Adopting a bouffant hairdo and Motown-like backing, she makes an instant mark with *I Only Want to be with You.*

SPORT

Football in the freezer

The UK's terrible winter plays havoc with the football fixtures, forcing a twelve-week shutdown and the creation of the Pools Panel by the football pools operators to predict what the scores would have been. Everton eventually beat Spurs to the league championship and Manchester United win the FA Cup by beating Leicester 3-1. But the most spectacular day in the football year is Boxing Day which delivers a series of unbelievable scorelines including Fulham beating Ipswich 10-1. An incredible 66 goals are scored in ten first division games.

Spurs win in Europe

15th May 1963 Tottenham Hotspur win the European Cup Winners Cup in fine style, beating Atletico Madrid 5-1 in Rotterdam. It is the first trophy for a British side in European competition.

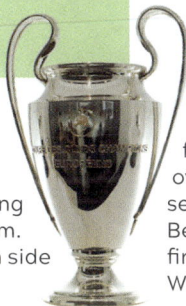

Cooper v. Clay

18th June 1963 British heavyweight champion Henry Cooper boxes the fight of his life at Wembley Stadium against world championship contender Cassius Clay. Against all expectations he puts a taunting Clay (later Muhammad Ali) on the canvas at the end of the fourth round, but Clay recovers and wins on a technical knockout when Cooper is forced to retire with a cut eye. Cooper's gallant challenge makes him a national hero overnight.

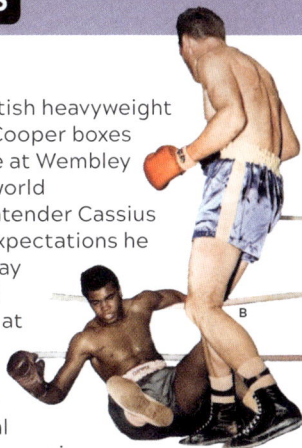

First ever Gillette Cup

7th September 1963 The Gillette Cup, English cricket's first one-day competition, climaxes with a final between Sussex and Worcestershire at Lord's. Led by England captain Ted Dexter, Sussex win by 14 runs.

Two auspicious debuts

The year sees two notable footballing debuts. In May, West Ham's Bobby Moore is Alf Ramsey's choice to lead his new-look England team and makes his first appearance as captain in a 1-0 victory over Czechoslovakia. In September, seventeen-year old Belfast boy George Best plays for Manchester United for the first time in a first division fixture against West Bromwich Albion.

Chester the champion

5th June 1963 Essex teenager Chester Barnes becomes the youngest ever winner of the England table tennis championships. He goes on to win the next three championships in a row and remains synonymous with UK table tennis until his retirement in 1975.

14 JAN 1963

Legendary locomotive *Flying Scotsman* is withdrawn from service.

9 FEB 1963

Maiden flight of Boeing 727 aircraft.

16 MAR 1963

Death of William Beveridge, pioneer of welfare state in UK.

DOMESTIC
NEWS

Big freeze
January - March 1963 Britain's 'Big Freeze' continues as snow blankets the country. January sees an average temperature of -2.1 degrees centigrade, and in some areas even the sea freezes. February sees a 36-hour blizzard and winds of up to 81 miles per hour, before the country finally starts to thaw in March.

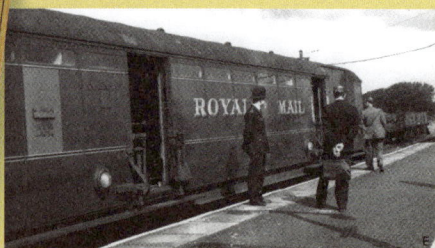

The Great Train Robbery!
8th August 1963 A gang of men waylay a Royal Mail train heading from Glasgow to London on the West Coast Mainline and steal the £2.6 million carried on board. The police offer a £10,000 reward for information, which leads to the thieves being identified, but not before they go to ground. Eight are arrested and seven found guilty at trial in 1964, with a further five arrested at later dates. There seem to be at least four others involved who are never caught.

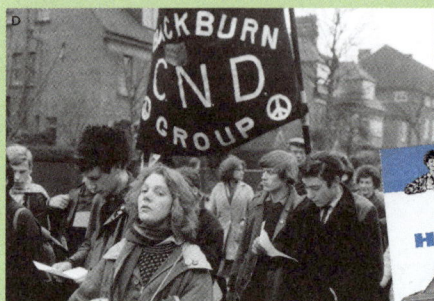

Hillman Imp launched
2nd May 1963 The Hillman Imp goes into production at the new Rootes Group car plant in Linwood in Scotland. The Imp is designed specifically to compete with the Mini Cooper and features both rear-wheel drive and a rear-engine layout. It also makes the most of its small size with a rear bench seat that folds down. The Imp would later become a successful rally car.

Nuclear in the news
6th April 1963 The UK agrees to purchase Polaris nuclear missiles from the United States, leading to protests across the country. The CND's annual Aldermaston to London march sees numbers swell to over 70,000 on the 15th April.

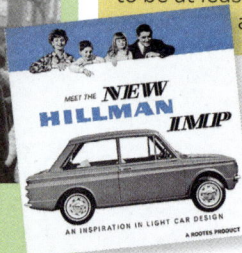

All change in the leadership
In a tumultuous political year, Labour leader Hugh Gaitskell dies on 18th January and is succeeded by Harold Wilson. The tawdriness of the Profumo affair undermines Harold Macmillan's government and he resigns as Prime Minister in October. Foreign Secretary Lord Home leaves his seat in the House of Lords to succeed him. By the end of the year, the whole political climate has changed.

7 APR 1963
Yugoslavian leader Tito made President for life.

15 MAY 1963
Weightwatchers slimming company founded in New York.

16 JUN 1963
Soviet cosmonaut Valentina Tereshkova is the first woman in space.

Say hello to Sindy!
September 1963 Pedigree Dolls and Toys launch their famous 'Sindy' fashion doll. Designed as the British answer to Barbie, which was not particularly popular in the UK at the time, Sindy was designed with the British audience in mind. Instead of Barbie's American glamour, Sindy was given a more 'girl-next-door' style that appealed to UK consumers, and she would become the best-selling toy of 1968 and 1970.

F

DO YOU REMEMBER THIS?

Glass Coca Cola bottle

Dartford Tunnel opens
18th November 1963 The Dartford Tunnel finally opens after the completion of a 57-year construction project disrupted by the Second World War. The toll is two shillings and sixpence.

The Profumo affair
25th September 1963 The Denning Report on the Profumo affair is published, concluding that there have been no security breaches and that government ministers and security services acted 'appropriately'. The scandal saw John Profumo, Secretary of State for War, have an affair with Christine Keeler, a nineteen-year-old model, who was also involved with a Soviet naval attaché, creating a love-triangle that was potentially damaging for national security.

Kenya and Zanzibar
Kenya and Zanzibar become the latest countries to gain independence from Britain, Kenya on 12th December, and Zanzibar on the 19th.

Lava lamps
Edward Craven-Walker, and his lighting company Mathmos, launch the 'Astro' lamp. These extraordinary lamps, featuring a wax mixture floating inside an illuminated, transparent liquid, become a design sensation. Also known as 'lava' lamps, they develop associations with hippie culture and remain a feature of fun-loving British shelves to this day.

ROYALTY & POLITICS

Macmillan signs test ban treaty
7th October 1963 A treaty banning the testing of nuclear weapons in the atmosphere is signed by the leaders of the US, USSR and UK. Harold Macmillan later refers to the signing of the treaty as the biggest achievement of his premiership.

30 JUL 1963
Kim Philby confirmed as Soviet spy now living in Moscow.

1 AUG 1963
Arthur Ashe becomes the first African-American tennis player in the US Davis Cup team.

15 SEP 1963
Bombing of Baptist Church in Birmingham, Alabama, kills four black children.

De Gaulle says *Non*

14th January 1963 In what is a personal humiliation for Prime Minister Harold Macmillan, President de Gaulle rejects the UK's application to join the Common Market. He claims that the UK's membership would be at odds with her Commonwealth links and that the UK would always value her relationship with the US over Europe.

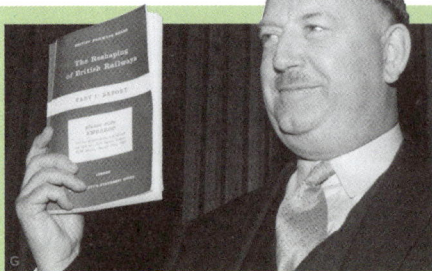

Beeching slashes the railways

27th March 1963 Dr Richard Beeching's report into 'modernising' the UK's railways is published, recommending the shutting down of half the existing railway lines and over 2,000 stations. The report is accepted by the government and closures are expected to begin within two years.

Princess Alexandra weds

24th April 1963 Princess Alexandra, cousin of the Queen and daughter of the late Duke of Kent, marries businessman Angus Ogilvy at Westminster Abbey. Princess Anne is chief bridesmaid. The televised wedding is watched by an estimated 200 million worldwide.

FOREIGN NEWS

White smoke

3rd June 1963 The death of Pope John XXIII sparks a wave of condolence for the simple farmer's son whose appeals for unity among all Christians, together with his humour and spontaneity, made him one of the twentieth century's best-loved religious leaders. On 21st June, after a two day papal conclave, the famous white smoke appears and Cardinal Giovanni Battista Montini succeeds him as Pope Paul VI (photo).

Communication line

30th August 1963 'The quick brown fox jumped over the lazy dog's back 1234567890' is the first message sent on the new teleprinter hotline between Washington and Moscow. Having a direct line of communication between the White House and the Kremlin is intended to prevent future escalations of the Cold War.

Dam catstrophe

9th October 1963 After heavy rainfall and landslides, a wave of water over 100 metres high flows over the Vajont Dam in Italy, killing 3,700 people in the towns and villages below.

---

30 OCT 1963
Lamborghini motor company founded in Italy.

15 NOV 1963
Valium is approved in the US and becomes the most prescribed drug in the world between 1969 and 1982.

12 DEC 1963
Kenya gains independence.

'Ich bin ein Berliner!'

26th June 1963 West Berlin has been a western enclave inside East Germany for eighteen years. In a powerful speech in front of the City Hall in West Berlin, President John F. Kennedy delivers words of hope to beleaguered peoples everywhere: 'All free people, wherever they live, are citizens of Berlin, and therefore I, as a free man, am proud to be able to say: 'I am a Berliner!'

Nuclear-free space

15th October 1963 Almost a year on from the Cuban Missile Crisis, the US and Soviet Union agree to a United Nations resolution banning the placing of nuclear bombs in space.

'I have a dream!'

28th August 1963 In the largest demonstration ever seen in the US, more than a quarter of a million demonstrate for 'jobs and freedom' for African-Americans in Washington DC. The masses gather at the Lincoln Memorial, where Mahalia Jackson, Bob Dylan and Joan Baez perform *We Shall Overcome* and *Blowin' in the Wind* and numerous speakers take the floor. Rev. Martin Luther King Jr. shares his dream of a world without racism with the words: 'I have a dream that one day my four little children will live in a nation where they will not be judged by the colour of their skin but by the content of their character. I have a dream today.' King's 'I Have a Dream' speech becomes a huge source of inspiration for the civil rights movement and is considered one of the finest speeches ever made.

Kennedy assassinated

22nd November 1963 In Dallas, Texas, to bolster support for his re-election, President John F. Kennedy is driven through the city in an open limousine accompanied by his wife Jackie and Texas governor John Connally and his wife Nellie. When the car passes the Texas School Book Depository, Kennedy is shot in the back and head. Lee Harvey Oswald, an ex-marine who once lived in Moscow, is arrested around 90 minutes later. On Air Force One, Vice President Lyndon B. Johnson is sworn in with Jackie Kennedy, still in her blood-stained pink dress, looking on. Oswald denies the murder and is himself shot and killed two days later by a known Mafia associate, Jack Ruby, as he is escorted out of Dallas police headquarters. A month of national mourning begins. The subsequent Warren Commission investigations produce more questions than answers and conspiracy theories remain. Was Castro or the KGB responsible? Did the CIA secretly prepare the assassination attempt? Was the Mafia behind it all? More than 60 years later, the debate goes on.

Exit Adenauer

16th October 1963 In West Germany, the fourteen-year reign of Chancellor Konrad Adenauer comes to an end. Adenauer has turned the country into a reliable and very successful Western nation after the war. Adenauer is succeeded by Ludwig Erhard, under whom Germany experiences a period of low inflation and enormous industrial and economic growth.

Snap happy

Kodak release their Instamatic 50 camera in the UK in February, an instant-loading, point and snap camera that even the most technically inept person can use. Film manufacturers can barely keep up with demand.

ENTERTAINMENT

Diana

DC Thomson launches *Diana* magazine, which runs until 1976 (when it merges with *Jackie*). *Diana*'s target audience is girls from around 11 to 14, and its picture stories include *Jane - Model Miss*, *Mary Brown's Schooldays* and the sci-fi strip cartoon, *The Fabulous Four*. *Diana* also publishes *The Avengers* comic strip from issues 199 to 224 to coincide with the popular television series.

Ready Steady Go!

Ready Steady Go! bursts on to screens on ITV at 6pm on Friday 9th August, a new music show that quickly becomes the TV embodiment of the Swinging Sixties. With the introductory catch-phrase, 'the weekend starts here' *Ready Steady Go!* (or *RSG!*) attracts all the best pop acts and fills the studio with the most fashionable crowd of hip dancers, invited after being scouted in the nightclubs of London. Anchoring the show is Cathy McGowan - Queen of the Mods - who was plucked from obscurity to front the show along with Radio Luxembourg DJ Keith Fordyce.

National treasure

The National Theatre Company, destined to be the official dramatic company allied to the National Theatre on the South Bank, open their first season at the Old Vic, which the company leases while their permanent home is under construction. The first play is *Hamlet* with Peter O'Toole, fresh from his success in *Lawrence of Arabia* and only available for 27 performances due to prior filming commitment.

Sharp cut

Snipper du jour Vidal Sassoon cuts American actress Nancy Kwan's long hair into a sharp, glossy bob prior to her filming *The Wild Affair*. Kwan is so nervous during the haircut she plays chess with her manager to distract her. The result is a sensation.

Ruling the air waves

Plans are well under way for the launch of Radio Caroline from a converted merchant vessel anchored off Felixstowe, just outside the UK's territorial limit. As a pirate radio station, Caroline will offer the wall-to-wall pop music that BBC radio does not, besides becoming the launchpad for many future stars of mainstream radio such as Tony Blackburn, Johnnie Walker and Dave Lee Travis. Caroline finally takes to the air on 28th March 1964.

Doctor who?

On 23rd November, *The Unearthly Child*, the first episode of a new science-fiction drama called *Doctor Who*, is shown on the BBC, starting eighty seconds behind schedule due to the news reporting on the assassination of President Kennedy. William Hartnell plays 'The Doctor, a humanoid alien who travels through time and space in a shape-shifting spaceship, the TARDIS. Due to a malfunction the TARDIS is permanently in the form of a police call box, but miraculously is vast inside despite its compact exterior dimensions.

Busman's holiday

Cliff Richard is Britain's most bankable star when he appears in *Summer Holiday*, his fifth film since 1959. Cliff plays Don, a mechanic at London Transport's service bus depot, who along with his pals, borrows a London double-decker bus and drives through Europe, meeting girls and singing and dancing along the way. It's no surprise that the film is a hit (coming only second to the Bond film *From Russia with Love* this year), and it generates four no. 1 singles, *Bachelor Boy*, *The Next Time*, *Foot Tapper* (for the Shadows) and the title track, *Summer Holiday*.

Ooh, you are awful!

After his role in TV's *The Army Game*, Dick Emery fronts his own BBC comedy sketch show, *The Dick Emery Show*. Emery's parade of characters become household favourites, from the hopeless Bovver Boy (whose long-suffering dad is played by Roy Kinnear) to Mandy, a flirtatious blonde who can't help but read sexual innuendo into every conversation, usually leading her to nudge her interviewer and utter the words, 'Ooh, you are awful!'.

Tom Jones

Many of actor Albert Finney's roles to date, from the film *Saturday Night, Sunday Morning*, or the Royal Court play, *Luther*, have been of the challenging and introspective nature, but in *Tom Jones*, Finney breaks the mould and has the time of his life as the pony-tail wearing, rambunctious womaniser roistering around the hostelries and haystacks of eighteenth-century England. As the posters state, 'Everybody loves Tom Jones!'

Mint mouthful

After Eight Wafer Thin Mints are new from Rowntree and Company and marketed as the ultimate in dinner party sophistication, guaranteed to 'turn any event into an occasion'.

Five o'Clock Club

150 kids form the raucous audience for twice a week show *Five o' Clock Club* which is first shown on ITV on 1st October. *Five o' Clock Club* mixes segments on hobbies such as pets, model-making and cooking, with puppets Fred Barker (a woolly dog) and a Liverpudlian owl Ollie Beak a music act in every show.

1963

Save your stamps
Tesco offers its shoppers the chance to collect Green Shield stamps at its stores. It's one of Green Shield Stamps' most important partnerships, and one of the first loyalty schemes introduced by a major retailer in the UK. At the end of each shop, stamps are issued which are stuck into a saver book and later exchanged for products in the Green Shield Stamps catalogue.

The Great Escape
Of the seventy-six POWs who attempted to escape from Stalag Luft III, fifty were shot on the orders of Hitler, and only three successfully made it home. *The Great Escape* takes a considerable amount of artistic licence in re-telling the original story, not least the inclusion of American soldiers in the escape attempt, done to appeal to US audiences, nevertheless it is an enthralling tribute to the bravery of those who lost their lives in a bid for freedom.

Jason & the Argonauts
Released in the US on 15th August, Ray Harryhausen's pioneering stop-motion visual effects are the real star of this mythological fantasy, from the merciless bronze giant Talos to the chilling sword-wielding skeletons that *Jason and the Argonauts* must battle. Harryhausen said it was the film he was most proud of almost thirty years later, when he was honoured with a Lifetime Achievement Award at the Academy Awards.

The Birds
It's a mystery why birds begin viciously attacking the people of Bodega Bay in Hitchcock's avian horror, released in the UK on 10th September, but the puzzling nature of the attack is perhaps why the film is so unsettling. Tippi Hedren is reportedly close to breakdown during filming due to Hitchcock's unrelenting demands. As for cinema audiences, nobody looks at a flock of starlings in the same way again.

MUSIC

The Stones start to roll
14th May 1963 Still smarting from passing up the Beatles, Decca Records sign a group that is well placed to challenge them. The Rolling Stones have cut their teeth in London's rhythm and blues clubs and play the music of Chuck Berry, Howlin' Wolf, Jimmy Reed et al with authenticity and insolence. They're managed by ex-Beatles publicist Andrew Oldham, whose strategy is to portray them as the anti-Beatles, with longer hair, a hard blues-based sound and lots of threat.

Beach Boys catch a wave
3rd August 1963 Surfin' USA marks the first appearance of a soon to be regular name on the UK record chart - the Beach Boys. In the US, 'surf' music is all the rage, a marriage of clanky guitars and high-voiced harmonies that's redolent of sun-kissed beaches, high waves, tanned muscle men and bikini-clad girls. Brian Wilson is the chief songwriter of the group and bases the song on Chuck Berry's *Sweet Little Sixteen*. Berry responds with a writ.

Freewheelin' Bob

27th May 1963 Bob Dylan already has one album under his belt but it's *The Freewheelin' Bob Dylan* that is really turning heads. It's the outcome of a burst of songwriting activity encouraged by girlfriend Suze Rotolo, who is pictured with Bob on the iconic album cover.

Beatlemania begins

As the year dawns, the Beatles are a little-known Liverpool group with one small hit to their name. Twelve months later, they are not just the biggest group in UK music but an all-consuming part of British life and culture. The journey starts with the No. 2 hit *Please Please Me*, showing off their harmonies and the songwriting skills of Lennon and McCartney. An LP follows, a collection of their stage numbers, then a first No. 1 with *From Me to You*, a second with the style-defining *She Loves You*, and a summer of 'Beatlemania' - girls swamping city centres wherever the Fab Four perform, boys sent home from school to get their hair cut, night after night of concerts where the band cannot hear themselves for screams, and press report after press report where they emerge as intelligent, funny spokesmen for a generation of post-war kids that has found a voice at last. Come the autumn there's another LP, *With the Beatles*, packed with John and Paul originals, plus a fifteen-minute performance on the Royal Variety Show that sends the country's love affair with the Fab Four into overdrive. Could an unwitting US be next for conquest?

Twelve-year-old genius

24th August 1963 Stevie Wonder becomes the first ever artist to top the US singles, LP and R&B charts during the same week. Stevie makes his first visit to the UK during December, where word about Motown is spreading fast, helped by the Beatles' LP versions of Smokey Robinson and Barrett Strong hits.

Epstein builds his stable

Not content with managing the greatest thing ever to happen to the UK music industry, Brian Epstein builds a stable of Liverpool talent. Gerry and the Pacemakers achieve what even the Beatles couldn't with three consecutive No. 1s with their first three releases, while John and Paul supply songs to Billy J. Kramer and the Fourmost. The Swinging Blue Jeans, one of the first Liverpool bands to switch from skiffle to rock, also score with *Hippy Hippy Shake* and *Good Golly Miss Molly*. Epstein does miss out on the Searchers who by common consent are the most musically gifted group on Merseyside. They have two years of hits but lack the songwriting ability to keep them at the top.

Patsy Cline RIP

5th March 1963 Tragedy strikes deep at the heart of country music with the death in a plane crash near Nashville of singing legend Patsy Cline.

Spector reveals his 'wall of sound'

19th October 1963 In Los Angeles, sharp-shooter producer and label owner Phil Spector is making his reputation by loading his productions for the Crystals and the Ronettes with what becomes known as a 'wall of sound' - layer after layer of earthquake-inducing drums and strings. Best of the lot is *Be My Baby* for the Ronettes, featuring his future wife Ronnie Bennett on lead vocal. It's said to be the Beatles' favourite record of the year. Spector spends the whole summer recording a Christmas album featuring all his groups, then withdraws it after President Kennedy is assassinated on its day of release.

MY FIRST 18 YEARS
TOP 10 — 1963

1. **She Loves You** *The Beatles*
2. **If You Gotta Make a Fool ...** *Freddie and the ...*
3. **Summer Holiday** *Cliff Richard*
4. **Dance On** *The Shadows*
5. **Be My Baby** *The Ronettes*
6. **Da Do Ron Ron** *The Crystals*
7. **Do You Love Me** *Brian Poole and the Tremeloes*
8. **Do You Want ...** *Billy J. Kramer and the Dakotas*
9. **Come On** *The Rolling Stones*
10. **You'll Never Walk Alone** *Gerry and the Pace...*

Open | Search | Scan

From *Carousel* to the Kop

31st October 1963 After two No. 1s, Gerry Marsden of Gerry and the Pacemakers pleads with producer George Martin to release *You'll Never Walk Alone* as a single. Martin isn't convinced but trusts Gerry's hunch that this arms-in-the-air highlight of their stage act can give him a third chart topper. As a hymn-like Rodgers and Hammerstein song from the show *Carousel*, it is hardly classic Merseybeat, yet Gerry's soaring vocal and George's rolling strings turn it into an anthem for the ages - and one that is swiftly adopted by the famous Kop at Liverpool FC on their way to championship glory.

The little sparrow is dead

14th October 1963 The death is announced of the legendary singer Edith Piaf, following a long period of illness, aged 47 years. Three days later, a crowd of over 40,000 gather in Paris for the funeral of 'the little sparrow'. Her tiny frame, powder keg voice and heart-churning songs of passion and tragedy made her the single most influential vocal talent ever to come out of France.

SPORT

1964 37 1964 RALLYE MONTE-CARLO

Paddy wins at Monte Carlo

21st January 1964 Driving for the British Motor Corporation, Paddy Hopkirk and co-driver Henry Liddon win the Monte Carlo Rally in a Mini Cooper S. The win cements the Mini in the affections of the UK public and gives a massive boost to its overseas reputation and sales.

DO YOU REMEMBER THIS?

Ken (Barbie) doll

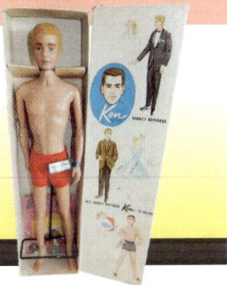

Clay defeats Liston

25th February 1964 In one of boxing's biggest shocks, brash contender Cassius Clay takes the world heavyweight boxing title from the seemingly immovable Sonny Liston. The fight drips with controversy and the outcome is in doubt until the start of the seventh round, when Liston claims a shoulder injury and fails to come out of his corner. Clay is declared the winner by a technical knock-out. The fight marks the real beginning of the Cassius Clay/Muhammad Ali legend, as he joins the Nation of Islam movement two days later and adopts his new name in early March.

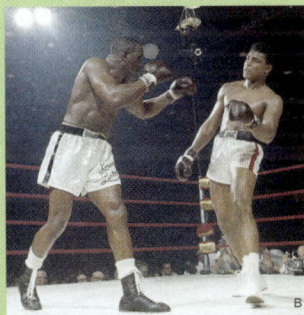

Lifetime ban for Swan

13th April 1964 A match-fixing scandal unveiled by *The People* newspaper leads to the banning of Sheffield Wednesday and England international Peter Swan for life and his imprisonment for four months for fraud. Club teammates Tony Kay and David Layne receive similar punishments. All are convicted for placing bets on the outcome of their club's match against Ipswich Town in December 1962. The bans last until 1972, when Swan returns to playing and managing in the lower leagues.

300 up for Fred

15th August 1964 While bowling for England against Australia in the fifth Test match, Fred Trueman becomes the first player to take 300 Test wickets. It is one of the few bright spots in a disappointing Test series in which Australia retain the Ashes.

27 JAN 1964

Mary Whitehouse launches Clean Up TV campaign

3 FEB 1964

Warren Commission convenes to investigate Kennedy assassination.

27 MAR 1964

Great Train Robbers are sentenced.

Olympics in Tokyo

10th - 24th October 1964 In an Olympic Games in Tokyo that reaches more people across the world than ever before thanks to new satellite technology, the UK team achieves some notable successes. Its four golds go to long jumpers Lynn Davies and Mary Rand, Ken Matthews in the 20-kilometre walk and Ann Packer in the 800 metres, who also wins silver in the 400 metres. Ann is one half of Britain's golden couple of the Games: her husband Robbie Brightwell wins silver in the 4 x 400-metre relay.

DOMESTIC NEWS

Springtown march

28th January 1964 Families living in the Springtown Camp in Derry, Northern Ireland, march through town to demand they are rehoused. Around 400 families have been living in the camp, in buildings made largely from corrugated iron, since the 1940s. The failure of the Protestant local authority to rehouse the predominantly Catholic families in proper houses gives rise to several civil rights protests in Northern Ireland.

Mods and Rockers

30th March 1964 Britain becomes embroiled in a culture war as two opposing groups, 'Mods' and 'Rockers', clash. The first physical conflicts occur at Clacton Beach and Hastings over Easter, followed by more disturbances in Brighton in May. 'Mod' culture focuses on a clean-cut image, with members wearing suits and riding scooters, listening to jazz and soul. 'Rockers' in contrast wear leather jackets and ride motorcycles, favouring rock 'n' roll and R&B.

Hello Habitat!

11th May 1964 The very first Habitat store is opened by designer Terence Conran in London. The Fulham Road store becomes famous for its modern aesthetic, featuring whitewashed brick walls and spotlights. The brand grows quickly and is soon found across the country.

habitat

Chunnel go ahead!

6th February 1964 Proposals to create a Channel tunnel connecting Britain to the continent are agreed upon by the British and French governments. The new rail tunnel is to pass 31 miles under the sea and connect Folkestone to Coquelles. Whilst an agreement is reached in 1964, studies and planning mean construction will not start for another decade.

21 APR 1964	28 MAY 1964	8 JUN 1964
BBC2 is launched.	The Palestine National Congress forms the PLO in Jerusalem.	Christine Keeler released from prison.

Shopping undercover!
29th May 1964 A new building opens at the Bull Ring, Birmingham. Alongside traditional outdoor market stalls, a large indoor shopping centre is developed, the first of its kind in the country.

More Moors murders
17th June 1964 Moors Murderers Ian Brady and Myra Hindley claim their third victim, twelve-year-old Keith Bennett, who is snatched on his way to his grandmother's house. Bennett's body is never found. In December their fourth victim, ten-year-old Lesley Ann Downey, is taken from a fairground near her home. It would be another year before their crimes would be uncovered.

Brook Advisory Centres
July 1964 The first Brook Advisory Centre is opened by Helen Brook, offering contraception and sexual health advice to teenagers. Other services, such as the Family Planning Association, had served only married, or soon-to-be-married, women. The Brook Centres play an important role in preventing teenage pregnancy and became synonymous with the sexual revolution of the 60s. By 1969 they are advising more than 10,000 young people.

Malawi, Malta and Zambia
6th July 1964 Malawi gains its independence from Britain, followed on 21st September by the island of Malta. On 24th October, Northern Rhodesia also gains independence and becomes the Republic of Zambia.

TV Innovations
1964 sees changes in the British television experience as BBC2 launches, with technical difficulties, in April. The 60s has seen television ownership rocket, with 90% of households now owning a set.

Forth Road Bridge
4th September 1964 The Forth Road Bridge opens across the Firth of Forth, and becomes the longest steel suspension bridge in Europe. The bridge replaces a centuries-old ferry service carrying 1.5 million passengers annually, and significantly cuts the journey time between Edinburgh and Fife.

HOW THE BROOK HELPS TEENAGERS NEEDING ADVICE ABOUT SEX

BROOK ADVISORY CENTRES
helpful people with helpful answers

Japanese cars
Japanese motor company Daihatsu launch their Compagno model car in Britain, becoming the first Japanese carmaker to export their vehicles to Europe. Despite curiosity in Japanese products, they do not welcome much sales success until the 1980s.

14 JUL 1964
Jacques Anquetil of France wins fourth consecutive Tour de France.

12 AUG 1964
Death of Ian Fleming, creator of James Bond.

4 SEP 1964
Forth Road Bridge opens in Scotland.

ROYALTY & POLITICS

Sir Alec gives way to the Beatles
12th February 1964 Sir Alec Douglas-Home makes his first visit to the US as UK Prime Minister and meets President Johnson for talks. Extraordinarily, the talks were scheduled for a week earlier but were postponed due to the Beatles' visit to New York.

Prince Edward born
10th March 1964 Prince Edward is born at Buckingham Palace. He is the fourth child of the Queen and the Duke of Edinburgh and is third in line to the throne. According to reports, his is the first royal birth to be witnessed by his father.

Wilson is Prime Minister
15th October 1964 One of the most anticipated general elections this century leads to the Conservatives losing power and the first Labour government for thirteen years, under the stewardship of Prime Minister Harold Wilson. The majority of just four seats over all other parties gives the new government little room for manoeuvre in its plans for legislation.

Churchill retires
27th July 1964 Sir Winston Churchill announces that he is retiring from Parliament after serving as MP for the constituency of Woodford since 1945. He is now 89 years old and in ill health.

Capital punishment suspended
21st December 1964 Four months after the last execution by hanging, Parliament votes to end the death penalty by 355 votes to 170. The vehicle for abolition is a Private Member's Bill proposed by Sydney Silverman MP which will reach the statute book in a year's time. No executions are carried out in the meantime.

FOREIGN NEWS

Tobacco warning
11th January 1964 A report commissioned by the US Surgeon General from leading scientists warns that smoking is a hazard to bronchial and cardiac health. Cigarette consumption in the US drops by almost twenty per cent during 1964 as a direct result.

14 OCT 1964
Philips begins experimenting with colour TV.

18 NOV 1964
FBI director J. Edgar Hoover calls Martin Luther King Jr. a 'most notorious liar'.

22 DEC 1964
Denis Law wins award for best European football player, the Ballon d'Or.

Primitive mouse

US engineer Douglas Engelbart invents the computer mouse. He demonstrates the device at a conference in San Francisco in 1968 and obtains a patent two years later. The primitive mouse is a wooden box with a thick electrical cord and two metal wheels that allow the X/Y position to be displayed on the screen.

Nehru is dead

27th May 1964 Jawaharlal Nehru, Prime Minister of India since partition in 1947 and a creator of the Non-Aligned Movement, dies in New Delhi.

Mandela's defence

12th June 1964 Nelson Mandela is sentenced to life imprisonment on Robben Island for organising a guerrilla war against South Africa's apartheid regime. At the start of his defence he speaks for three hours about an ideal society in which everyone lives together in harmony and with equal opportunities. His speech ends with the historic words 'My Lord, if needs be, it is an ideal for which I am prepared to die.'

Khruschev deposed

15th October 1964 There is an unexpected change of the guard in the Kremlin. Soviet leader Nikita Khrushchev is deposed by the Politburo, partly because of the loss of face that the Soviet Union suffered over the Cuban Missile Crisis. Khrushchev is placed under house arrest as the more conservative Leonid Brezhnev (photo) replaces him as the new Communist Party leader and Alexei Kosygin is made Prime Minister.

A second emancipation

2nd July 1964 The historic Civil Rights Act is signed into law by President Johnson. It abolishes racial segregation in schools, hotels and transport, and makes discrimination in employment on grounds of race illegal. Martin Luther King Jr describes it as 'a second emancipation'. The Act comes just over a year after his 'I have a dream' speech in Washington DC.

Gulf of Tonkin incidents

2nd - 4th August 1964 Two incidents in the Gulf of Tonkin precipitate a major escalation of the Vietnam conflict. US Congress approves President Johnson's use of war powers to combat attacks, clearing the way for the rapid intensification of US involvement.

LBJ re-elected

8th November 1964 As his campaign slogan goes, it's 'all the way with LBJ'. Lyndon Johnson is re-elected President of the US, defeating his Republican challenger Senator Barry Goldwater with a record 61 per cent share of the popular vote.

King recognised

10th December 1964 Dr Martin Luther King Jr becomes the youngest ever recipient of the Nobel Peace Prize, which is awarded to him in recognition of his work in leading non-violent resistance to racial discrimination in the US.

📺 ENTERTAINMENT

Lest we forget

The Great War, a landmark, 26-part documentary marking the fiftieth anniversary of the outbreak of the First World War, begins on the BBC on 30th May. The series, which is narrated by Michael Redgrave, includes interviews with a number of veterans who had responded to requests in the press, and attracts an average audience of eight million per episode.

Jackie

DC Thomson launch *Jackie* magazine, packed with features on fashion and make-up, advice on boys and splashes about the latest teen pop stars. Its agony aunts, Cathy and Claire, prove to be a lifeline for teenage girls negotiating the complexities of love and teenage angst. The first issue on 11th January features (who else but?) Cliff Richard on the cover.

Power shifts on Fleet Street

In the world of newspapers, the *Daily Herald*, a paper which had begun in 1912 as an organ in support of the trade union and Labour movement, closes and relaunches as *The Sun*, although *The Sun's* circulation is, for a time, even lower than its ailing predecessor. It is purchased by Rupert Murdoch in 1969 for £800,000, with a promise to publish an 'honest, straightforward newspaper'. In time, Murdoch's *Sun* will have radically opposed political views to the original *Daily Herald*, and he remarks on 'the ease with which I entered British newspapers'.

GOOD MORNING! YES, IT'S TIME FOR A NEW NEWSPAPER

A Hard Day's Night

Beatlemania is reaching a crescendo when *A Hard Day's Night* premieres at the Pavilion Theatre on 6th July and several hundred perspiring policemen battle to hold back 12,000 screaming fans who have descended on Leicester Square to see their heroes in the flesh. Directed by Richard Lester, who also directs *Help!* the following year, it's a nimble, off-beat mockumentary in which the band members play themselves, helped (or rather hindered) by Paul's on-screen grandfather, Wilfred Brambell. A critical as well as commercial success, the boys' screen debut is widely praised.

On the ball

Match of the Day, television's first regular football programme, is transmitted on BBC2 on 22nd August, kicking off the 1964-5 football season, but the BBC agree with the Football League to keep the match chosen (Arsenal v. Liverpool) secret until 4pm for fear fans will stay at home rather than attend in person.

MATCH OF THE DAY

Play School

'Here's a house, here's a door. Windows: 1, 2, 3, 4. Ready to knock? Turn the lock. It's Playschool.' For pre-school children of the next three decades, *Playschool*, which is first shown on 21st April, is part of their daily routine, a show in which presenters sing songs, dance, tell stories and urge you to guess which shaped window (the round, the square or the arched) will be showing the day's film. *Playschool* has a pool of presenters who, if not already well-known, will go on to become so due to their association with the show; actor Paul Danquah is television's first black children's presenter, then there is Johnny Ball, Chloe Ashcroft, Floella Benjamin, Toni Arthur and the loose-limbed Derek Griffiths. At his audition, Brian Cant, who presents the show for twenty-one years, used a box to pretend he was rowing out to sea. The real stars of course are the toys, Humpty; the dolls, Jemima and Hamble; Big and Little Ted.

Apology accepted

I'm Sorry, I'll Read That Again is first broadcast on the BBC Home Service (later Radio 4) on 3rd April. Derived from a sketch show created by members of the Cambridge University Footlights Revue, the cast includes John Cleese, Graeme Garden, Tim Brooke-Taylor and Bill Oddie. The show's title, referencing the apology given by announcers when fluffing lines on live radio, set the tone for its irreverent and off-the-cuff brand of humour.

Charlie and the Chocolate Factory

Roald Dahl's timeless tale of Charlie Bucket and his eventful trip to the marvellous chocolate factory of Mr Willy Wonka is published in the UK by Allen and Unwin on 23rd November, with illustrations by Faith Jacques.

Top of the Pops

ITV has *Ready Steady Go!* and now it's time for BBC to get down with the kids. *Top of the Pops* is first broadcast on New Year's Day from a converted church in Dickenson Road, Rusholme, Manchester and fires a salvo to the competition with a prestigious line-up of music makers; Dusty Springfield is the first act to perform in a show that also boasts the Rolling Stones, the Hollies, the Swinging Blue Jeans and the Dave Clark Five. With music performances introduced by popular DJs of the day and a studio full of shimmying local audience members, *Top of the Pops* becomes the UK's longest-running music programme and hosts some of pop and rock's greatest moments.

Seven Up

Aristotle's challenge, 'Give me a child when he is seven and I will show you the man' is the premise for this ambitious and groundbreaking social experiment as documentary, in which fourteen children from different backgrounds are selected to be filmed every seven years. The first, *Seven Up* introduces audiences to the seven-year-olds including Tony, the east end lad with ambitions to be a jockey and sweet Liverpudlian, Neil, who wants to be an astronaut, but audiences must wait until 1973 to meet them again.

Bond strikes gold

Agent 007, played with unerring sang-froid by Sean Connery, comes into his own when *Goldfinger*, the third in the series of film adaptations of Ian Fleming's novel opens at the Odeon Leicester Square on 17th September. Goldfinger's budget is more than that of *Dr. No* and *From Russia with Love* combined, and for the first time, MI6 gadgetry and technology become an essential part of Bond's arsenal as he globetrots around the world determined to outwit Auric Goldfinger while wearing a succession of immaculate Anthony Sinclair suits.

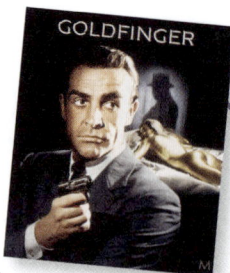

Meccano makes it

Construction toy Meccano has been part of children's toy cupboards since it was first introduced in 1898, but the company fall into financial difficulties and is purchased by Lines Brothers, who operate under the brand name, Tri-Ang. Under its new owners, Meccano undergoes a revamp with pieces now made in black and yellow to mirror the colour scheme of most construction vehicles.

Doolittle vs. Poppins

Despite her huge success in the Broadway and West End productions of *My Fair Lady*, Warner Brothers boss Jack Warner thinks Julie Andrews isn't a big enough name to play Eliza Doolittle in the film version, and casts Audrey Hepburn (albeit with her songs dubbed by Marni Nixon). Andrews instead lends her cut-glass British accent and impressive vocal cords to Disney in *Mary Poppins* and scoops an Academy Award, while Hepburn doesn't even receive a nomination for *My Fair Lady*.

MUSIC

Here's the Tottenham sound!

16th January 1964 After Merseybeat, what price the Tottenham sound? The Dave Clark Five are the resident quintet at a ballroom in Tottenham, North London, who mix organ, guitar, saxophone and stomping drums with the half-shouted vocals of singer Mike Smith. Their No. 1 with *Glad All Over* is enough to cause a flutter of worry in the Beatle ranks that they might have a serious rival.

The Beatles invade!

7th February 1964 The Beatles land in New York where astute promotion has helped *I Want to Hold Your Hand* become the fastest-ever million seller in US history. Over 73 million tune in to *The Ed Sullivan Show* for their first glimpse of the group two days later. By the end of the month they have five singles in the US Hot 100 and three LPs in the album chart. The Beatles' impact on the home of rock'n'roll is seismic as they open the floodgates for a other UK groups to rush through - most controversially, the Rolling Stones. So complete is the 'British invasion' that home-grown bands have to look and sound British to get noticed.

Bachelor boys

20th February 1964 In the middle of a beat group bonanza, who should sit at No. 1 in the UK but a trio of cardigan-clad Irishmen with *Diane*, a song from 1927. The Bachelors - brothers Con and Dec Cluskey and their pal John Stokes - will finish the year as Decca Records' top chart act, ahead of even the Rolling Stones.

Cilla has a heart

27th February 1964 Cilla Black is the fourth of Brian Epstein's acts to reach No. 1, with her George Martin produced cover of Dionne Warwick's *Anyone Who Had a Heart*. Cilla (real name Priscilla White) was formerly the cloakroom girl at the Cavern. *You're My World* gives her another No. 1 during May.

Bluebeat comes to Britain

14th March 1964 Determined to bring the bluebeat and ska sounds of his native Jamaica to the world, Chris Blackwell created his Island label in 1959 to record local artists and license the discs overseas. Millie Small's delightful *My Boy Lollipop* is the international breakthrough that Jamaican music has been waiting for.

Girl power 1960s style

21st May 1964 Following the trail blazed by Dusty Springfield and Cilla Black, pint-sized fifteen-year-old Lulu arrives with a sizzling cover of the Isley Brothers' *Shout*. Glaswegian Lulu (real name Marie McDonald Lawrie) has not even left school yet. Also waving the flag for 1960s girl power is Dagenham's Sandie Shaw who raids the Dionne Warwick songbook for *Always Something There To Remind Me* and upsets Britain's chiropodists by performing in her bare feet.

Mancs on the march

Now that London's record labels have raided Liverpool of its groups they turn their attention to Manchester, 30 miles east. The wacky Freddie and the Dreamers are the first scalps, followed by the Hollies, Mindbenders and Herman's Hermits, whose toothy lead singer Peter Noone once played a scallywag in *Coronation Street*.

The Stones roll on

16th July 1964 The bad boys of UK pop score their first No. 1 with It's All Over Now, a song by Bobby and Shirley Womack of the Valentinos that they recorded at Chess studios in Chicago, home of their blues heroes Chuck Berry and Muddy Waters. So far they have no original material, but that changes when Andrew Oldham locks Mick and Keith in a kitchen and tells them to write a song for new protégé Marianne Faithfull. As Tears Go By is the result. For the moment, they're sticking to covers for singles, with Willie Dixon's Little Red Rooster the next in line for No. 1.

Animal tracks

9th July 1964 UK pop's hottest producer is Mickie Most, who's behind hits for Herman's Hermits (*I'm Into Something Good*), Lulu (*Shout*) and Newcastle blues band the Animals. The combination of Eric Burdon's coalmine-deep blues voice and Alan Price's swirling organ playing make *House of the Rising Sun* one of the grittiest No. 1s ever - and, at well over four minutes, one of the longest.

Sam Cooke shot dead

11th December 1964 Sam Cooke is shot dead in a Los Angeles motel. Originally the handsome, honey-voiced lead man of gospel group the Soul Stirrers, he left to find pop success with *Only Sixteen*, *Wonderful World* and *Another Saturday Night*. The recent *A Change is Gonna Come*, a powerful plea for black civil rights, signalled a shift towards the gospel/rhythm and blues blend pioneered by Ray Charles.

Hitsville USA

Motown's releases this year include such imperishable pop classics as Mary Wells' *My Guy*, Martha and the Vandellas' *Dancing in the Street* and the Supremes' *Baby Love*, all the products of a crack team of musicians, writers and producers in a Detroit studio working under the shrewd eye of owner Berry Gordy. The Motown sound oozes glamour and gospel-like feeling - and it's only just getting started.

MY FIRST 18 YEARS
TOP 10 — 1964

1. **Baby Love** *The Supremes*
2. **Can't Buy Me Love** *The Beatles*
3. **I Get Around** *The Beach Boys*
4. **A World Without Love** *Peter and Gordon*
5. **Goldfinger** *Shirley Bassey*
6. **It's All Over Now** *The Rolling Stones*
7. **You Really Got Me** *The Kinks*
8. **Oh Pretty Woman** *Roy Orbison*
9. **The Times They Are A' Changin'** *Bob Dylan*
10. **Dancing in the Street** *Martha and the Vandellas*

Open | Search | Scan

The big O

British pop's US invasion isn't all one way. In a class all his own is Roy Orbison, once a label mate of Elvis at Sun Records and latterly the purveyor of unbearably sad self-composed ballads. Famously static in live performance, his towering falsetto and dark glasses give 'the big O' an almost ghostly stage presence. Roy's two No. 1s of 1964 are the angst-laden *It's Over* and the frankly lascivious *Oh Pretty Woman.*

SPORT

Arise, Sir Stanley

1st January 1965 Stanley Matthews becomes the first ever professional football player to receive a knighthood. He will be 50 years old in February, shortly before he plays his last competitive match for Stoke City.

Dawn Fraser banned

1st March 1965 Triple Olympic gold medal-winning Dawn Fraser is suspended by Australia's Amateur Swimming Association for ten years for misconduct during the previous year's Olympic Games in Tokyo. It is punishment for her decision to march in the opening ceremony against their instructions, and for an incident in which she was alleged to have stolen a flag from outside Emperor Hirohito's palace.

An American first

27th March 1965 It's an all-American triumph in the 119th running of the Grand National. Crompton 'Tommy' Smith becomes the first American jockey to win the race, on the US-owned and trained horse Jay Trump, who defeats Freddie in a close finish at 100/6.

DO YOU REMEMBER THIS?

Ministeck

Double triumph for Clark

31st May 1965 Jim Clark is the first non-American driver in 49 years to win the Indianapolis 500. Two months later he wins the German Grand Prix at Nürburgring to take the second of his Formula One World Drivers' Championships, so becoming the only driver in history to win the Indy 500 and the Formula One championship in the same year.

Ali v Liston

25th March 1965 In a rematch to decide the world heavyweight championship, Muhammad Ali (formerly Cassius Clay) beats Sonny Liston once again. Liston falls to the canvas after two minutes of the second round and does not get up.

20 JAN 1965

Lyndon Johnson inaugurated as US President for second term.

23 FEB 1965

Death of Stan Laurel, one half of Laurel and Hardy comedy team.

7 MAR 1965

US Marines arrive in Vietnam as conflict intensifies.

1965

Football firsts

The end of the 1964-65 season sees Manchester United win the league championship for the first time since the 1958 Munich air crash that decimated their playing squad. Liverpool beat Leeds United 2-1 to win the FA Cup for the first time, this in a match that sees Albert Johanneson of Leeds become the first black player to grace a cup final. Debuting in the European Cup Winners' Cup, West Ham beat 1860 Munich 2-0 in the final. An innovation for the 1965-66 season is the allowance of one substitution per side per game, the very first player to take the field as a 'sub' being Keith Peacock (Illustration) of Charlton Athletic. After all these firsts there is a last: the very last Christmas Day fixture is played in England, a derby match between Blackpool and Blackburn Rovers. From now on festive games will be restricted to Boxing Day

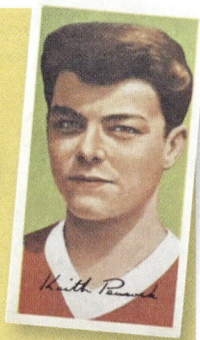

DOMESTIC NEWS

NHS charges end

31st January 1965 The Labour government ends charges for prescriptions available on the National Health Service. The charge had been 2 shillings, but for the next three years prescriptions are free to all, before charges are reintroduced in 1968.

Goldie the Eagle

11th March 1965 The nation is gripped as the infamous 'Goldie the Eagle is finally recaptured by his London Zoo keepers after eleven days on the run'. Goldie's brief bid for freedom dominates the news for a fortnight, after his escape during a routine cage clean. Goldie wasn't done with his life on the run, however, escaping again for five days in December.

Famous foods

1965 sees the launch in the UK of several famous brands, including the very first Pizza Express restaurant, a British brand, which opens in Soho, London, on 27th March. American brand KFC launches in Preston, Lancashire, in May, and in the same month the Asquith brothers launch their new supermarket chain with Associated Dairies, taking the 'As' from Asquith and the 'Da' from dairies to create British brand 'ASDA' (photo).

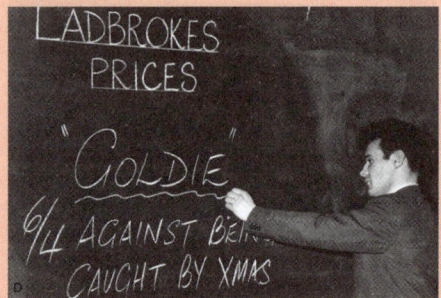

6 APR 1965	12 MAY 1965	1 JUN 1965
UK government's TSR-2 bomber aircraft project is abandoned.	West Germany and Israel establish diplomatic relations.	The first Certificate of Secondary Education (CSE) examinations take place.

Little Baldon air crash

6th July 1965 Tragedy strikes as a Handley Page Hastings crashes shortly after take-off from RAF Abingdon. The flight is carrying 41 service personel on a parachute training mission and comes down in Little Baldon with no survivors.

Ronnie Biggs escapes!

8th July 1965 Ronnie Biggs, one of the thieves convicted of the Great Train Robbery, escapes from Wandsworth prison. Biggs is on the run for 36 years, spending time in Australia and South America, before returning to the UK, and prison, in 2001.

No smoking adverts

1st August 1965 Advertisements for cigarettes are banned from British television, forming the first step in measures designed to curb the nation's smoking habit. Anti-smoking campaigners must wait until the 1990s for further restrictions to be enacted.

Moors Murderers caught

7 October 1965 Ian Brady is charged with the murder of seventeen-year-old Edward Evans. Over the next month the police arrest Brady's girlfriend, Myra Hindley, and 150 police officers comb Saddleworth Moor, looking for the bodies of further victims. Eventually the remains of Lesley Ann Downey and John Kilbride are discovered, along with tape recordings of the murders, and a horrified nation learns the extent of the pair's crimes.

Television morality fears

13th November 1965 Theatre critic Kenneth Tynan becomes the first person to clearly say the F-word on British television. The live debate he is partaking in discusses issues relating to censorship in the theatre, and morality in entertainment becomes a hot topic in 60s Britain.

Sea Gem collapses

27th December 1965 The Sea Gem oil rig collapses in the North Sea killing thirteen people. The rig is in the process of being moved to a new location when two of its ten legs collapse, sending men and equipment into the cold North Sea.

Mary's minis!

The world of fashion gets mini skirt fever as designer Mary Quant introduces her shockingly short designs to London's streets. Her shop on the King's Road in Chelsea, 'Bazaar', does a roaring trade and soon the mini skirt becomes synonymous with the 'Swinging' Sixties.

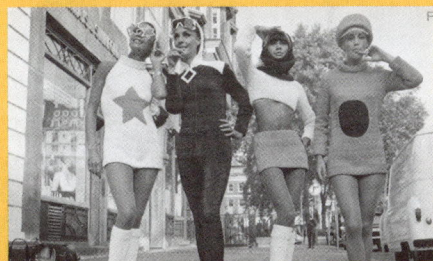

19 JUL 1965
Mont Blanc Tunnel is opened between France and Italy.

5 AUG 1965
A five month war begins between India and Pakistan.

27 SEP 1965
Death of Clara Bow, icon of the silent movie era.

ROYALTY & POLITICS

Churchill is dead
24th January 1965 Britain's wartime Prime Minister Sir Winston Churchill dies at his London home at the age of 90. He is accorded a huge state funeral at St Paul's Cathedral six days later and is buried in Bladon churchyard in Oxfordshire.

DO YOU REMEMBER THIS?

Hand mixer

Sir Alec resigns
2nd July 1965 Alec Douglas-Home surprises even his closest colleagues by resigning as Conservative Party leader. Attention turns immediately towards his successor. For the first time Conservative MPs will be able to choose their own leader by secret ballot. The winner is Edward Heath (photo), the first Conservative leader not to have had a public school education.

Death of the Princess Royal
28th March 1965 Mary, Princess Royal, dies at her home, Harewood House in Yorkshire, aged 67. The only daughter of King George V and Queen Mary, sister of King Edward VIII and King George VI and aunt of Queen Elizabeth II, she was known for her strong advocacy of higher education for women.

Race Relations Act
8th December 1965 The Race Relations Act comes into force making it a civil offence to discriminate against people on grounds of colour, race or ethnic or national background.

Government agenda
May - July 1965 With the partial nationalisation of the steel industry narrowly secured, the Labour government's legislative programme includes a promise to introduce a blood alcohol limit to combat drink driving. Further measures include the introduction of a 70 mph speed limit on UK roads and, after the appointment of Roy Jenkins as Home Secretary in December, a raft of social reforms including the planned decriminalisation of homosexuality.

7 OCT 1965
Post Office Tower opens in London.

27 NOV 1965
First major anti-Vietnam war protest in Wahington DC.

22 DEC 1965
Barbara Castle becomes Minister of Transport.

FOREIGN
NEWS

Malcolm X shot dead

21st February 1965 Black Power leader Malcolm X is assassinated in New York. Formerly an advocate of black separatism and a member of the Nation of Islam, his formation of the Organisation of Afro-American Unity and his growing advocacy of world brotherhood made him a hate target for black militants.

Arafat's new force

1st January 1965 Palestine Liberation Movement leader Yasser Arafat announces the formation of a military wing to pursue a guerilla war against Israel.

War in Kashmir

5th August 1965 Pakistan sends thousands of troops disguised as civilians into India and sparks conflict in Kashmir that will lasts five months.

Rolling Thunder begins

22nd March 1965 Operation Rolling Thunder begins - aerial bombing of North Vietnam on a daily basis. Over 55,000 missions will be mounted over the next three years and will bring an end to the war no closer. In October, the war escalates with the US bombing of Viet Cong positions in neighbouring (and neutral) Cambodia.

First space walker

18th March 1965 Soviet cosmonaut Alexei Leonov is the first man to walk in space. He floats outside Voskhod 2 for twelve minutes. 'You just can't comprehend it. Only there can you feel the grandeur, the enormous scale of everything around us,' he says later.

Voting Rights Act

6th August 1965 President Johnson signs the Voting Rights Act into law, removing obstacles such as literacy tests that disqualified African-Americans from voting.

Dolby system

At his London laboratory, US engineer Ray Dolby develops a system to suppress tape noise that will become a movie and recording industry standard.

Watts aflame

11th August 1965 Mass rioting breaks out in Watts, a poor black neighbourhood of Los Angeles, following a minor traffic incident. The riots last for six days and cause 34 deaths and over a thousand injuries.

ENTERTAINMENT

Short life for London Life

London Life magazine is launched on 9th October by the Thomson organisation, intended as a hip and happening replacement for the *Tatler*. Contributions include fashion advice from Terence Stamp and Jean Shrimpton, Marc Bolan writes the music reviews one issue, photographs are by Terence Donovan and Duffy, and artwork is supplied by a young artist called Ian Dury. By the end of 1966, staff turn up to work one day to be told the title is closing with immediate effect.

Pipe Up

Unusual pipes and long cigarette holders are all the rage with mods in London this year, who keep one 150-year-old Soho tobacconist in business with their demand for strange smoking accoutrements, or 'kinky gear'.

The hills are alive…

Nuns! Nazis! Lederhosen! Singing siblings! It's all here in what many consider the ultimate musical as Julie Andrews takes on the career-defining role of Maria, a novice nun whose restless character leads the Mother Superior at her Austrian convent to send her to become governess to the motherless offspring of gruff disciplinarian Captain von Trapp (Christopher Plummer). Rodgers and Hammerstein's sing-a-long score seals the film's reputation as a future classic.

Big move for Biba

Around sixty models and well-known personalities, including *Ready, Steady Go!* presenter Cathy McGowan and singer Cilla Black, help the cult London fashion store Biba move premises from Abingdon Road to Kensington Church Street in what is a carefully orchestrated publicity stunt.

Magic Roundabout

Adapted from the stop-motion animation French original, the psychedelic world of *The Magic Roundabout* is first introduced to the British public on 18th October. When the programme is moved the following year, from its slot before the 6 O' clock News to an earlier time, the BBC receives a flood of complaints from adults who are unable to get home from work in time to watch it, proving the cross-generational appeal of Florence, Zebedee, Dougal and Brian the Snail.

Ladybird, ladybird

Ladybird is one of the best-selling childrenswear brands in the 1960s and most children will be dressed in at least one or two Ladybird garments, whether it's dresses and coats for Sunday best, or vests, baby clothes, pyjamas and playsuits from the more affordable Woolworth's range.

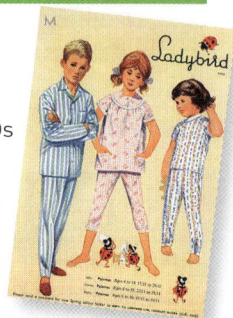

Round the Horne

Created by Barry Took and Marty Feldman, radio sketch show *Round the Horne* is first broadcast on 7th March and includes a number of the cast from its predecessor show, *Beyond our Ken*, among them Kenneth Williams and Hugh Paddick. Blazing a trail for shows such as *The Goodies* and *Monty Python's Flying Circus*, *Round the Horne's* cast of nonsensical characters has the urbane straight man Kenneth Horne at its centre, whose smooth patter is liberally laced with innuendo.

Exterminate!

With *Doctor Who* now firmly established as essential viewing, Whovian playthings are in demand from miniature replicas of the Doctor's most dangerous foe to the AstroRay Dalek Gun made by Bell Toys, essential for keeping at one's side while hiding behind the sofa.

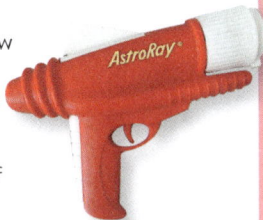

Up the Junction

The launch of *Wednesday Playhouse* the previous year provides a platform for some of the decade's most influential dramas, including *Up the Junction* written by Nell Dunn and directed by Ken Loach who shoots it in a drama-documentary style. Following the lives of three female friends from south London, *Up the Junction* tackles some challenging themes, notably back-street abortion, and after it is broadcast on 3rd November, the BBC receives 400 complaints.

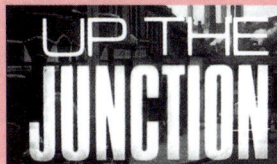

Call My Bluff

Call My Bluff, the much-loved panel game in which participants attempt to explain the meaning of an obscure word in the English dictionary, with only one definition actually true, is broadcast for the first time on 17th October. Debonair wit Frank Muir captains one team, while the magisterial Robert Morley heads the other; the host is Robin Ray, later succeeded by Robert Robinson. For viewers, the show's lasting appeal is not only the amusing banter among contestants but the chance to expand one's vocabulary with a wondrous array of new words from hickboo to ablewhacket.

Telling tales

The very first story - Cap of Rushes - is told on Jackanory on 13th December by Lee Montague. *Jackanory's* simplicity is also its power. Storytellers, recruited from the realms of theatre, film and literature, sit in a chair in front of the camera as they read the autocue and captivate kids with their energetic and characterful readings of stories old and new. Over the years, Kenneth Williams, Michael Hordern, Alan Bennett and Rik Mayall are just some who sit in the Jackanory chair, with Bernard Cribbins (photo) boasting a record-breaking 111 appearances.

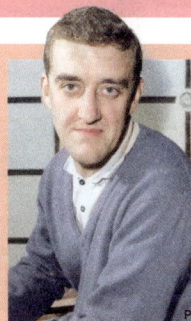

A Bright Future

Wannabe science boffins (and anyone quite simply interested in new technology) gets their first taste of *Tomorrow's World* presented by Raymond Baxter on the BBC on 7th July 1955.

Darling Julie

Julie Christie, gorgeous and gifted, is swiftly becoming the 'it' girl of sixties cinema. This year she stars as Lara opposite Omar Sharif, Tom Courtenay and Geraldine Chaplin in *Dr Zhivago*, David Lean's sweeping, Russian revolution romance based on Boris Pasternak's novel. But it's the John Schlesinger film *Darling*, in which she plays a model and actress juggling the attentions of two older men, that bags her an Academy Award. *Darling* has its finger on the pulse of swinging London and Julie Christie is at its beating heart.

Sex a-Peel

Diana Rigg joins the cast of *The Avengers* as Emma Peel, replacing Honor Blackman's Cathy Gale (who leaves to film *Goldfinger*). In partnership with Patrick Macnee's Steed, she's a brilliant secret agent and martial arts expert, rescuing him from a succession of scrapes wearing the best outfits any crime-fighting heroine could wish for.

Thunderbirds are GO!

Tracy Island in the Pacific Ocean is the base for International Rescue, headed by Jeff Tracy whose five sons, Scott, Virgil, John, Gordon and Alan (aided by brilliant scientist Brains) can scramble their high-performance Thunderbird craft at a moment's notice to rescue those in need. Created by Gerry Anderson, also renowned for supermarionation productions *Captain Scarlett*, *Joe 90* and *Stingray*, the Thunderbirds' special British agent, the glamorous Lady Penelope Creighton-Ward, is voiced by Sylvia Anderson, Gerry's wife and co-creator of the show.

Charlie Girl

Singing star Joe Brown co-stars with Anna Neagle in the musical *Charlie Girl*, which opens at the Adelphi Theatre on the 15th December. The show is one of the most successful of the 1960s, running for 2,202 performances until March 1971.

MUSIC

The Byrds take flight

20th January 1965 By setting an acoustic song to a rock accompaniment, California band the Byrds create a whole new style called folk-rock. The song is Dylan's *Mr Tambourine Man*, which former folk singer and twelve-string guitarist Roger McGuinn has embellished with gorgeously dense harmonies. The record tops the US and UK charts and encourages Dylan to embrace rock.

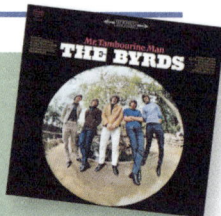

The best of British blues

14th January 1965 In the wake of the Rolling Stones, London's rhythm and blues club scene is awash with talent. Scoring the year's first new No. 1 are Georgie Fame and the Blue Flames, resident band at the Flamingo in Soho, with the Mose Allison song *Yeh Yeh*. Manfred Mann, with Jagger's pal Paul Jones on vocals, are already Top Ten regulars. Cream of the crop are the Yardbirds, whose guitarist Eric Clapton (photo) joined from John Mayall's Bluesbreakers and has an almost messianic following. He leaves the group in March rather than promote what to him is the distastefully commercial *For Your Love*. Another much-talked-about guitar hero, Jeff Beck, joins in his place.

A righteous No. 1

4th February 1965 Produced and co-written by Phil Spector, the Righteous Brothers' *You've Lost That Lovin' Feelin'* spotlights the cavernous bass voice of Bill Medley and the high counter singing of Bobby Hatfield, who make the most convincing 'white soul' sound yet heard in pop music.

Jones the voice

13th March 1965 New at No. 1 in the UK is Pontypridd-born Tom Jones with *It's Not Unusual*. Tom's steamroller voice and Presley-like movements stand out in a group-saturated music scene.

Stones across the water

18th March 1965 After a series of covers, the Rolling Stones finally hit No. 1 with a Jagger-Richards song. They record *The Last Time* with Phil Spector guesting on acoustic guitar but it's just the appetiser for *(I Can't Get No) Satisfaction* on which Jagger rages with frustration and Keith Richards plays a fuzz-toned guitar riff to die for.

Beatles work it out

Another non-stop Beatle year finds Liverpool's best receiving MBEs from the Queen at Buckingham Palace, filming *Help!* in the Bahamas and meeting Elvis at Graceland. The joyless title of the *Beatles for Sale* LP suggests that some world weariness is creeping in, but their music is evolving, influenced by Bob Dylan's iconoclasm and the new musical adventurism of the Byrds and the Beach Boys. Paul even spreads his wings with *Yesterday*, soon to become the most recorded song in history. On the *Rubber Soul* album they start to edge away from boy-girl love songs to reflective pieces like *In My Life* and *Nowhere Man*, while augmenting their instrumentation with piano, organ and even a sitar.

A world of their own

2nd December 1965 Voted best new group by *New Musical Express* readers are an Australian folk group without an electric guitar in sight. The Seekers have had two UK No. 1s so far - I'll *Never Find Another You* and *The Carnival is Over*.

Provincial pop

What Liverpool, Manchester and London can do, so can the rest of Britain. As a full scale Beatles- and Stones-stoked music boom gathers pace, the Moody Blues (photo) and the Spencer Davis Group emerge from the Midlands. From Hertfordshire come the Zombies - bigger stars in the US than in the UK - and Unit Four Plus Two with the chart topping *Concrete and Clay*. Every town and city seems to have its own group scene, making the future of British pop music look very bright indeed.

Doddy beats the Beatles

30th September 1965 The biggest selling single of the year - now at No. 1 for the first of five weeks - is not a Beatles track but the gushing *Tears* by another famous Liverpudlian export, comedian Ken Dodd.

Dylan goes electric

25th July 1965 The Newport Folk Festival witnesses an electrifying moment in every sense. Bob Dylan, enfant terrible of folk music, takes to the stage with a rock band, plugs in and lets rip with *Maggie's Farm* and the rambling but unignorable *Like a Rolling Stone*. Crowd reaction is split between bemused and enraged, someone cuts the power supply but there's no going back.

Protest pop

28th August 1965 A vogue for protest pop begins when Dylan soundalike Barry McGuire of the New Christy Minstrels tops the US chart with *Eve of Destruction*, which rants about everything from segregation to fallout shelters. Almost simultaneously, Sonny and Cher - Phil Spector acolyte Sonny Bono and backing singer Cherilyn Sarkisian - dress like anti-war protesters and declare their mutual besottedness to the world in *I Got You Babe*.

SPORT

European gold
30th August - 7th September 1966 Great Britain's only two medals in the European Athletics Championships in Budapest are both golds and go to Lynn Davies in the long jump and Jim Hogan in the marathon.

Billie Jean's at our door
1st July 1966 Having defeated reigning champion Margaret Smith in the semi-final, Billie Jean King of the US wins the first of her six Wimbledon tennis championships at the age of 22. She beats Brazilian Maria Bueno 6-3 3-6 6-1.

Ali v. the Brits
Reigning world heavyweight boxing champion Muhammad Ali takes on two British opponents during the course of the year. May sees a rematch with Henry Cooper, who three years earlier had put the then Cassius Clay on the canvas before losing to a technical knockout. Ali wins the fight at Arsenal's Highbury stadium by a sixth round technical knockout. while August finds Ali pitched against Geordie fighter Brian London at Earl's Court. The outclassed London lasts for nearly three rounds before succumbing to a knockout punch.

England's greatest day
30th July 1966 On the greatest day in England's football history, the national team defeat West Germany 4-2 at Wembley to win the FIFA World Cup. England are the tournament hosts and overcome Argentina 1-0 in the quarter final and Portugal 2-1 in the semis to reach the final. The star of the final is striker Geoff Hurst who scores a hat trick, his last goal coming at the very end of extra time. As BBC television commentator Kenneth Wolstenholme famously tells the watching millions, 'Some people are on the pitch, they think it's all over … it is now.' Manager Alf Ramsey will be rewarded with a knighthood in the New Year honours list.

12 JAN 1966
Lyndon B. Johnson says US should stay in South Vietnam until communist aggression ends.

3 FEB 1966
Unmanned Luna 9 is first spacecraft to make rocket-assisted landing on the Moon.

8 MAR 1966
An IRA bomb damages Nelson's Pillar in Dublin.

DOMESTIC NEWS

Action Man launched!
30th January 1966 Palitoy launches 'Action Man' a British licensed version of the American toy 'G.I. Joe'. This posable, dress-able soldier doll initially comes in three versions, 'Action Soldier', 'Action Sailor', and 'Action Pilot'.

Panda on a plane
11 March 1966 London Zoo's panda Chi Chi makes the news as she is flown to Russia to mate with An An at Moscow Zoo. Sadly, the two do not take to each other and the attempts are unsuccessful. Chi Chi proves one of the most popular animals at London Zoo, and her image is immortalised as the logo of the World Wildlife Fund.

Britain goes on safari!
11th April 1966 Britain gets its first safari park as the Marquess of Bath opens one on his estate at Longleat. It is the first such experience, outside of Africa, in the world and allows visitors to drive their cars through enclosures containing the 'Longleat lions' and other animals.

Murderers convicted
6th May 1966 The Moors Murderers Ian Brady and Myra Hindley are final-ly brought to justice for their crimes following a trial that grips and revolts the nation. Both killers receive multiple concurrent life sentences and are never released, Hindley dying in jail in 2002, and Brady in 2017.

Barclaycard launches
29th June 1966 The Barclaycard is launched as Britain's first creditcard. Initially it is a 'charge' card, meaning the balance must be paid in full every month to avoid penalties, but by the end of 1967 it becomes a full credit card. This allows shoppers to purchase items throughout the month and pay their bills on payday, revolutionising shopping.

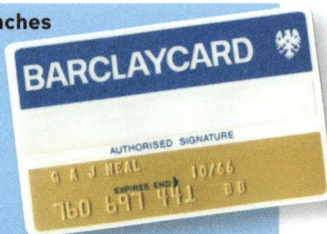

Pickles saves World Cup!
27th March 1966 Pickles the dog is applauded as a national hero as he sniffs out the stolen FIFA World Cup trophy. The Jules Rimet trophy had been stolen seven days before whilst on display. With the World Cup just four months out, the search is desperate, and Pickles is the hero of the hour as he finds the trophy under a hedge in South London.

6 APR 1966	30 MAY 1966	30 JUN 1966
Cross-Channel hovercraft service inaugurated between Ramsgate and Calais.	Graham Hill wins the Indianapolis 500.	France leaves NATO.

Independence spreads

More former British colonies and territories gain independence, as British Guiana becomes Guyana, the Bechuanaland Protectorate becomes Botswana, Basutoland becomes Lesotho, and Barbados becomes a Commonwealth realm.

Wage freezes and unemployment

20th July 1966 The government's Prices and Incomes Board gets the legal power to control wages, announcing the beginning of a six-month wage and price freeze. The country's economic troubles continue as unemployment rises by around 200,000 between September and November.

Shepherd's Bush murders

12th August 1966 The country is rocked by the murder of three Metropolitan Police officers. The officers are shot dead in East Acton as they approach a suspicious vehicle. The murderers go on the run. Whilst two are apprehended a few days later, one of them evades a large manhunt that lasts until November, when he is finally apprehended. All three receive life sentences of 30 years.

Plaid Cymru's first seat

14th July 1966 A by-election in Carmarthen occasioned by the death of sitting MP Megan Lloyd George brings Gwynfor Evans, leader of the Welsh Nationalist party Plaid Cymru, to Parliament. He defeats his Labour opponent and becomes Plaid Cymru's first ever Member of Parliament. The result is a catalyst for the growth of Plaid as a party and suggests that Labour's hold on its heartland of Wales may be under threat.

Pirate radio to be outlawed

27th July 1966 The government introduces the Marine etc Broadcasting Offences Bill to make illegal the unlicensed pirate radio stations operating around the UK coast. It will become law in a year's time. The move is unpopular, given the high broadcasting figures that stations such as Radio Caroline and Radio London attract.

ROYALTY & POLITICS

Labour landslide

31st March 1966 With the Labour government's majority reduced to two by recent by-elections, Prime Minister Harold Wilson calls a general election. It is the last to be held with a minimum voting age of 21. Labour returns with a landslide victory over Edward Heath's Conservatives, gaining 48 seats and achieving a majority of 98.

31 JUL 1966	22 AUG 1966	6 SEP 1966
31 drown as pleasure cruiser MV Darlwyne sinks off Cornish coast.	London's Centre Point office block completed and left empty for ten years.	South African premier Hendrik Verwoerd assassinated.

1966

The Queen at Aberfan
29th October 1966 The Queen visits Aberfan in South Wales, eight days after the village school is engulfed by a coal tip landslide causing over 140 deaths, the majority of them children.

France leaves NATO
30th June 1966 Having withdrawn French forces from NATO's Mediterranean fleet and refused to place American nuclear weapons on French soil, President Charles de Gaulle makes good his threat to leave NATO, which is now obliged to move its headquarters from Paris to Belgium.

Democratic fashion
15th September 1966 Having set the tone in haute couture during the 1950s with his trapeze dress with a free waist, Yves Saint Laurent opens a Paris boutique to sell ready-made clothes aimed at democratising fashion, challenging the assumption that London is now the centre of the fashion world thanks to Carnaby Street, Mary Quant and the mini skirt.

FOREIGN NEWS

Nigerian coup
15th January 1966 The government of Nigeria is overthrown and its Prime Minister murdered in a military coup. In July, a different section of the military seizes power under General Yakubu Gowon. A bloody civil war soon erupts as the eastern province of Biafra fights for independence.

Gandhi elected
19th January 1966 Indira Gandhi, daughter of the late Jawaharlal Nehru, is elected Prime Minister of India in succession to Lal Bahadur Shastri, who died nine days earlier after signing the Tashkent peace agreement with Pakistan.

Let's twist again
Twister, the game where humans are the pieces, and bodily entanglement is an unavoidable result of taking part, is launched this year. Store buyers are initially reluctant, expressing concerns the game is too risqué but the following year, *Twister* (which was originally called *Pretzel*) sells three million units.

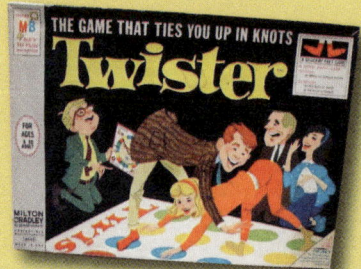

THE GAME THAT TIES YOU UP IN KNOTS
Twister

---

22 OCT 1966
Soviet spy George Blake escapes from prison and is next seen in Moscow.

4 NOV 1966
Devastating floods strike Florence and Venice.

15 DEC 1966
Death of animation pioneer Walt Disney.

Emperor Cannibal?
1st January 1966 Colonel Jean Bodel Bokassa leads a military coup in the Central African Republic and declares himself President. Although he seems to have good intentions for the people of the poverty-stricken country, he soon has opponents eliminated and enriches himself and a small group of associates. A rumour then circulates that Bokassa feasts on the flesh of his political opponents.

Cultural Revolution
16th May 1966 An inflammatory article in the *Chinese People's Daily* calls for the destruction of 'all monsters and demons'. Chinese leader Mao Zedong demands that the country must be cleansed of any form of bourgeoisie and begins the Cultural Revolution, though which Mao, following Lenin's example, aims to secure total power. At least half a million are killed during the revolution, which lasts until Mao's death in 1976.

LSD is outlawed
6th October 1966 The drug LSD - lysergic acid diethylamide - is outlawed in California, though it will continue to be manufactured clandestinely and widely used within the state's hippie communities.

Pogles' Wood
First introduced to viewers as *The Pogles* in the TV programme *Clapperboard* in 1965, *Pogles' Wood* from Smallfilms begins a new series on 7th April under the *Watch with Mother* banner. Created in the barn belonging to Oliver Postgate, Mr and Mrs Pogle, along with their adopted son Pippin and Tog the squirrel, live in a tree hollow. Postgate narrated the series which usually began with the question, 'Now where will we find the Pogles?'

ENTERTAINMENT

DO YOU REMEMBER THIS?

Fondue set

The Frost Report
The Frost Report premieres on BBC1 on 10th March 1966 with writers and performers from the cream of British comedy talent, including John Cleese, Eric Idle, Graham Chapman, Terry Jones and Michael Palin, who find their Python writing style while working on the show.

Till Death Us Do Part

Alf Garnett, a bald, bigoted racist, railing against practically everything in modern Britain, is introduced to an unsuspecting public on 6th June and within two days, the Conservative Party have asked for a copy of the script due to Alf (played to perfection by Warren Mitchell) referring to Edward Heath as, 'a grammar school twit'. Scriptwriter Johnny Speight smartly turned Garnett into a parody of himself, exposing him as a character that embodies the worst aspects of the British.

It's a Knockout

From 7th July 1966, the battle for regional supremacy of the UK is thrashed out on BBC every Saturday evening as amateur athletic teams from around the country don outsized cartoon costumes and tackle obstacle courses, slippery slopes and avoid buckets of slime in a series of baffling races. Still, there is nothing the British population like better than seeing their fellow citizens making fools of themselves, and the slapstick carnage of It's a Knockout is regularly watched by 19 million viewers.

On the Margin

Alan Bennet writes and performs this satirical sketch show with the support of a regular cast including future BBC political commentator John Sergeant, and guest appearances from Michael Hordern and Prunella Scales. Bennett's sardonic comedy is contrasted with more serious poetry readings and, unusually, archive clips of nostalgic music hall performances.

Alfie

A serial womaniser, Alfie knocks around London, loving and leaving a trail of sexual conquests in his wake, until events cause him to examine his self-centred behaviour with a sense of remorse. Michael Caine, unconventionally but mesmerizingly handsome, breaks the fourth wall and talks to the camera and with that laconic expression and chipper attitude, you can see how he's such a successful seducer.

Cathy Come Home

Ken Loach directs another Wednesday Playhouse play, Cathy Come Home, a dramatic exposé highlighting the inhumanity of a social system in which one young woman finds herself trapped. Cathy Come Home follows the devastating descent of one couple into poverty and homelessness, as Cathy finds her marriage destroyed and her children taken from her. The searing impact of the film on the British public means huge support for the charity Shelter which forms shortly afterwards.

Icon of an era

Model Lesley Hornby is 'discovered' when her photograph by Barry Lategan, sporting a chic cropped hairdo by the hairdresser Leonard, is seen by *Daily Express* journalist Deirdre McSharry and published under the headline, 'The Face of 1966'. Aged just 16, Twiggy's androgynous look with her inimitable, gangly frame, freckles, saucer eyes and spider lashes, becomes synonymous with the Swinging Sixties.

Born Free

Virginia McKenna and Bill Travers play real-life couple George and Joy Adamson, who attempt to introduce an orphaned lion called Elsa back into the wild in Kenya.For McKenna and Travers, the film has a life-changing effect and they go on to become wildlife campaigners, and found the Born Free Foundation. John Barry's song, *Born Free*, sung by Matt Munro with lyrics by Don Black, wins an Academy Award for best original song.

Carry on Screaming

The *Carry On* juggernaut continues with *Carry On Screaming*, the franchise's thirteenth film: a barely-disguised parody of the Hammer Horror genre in a riff on the Frankenstein story.

Holy smoke Batman!

DC Comics superhero Batman and his sidekick Robin first hit TV screens in America on 12th January. Adam West dons the cape as Bruce Wayne/Batman with Dick Grayson/Robin played by Burt Ward. Together they run around Gotham City fighting crimes committed by an inordinate number of dastardly villains. The series has its tongue firmly in its cheek and Batman's comic-book roots are never forgotten. Lines are delivered with hammy drama and the fight scenes cut with cartoon graphics of punch-up noises. Wham! Ker-pow!

Live long and prosper

The multi-racial, multi-species crew of the 23rd-century starship, USS *Enterprise*, led by Captain James T. Kirk (William Shatner) are on a mission to 'boldly go where no man has gone before' patrolling the galaxies as a kind of inter-planetary peace-keeping force, but with groovier coordinated uniforms. *Star Trek* ensures that beneath the action and sci-fi kitsch, is a moral and philosophical message in storylines that act as metaphors for current global issues like feminism or the Vietnam War. *Star Trek* gains a cult following and flowers into one of the most successful TV and film franchises of all time.

Prehistoric pin-up

Nobody seems to care much that prehistoric man and dinosaurs are co-existing in *One Million Years B.C.* a fantasy adventure which is released on 25th October, even though dinosaurs died out about 65 million years before early man made an appearance. All eyes instead are on Raquel Welch, who strides around with only a fur bikini cladding her voluptuous frame. The image of Welch as the ultimate in sexy prehistoric womanhood becomes a cultural phenomenon.

MUSIC

What's it all about?

22nd February 1966 Composer Burt Bacharach is a name on everyone's lips. He and lyricist Hal David record mainly with their discovery Dionne Warwick, but Dusty Springfield (*Wishin' and Hopin'*), the Walker Brothers (*Make It Easy on Yourself*) and Tom Jones (*What's New Pussycat?*) have all had hits with their songs. Now Bacharach is in London to oversee Cilla Black's recording of the title song of the film *Alfie*.

Beatles quit performing

These are momentous months for the Beatles. In the middle of an exhausting US tour, John Lennon's opinion that 'we are more popular than Jesus now' provokes an anti-Beatle backlash, convincing the group that they should stop live performing altogether. Their last ever concert is at Candlestick Park in San Francisco in August. The plan now is to focus exclusively on making music in the studio, with a big project in mind that will eventually take shape as *Sgt Pepper*.

Sounds of Simon

1st January 1966 Paul Simon, who is touring UK folk clubs as a singer-songwriter, discovers that a track he made in New York with best pal Art Garfunkel called *The Sound of Silence* is sitting at the top of the US charts. Except it's not quite the same track: someone has added a rock backing to it. Within days he is back in the US and recording again with Art as avatars of the new folk-rock.

James Brown's solo show

11th March 1966 ITV's must-see music show *Ready Steady Go!* departs from its standard format to showcase the inimitable James Brown. The doyen of 60s soul music, Brown receives a Grammy for *Papa's Got A Brand New Bag*, while *It's A Man's Man's Man's World* tops the US R&B chart in May.

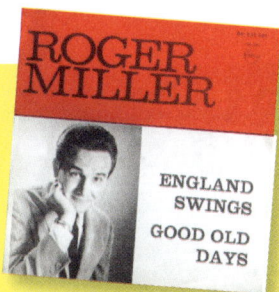

In praise of swinging England

16th April 1966 That the UK represents everything that is hip, young and swinging is confirmed by a famous article in *Time* magazine. On cue, Roger Miller's *England Swings* depicts the old country as a place of rosy-cheeked children and friendly bobbies. The tongue-in-cheek song is a gift to the tourist trade and confirms the current American passion for all things British.

Kink commentaries

7th July 1966 The Kinks came out of London's Muswell Hill in 1964 playing a primitive kind of heavy metal on the chart topping *You Really Got Me*. Gradually their sound has mellowed and leader Ray Davies's lyrics have become more observational and satirical, typified by the Carnaby Street send-up *Dedicated Follower of Fashion* and the lament of a bored rock star, *Sunny Afternoon*. Few songs better evoke the long, hot, enervating British summer of 1966.

Frank and Nancy

2nd June 1966 After several years of absence from the singles chart, Frank Sinatra is back with *Strangers in the Night*. He tops both US and UK charts, as does his daughter Nancy with the proto-feminist anthem *These Boots Are Made for Walkin'*, featuring the most famous descending bassline in pop music.

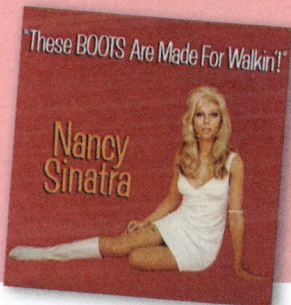

Comings and goings

1st August 1966 Can groups survive the loss of key members? Paul Jones leaves Manfred Mann to go solo and is replaced by Mike D'Abo from Band of Angels, while Jimmy Page joins the Yardbirds in place of Paul Samwell-Smith. Meanwhile the Animals, having already lost Alan Price and Chas Chandler, break up altogether in September, though Eric Burdon keeps the band name with a new line-up.

Spector's masterpiece

25th June 1966 Phil Spector has created another masterpiece. Credited to Ike and Tina Turner but with only Tina heard on the track, *River Deep Mountain High* is the ultimate 'wall of sound' record, made with over twenty musicians in multiple takes over many days.

Beach Boy brilliance

7th November 1966 Some call it the record of the year and even the decade. It may even be the record of the millennium. The UK's new No. 1 is *Good Vibrations* by the Beach Boys, who are now creating the most imaginative soundscapes in pop history. The genius behind this and the head-turning *Pet Sounds* LP is Brian Wilson, who roots the group's sound in sun-kissed harmonies and production techniques learned from Phil Spector.

MY FIRST 18 YEARS
TOP 10   1966

1. **Summer in the City** *The Lovin' Spoonful*
2. **My Generation** *The Who*
3. **Wouldn't it be Nice** *The Beach Boys*
4. **Reach Out, I'll Be There** *The Four Tops*
5. **Sunny Afternoon** *The Kinks*
6. **Eleanor Rigby** *The Beatles*
7. **Semi-Detached Suburban...** *Manfred Mann*
8. **The Sun Ain't Gonna S...** *The Walker Brothers*
9. **Homeward Bound** *Simon and Garfunkel*
10. **Walk Away Renee** *The Left Banke*

Open 🟢 | Search 🔍 | Scan 📷

Talkin' about their generation

Mod fashions and iconography are all over British pop at the moment, but one band in particular seems to have truly authentic Mod credentials. From the Mod heartland of Shepherds' Bush, the Who have a restless and questioning resident songwriter in Pete Townshend, whose songs like *My Generation*, *Substitute* and *I'm a Boy* distil the Mod experience. Such is the band's aggression on stage that their performances usually end with them destroying their equipment.

Folk-rock evolves

Out of the folk music hub of Greenwich Village burst the Lovin' Spoonful, with good-time songs like *Daydream* and *Do You Believe in Magic* written by John Sebastian and a style evoking old-time jug bands. Sebastian's chum John Phillips forms the Mamas and the Papas who de-camp to Los Angeles to add the sweetest of boy-girl harmonies to *Monday Monday* and *California Dreamin'*. Back in the UK, Donovan (photo) evolves from a guitar-playing troubadour with a Bob Dylan cap into a creator of whimsical, fey and faintly psychedelic hits such as *Sunshine Superman* and *Mellow Yellow*.

SPORT

Arise Sir Alf
1st January 1967 Alf Ramsey, manager of the victorious 1966 World Cup-winning England side, is recognised with a knighthood in the New Year honours list. The England captain, Bobby Moore, receives an OBE.

100/1 outsider wins the Grand National
Foinavon, ridden by John Buckingham, is a rank outsider at 100/1 at the start of the 1967 Grand National steeplechase at Aintree on 8th April. But the racing gods are smiling on him and when numerous horses and riders fall at the 23rd fence, Buckingham avoids the melee and takes the lead and romps home to victory.

Grand Slam queen
American Billie Jean King wins the second of her six Wimbledon singles titles against British player Ann Jones, as well as scooping the women's doubles and mixed doubles titles at the tournament.

Arise Sir Francis
Francis Chichester sails his yacht, the *Gipsy Moth IV*, back into Plymouth harbour on the evening of 28th May, 226 days and 28,500 miles after departing. In recognition of his achievement in becoming the first person to sail solo around the world from west to east, he is knighted by the Queen at Greenwich.

Knocked out
9th May 1967 Muhammad Ali is stripped of his World Heavyweight Champion titles and banned from boxing after refusing to be drafted into the US Army at the height of the Vietnam War. Ali argues that as a black Muslim, he is a conscientious objector, but his moral stand comes at great personal cost.

Our 'Enry
Heavyweight boxer Henry Cooper becomes the first person to win three Lonsdale belts outright after his victory over Billy 'Golden Boy' Walker on 7th November. A few weeks later, he wins the first of his two BBC Sports Personality of the Year Awards.

12 JAN 1967
Britain's latest new town is to be built on a 22,000-acre site in Buckinghamshire and called Milton Keynes.

2 FEB 1967
Nicotine-free Bravo cigarettes, made from cured lettuce, go on sale in Tesco supermarket in Brixton.

30 MAR 1967
Photographer Michael Cooper shoots the Peter Blake-designed album artwork for The Beatles' *Sgt. Pepper's Lonely Hearts Club Band*.

DOMESTIC NEWS

Campbell killed
4th January 1967 Donald Campbell, pioneering racing driver, is killed in an attempt to break his own Water Speed World Record in his craft Bluebird. A serial record breaker, Campbell heads to Coniston Water in the Lake District to attempt 300 mph but is killed as Bluebird lifts out of the water and backflips.

European Economic Community
15th January 1967 Britain enters negotiations to discuss joining the European Economic Community. Italy and the Netherlands signal their support for Britain's membership, and a formal application is made from the United Kingdom in May. However, President Charles de Gaulle of France vetoes the move in November.

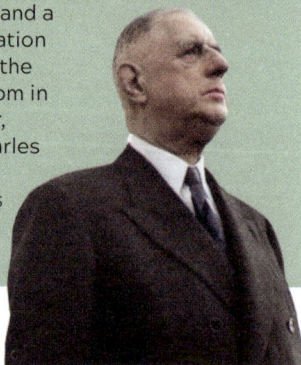

Outer Space Treaty
27th January 1967 The Outer Space Treaty is signed by the UK, United States, and the Soviet Union in a landmark agreement to prohibit nuclear weapons in space and ensure that no country can claim sovereignty of part of the cosmos. It is also agreed that celestial bodies such as the moon can be used only for peaceful purposes. In light of these agreements, the British launch their Ariel 3 satellite in May, the first satellite to be developed outside either the Soviet Union or the United States.

Torrey Canyon Disaster
18th March 1967 The oil tanker SS Torrey Canyon runs aground off Land's End near the Scilly Isles and begins shedding its cargo of crude oil. 170 miles of British and French coastline are contaminated in one of the world's most serious spills.

Stockport air disaster
4th June 1967 British Midland Flight G-ALHG crashes in Stockport killing 72 passengers and crew in one of Britain's worst air disasters. The crash occurs as the plane is heading into land at Manchester Airport, when two of its engines cut unexpectedly. 12 people survive thanks to the brave efforts of members of the public and police.

New Look Stamps
5th June 1967 British stamps receive a new look as the General Post Office unveils the new 'Machin' series of stamps, replacing the old Wilding series. The new stamps are much simpler than previous designs, and feature Arnold Machin's sculpture of the Queen.

APR 1967
Marion Boyers and John Calder are prosecuted under the Obscene Publications Act for publishing the novel, *Last Exit to Brooklyn*.

MAY 1967
Bird's launch *Angel Delight*, an instant dessert made by magically whipping a sachet of flavoured powder into milk.

27 JUN 1967
The UK's first cash machine opens at a branch of Barclay's Bank on Enfield High Street.

Gay and women's rights

4th July 1967 Following on from the Wolfenden Report's 1957 recommendations, acts of consensual male homosexuality between consenting adults are decriminalised in England and Wales. This first step in gay rights comes just a few months before the Abortion Act is passed in October, legalising abortions up to the 28th week of pregnancy.

Welsh Language Act

27th July 1967 The introduction of the Welsh Language Act takes a step towards protecting Welsh speakers, by enshrining their right to use Welsh in legal proceedings and in official documents in Wales. Alongside the protection of the Welsh language, the Act also importantly repeals an Act from 1746 which defines Wales as part of England.

Britain abroad

10th September 1967 A referendum held on British sovereignty in the Crown colony of Gibraltar returns a huge majority in favour of remaining a British territory. Of the island's 12,000 voters, only 44 vote to become part of Spain. In contrast, in November, British troops finally leave the State of Aden after 128 years, leading to the formation of the republic of Yemen.

Hither Green rail crash

5th November 1967 49 people are killed when the evening express from Hastings to London Charing Cross hits a broken rail and leaves the tracks at the Hither Green Depot.

DO YOU REMEMBER THIS?

Scooter

BBC radio changes

8th November 1967 A month after the BBC renames all its radio networks to accommodate its new pop music station, Radio 1, it launches a new local radio service, starting with BBC Radio Leicester. Both Radio 1 and these local radio stations are designed to replace the newly outlawed 'pirate' radio stations. Eight experimental local stations launch initially, with services to the rest of the country rolled out in the 1970s.

Pound devalued

19th November 1967 The deepening sterling crisis in the UK leads to Prime Minister Harold Wilson taking the drastic action of devaluing the pound by 14%, from $2.80 US dollars to $2.40. The decision is controversial, and Wilson attempts to reassure the nation, stating in a broadcast that the 'pound... in your pocket' will not be affected.

17 JUL 1967
The Keep Britain Tidy campaign launches a dedicated Anti-Litter Week.

2 AUG 1967
A second, southbound bore of the Blackwall Tunnel under the River Thames in east London is opened.

20 SEP 1967
The Queen names the new passenger ship, *Queen Elizabeth 2 (QE2)* at Clydebank.

1967

ROYALTY & POLITICS

FOREIGN NEWS

A royal reconciliation?

7th June 1967 Queen Elizabeth, the Queen Mother meets the Duke and Duchess of Windsor for the first time since the 1936 abdication after they had been invited to London for a dedication ceremony for a memorial plaque to Queen Mary at Marlborough House.

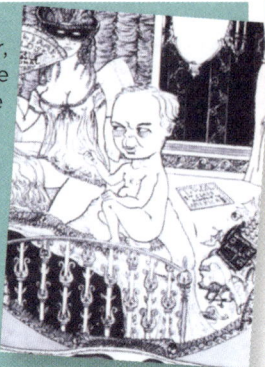

Moved to say sorry

On the 11th October, pop group the Move are obliged to issue a formal apology in the High Court to Prime Minister Harold Wilson after they had featured a caricature of the P.M. in the nude on a promotional postcard for their single, *Flowers in the Rain*. The band are ordered to pay all royalties from the single to a charity of the Prime Minister's choice.

Flower power's first shoots

14th January 1967 Something is brewing in San Francisco, where a 'Human Be-In' takes place in Golden Gate Park. It's a gathering of hippies who live in the city's bohemian district of Haight-Ashbury and reject what they see

as the bourgeois, well-behaved lifestyle of their parents' generation. The hippie movement has its roots in the nomadic west coast community led by Ken Kesey, author of *One Flew Over the Cuckoo's Nest*. Many hippies believe in free love, communal living and the mind-expanding drug LSD. They're against capitalism, materialism, and war. Their music as played by groups like the Grateful Dead and Jefferson Airplane is free form, unruly, loud and mind expanding. Everything is set for a legendary 'summer of love', as radio vibrates to the sounds of the Frisco bands and the cult of flower power goes international.

The student prince

9th October 1967 Prince Charles begins his first term as an undergraduate student at Trinity College where he reads Archaeology and Anthropology in his first year, followed by two years of History. Arriving in true sixties style as a passenger in a red Mini, the bashful eighteen-year-old is met by a crowd of vocal well-wishers and the inevitable flashbulbs of the press.

8 OCT 1967

Death of Clement Attlee, Britain's Prime Minister from 1945 to 1951.

27 NOV 1967

John Noakes gamely models a chest wig on Blue Peter while Valerie Singleton tells young viewers they are all the rage in the US.

4 DEC 1967

The Royal Smithfield Show opens at Earl's Court with no animals and mechanical exhibits only, due to an outbreak of foot-and-mouth disease.

Astronaut deaths
27th January 1967 A tragic setback in the space race: three astronauts are killed in a fire in their Apollo spacecraft during a test launch. Designated Apollo 1, this was to be the first attempt at a manned crew mission. Crewed flights are suspended for twenty months.

Oppenheimer dies
18th February 1967 Robert Oppenheimer dies of throat cancer aged 62. The director of the Manhattan Project that created the atom bomb, his concerns over nuclear proliferation and his earlier left-wing political affiliations led to the removal of his security clearance in 1954.

Svetlana defects
9th March 1967 In one of the Cold War's most surprising twists, Svetlana Alliluyeva, daughter of Joseph Stalin, defects to the west at the US Embassy in New Delhi.

Coup in Greece
21st April 1967 A military coup in Greece ousts Prime Minister Andreas Papandreou. The new regime headed by Colonels George Papadopoulos and Stylianos Pattakos imposes martial law, suspends democracy and even outlaws beards and mini skirts. The infamous Colonels rule until 1974.

Six-Day War
5th - 10th June 1967 To prevent encirclement by the Arab states, Israel launches what becomes known as the Six-Day War against Egypt, Syria, Iraq and Jordan. Virtually all of the Arab air defences are destroyed on the first day and Israeli forces sweep into Sinai and the West Bank. The war ends when Israel and Syria agree to a UN-mediated truce.

Che is dead
8th October 1967 Revolutionary leader Che Guevera, whose relations with Fidel Castro's Cuban regime have cooled, is captured and executed by government forces in Bolivia.

First heart transplant
3rd December 1967 In Cape Town, a team of surgeons led by Christiaan Barnard performs the first heart transplant. A 57-year-old Polish immigrant named Louis Washkansky receives the heart of a young woman who died in an accident. He will die eighteen days later from pneumonia due to a weakened immune system.

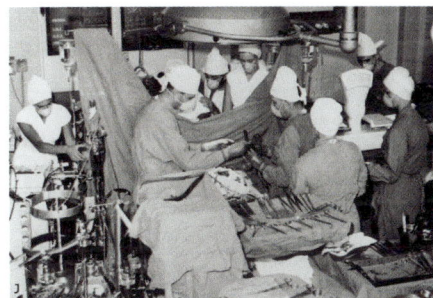

Ceaușescu in power

9th December 1967 Nicolae Ceaușescu becomes Chairman of the Romanian State, with dictatorial powers. Initially his regime seems liberal and mild compared to the rest of the Soviet Bloc, but by the late 1970s Ceaușescu is the strictest of Stalinist dictators running the most repressive regime in Eastern Europe.

Holt disappears

17th December 1967 Australian Prime Minister Harold Holt disappears while swimming near Portsea, Victoria. His body is never found.

ENTERTAINMENT

Eurovision winner

8th April 1967 After nearly a decade of trying, the UK finally wins the Eurovision Song Contest with *Puppet on a String* by Sandie Shaw. Sandie (real name Sandra Goodrich) has been a chart regular for three years and secretly feels that this song is beneath her, yet it is her most lucrative record ever.

Top *Trumpton*

The stop-animation children's series *Trumpton* first airs on 3rd January 1967, with gentle stories from Trumpton-shire, a place originally introduced to young viewers in *Camberwick Green* the previous year. Pivotal to each episode, narrated by Brian Cant, is an emergency call-out by Trumpton's trusty fire brigade led by Captain Flack, whose team dutifully responded to their memorable roll call of 'Pugh, Pugh, Barney McGrew, Cuthbert, Dibble, Grub.'

Derring done

Since its launch in 1879, the *Boy's Own Paper* has fed successive generations of young men with a diet of stirring tales of derring-do, public school stories and advice on wholesome, practical pursuits.

But in 1967, its publisher decides a paltry circulation of 24,000 (compared to 190,000 in its 1890s heyday) cannot justify its continuation in a vastly changed market.

The Jungle Book

Disney's full-length animation based loosely on the 1894 stories of Rudyard Kipling opens in the UK on 17th November 1967. With its lush artwork and uplifting jazz tunes including the toe-tapping *Bare Necessities*, *The Jungle Book* is a critical and commercial success.

Monkee business

It is Beatlemania all over again when manufactured pop foursome The Monkees touch down at Heathrow on 28th June to perform in Britain for the first time. They are greeted by what one news report describes as 'a highly trained team of hysterical mini-skirters' as Manchester-born frontman Davy Jones is rugby tackled by one particularly determined lovestruck fan. The following day, Davy, Peter, Mike and Mickey are woken to a dawn chorus of hundreds of screaming girls outside the Royal Garden Hotel in Kensington.

BBC2 embraces colour

Television viewers begin to see the world in glorious technicolour on 1st July 1967 when BBC2 is the first channel in Europe to show programmes in colour, starting with its coverage of the Wimbledon Lawn Tennis Championships. But with just 5,000 colour television sets in circulation among the population it will be a few more years before colour TV becomes the norm.

The test card girl

When BBC engineer George Hersee asks his daughter Carole to pose for photographs with a blackboard and her clown doll, Bubbles, little does she know it will make her one of the most recognisable faces in British television history. Her picture subsequently becomes the test card image for the BBC and it is Carole (and the rather sinister Bubbles) who viewers see on-screen until 1998.

Just a Minute

22nd December 1967 Three months after the launch of Radio 4, a new panel show, *Just a Minute*, takes to the airwaves, hosted by Nicholas Parsons. The show's insanely simple format - that contestants should speak on any given topic, 'without hesitation, repetition or deviation' proves to be a winning formula. Parsons remains the host until shortly before his death in 2020 at the age of 96.

Fiddler on the Roof

Fiddler on the Roof opens at Her Majesty's Theatre on 16th February 1967 starring Israeli actor Topol in the role of Tevye; he would later be nominated for an Academy Award for playing the same role in the 1971 film adaptation. The £80,000 production is the hit of the year, eventually running for 2030 performances.

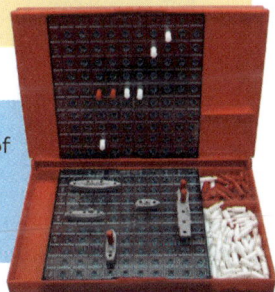

Calamity the Cow

Children's Film Foundation release *Calamity the Cow*, which stars a terribly well-spoken teenage Phil Collins three years before he joins prog-rock band Genesis.

Battleship is launched

Budding naval strategists can test out their skills with the launch of the board game *Battleship*. The aim of the game for two players is to hunt, sink or destroy your opponent's (imaginary) fleet of ships, using nothing more than a plastic board with pegs.

Fashion on film
Two major films of 1967, *Far from the Madding Crowd* starring Julie Christie, Alan Bates and Terence Stamp, and *Bonnie and Clyde* with Faye Dunaway and Warren Beatty, have a major influence on fashion, as trim silhouettes and mini skirts give some ground to hippysh Victoriana and Depression-era style dresses.

Blow Up!
For his first English-speaking film, Michaelangelo Antonioni plunges headfirst into a strange and sometimes seedy world of swinging London with a tale about a fashion photographer, played by David Hemmings, who thinks he witnesses a murder. The film's fashionable themes and sexual content quickly make it into a cult classic, with its racy reputation enhanced by a scene with Jane Birkin, in which female pubic hair is glimpsed for the first time in mainstream cinema.

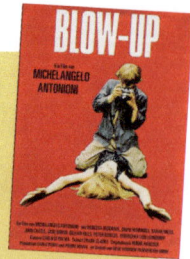

Sixties comedy favourite
Not in Front of the Children becomes one of the year's most popular sitcoms. Wendy Craig stars as Jennifer Corner in her first sitcom, playing the role of a harassed, middle-class wife and mother, a 'type' in she which comes to excel. *Not in Front of the Children* runs for 39 episodes over 4 series until 1970 and wins Craig a BAFTA for Best Actress in 1969.

Dee Time
Radio disc jockey Cyril Nicholas Henty-Dodd, better known as Simon Dee, attracts 18 million viewers with his early evening chat show *Dee Time* on BBC1. In a scene that is to become something of a sixties cliché, at the end of each programme, Dee is filmed driving off in a white E-type Jaguar beside blonde model Lorna Macdonald.

It happens in Monterey
16th - 18th June 1966 Monterey in California is the site of the first true rock festival, which showcases not just star names like the Who and the Byrds but also acts from the mushrooming San Francisco scene who haven't even signed with a record label yet. Janis Joplin (photo) and her band get a big-money deal, while Jefferson Airplane, the Grateful Dead, Moby Grape and a jaw-dropping Jimi Hendrix seize the chance to launch themselves on a bigger stage. Ending with Scott McKenzie singing his 'summer of love' hippie anthem *San Francisco*, Monterey is the start of a new rock era in which the music is louder, druggier and more provocative than ever.

Britain's Summer of Love

Between the 26th and 28th August, the Festival of the Flower Children takes place at Woburn Abbey in Bedfordshire, seat of the Duke of Bedford, where acts include the Small Faces, the Bee Gees and Eric Burdon from The Animals. Britain's Summer of Love is centred largely in London, where clubs like the UFO (where Pink Floyd play) or The Middle Earth Club attract hippies and musicians who embrace drug culture, psychedelic sounds and 'flower power'. While the Beatles and the Rolling Stones become steeped in the scene, for most young people, the Summer of Love is a news story in which they are observers rather than participants.

The Beatles

Beatles in Pepperland

Two very different but complementary songs about their Liverpool childhoods, *Penny Lane* and *Strawberry Fields Forever*, launch the Beatles as an exclusively studio-based band. Two months of recording produce *Sgt. Pepper's Lonely Hearts Club Band*, an all-bells-and-whistles, LSD-tinged album of songs inspired by news stories (*A Day in the Life*, *She's Leaving Home*), comic characters (*Lovely Rita*, *When I'm 64*) and even a child's drawing (*Lucy in the Sky with Diamonds*). The LP sets new standards in production and packaging and inspires all manner of bands to create their own *Pepper* equivalent. After this peak, the late-summer suicide of Brian Epstein leaves the band rudderless, while their self-made television movie *Magical Mystery Tour* is poorly received.

MUSIC

It's a mystery

One of the biggest records of the year is surely among the most mysterious in chart history. Based on a Bach organ fugue with lyrics referencing Chaucer and Greek mythology, *A Whiter Shade of Pale* is the first hit for Procol Harum (photo), who were once an Essex beat group called the Paramounts.

Hendrix unveiled

11th January 1967
At a press reception in Soho, ex-Animal Chas Chandler reveals his new discovery, blues guitarist Jimi Hendrix. Jimi is an instant sensation and charts with *Hey Joe* and *Purple Haze* before touring the UK as the Jimi Hendrix Experience. *Are You Experienced* is one of the albums of the year, while Jimi's festival-stealing appearance at Monterey shows his native US what they have been ignoring. A second album, *Axis Bold as Love*, keeps up the momentum in December.

1967

Stones are busted

12th February 1967 Mick Jagger and Keith Richards are arrested on drugs charges at Redlands, Keith's home. At the subsequent court hearing, Richards is sentenced to a year in prison while Jagger gets three months. On appeal, Richards' conviction is quashed and Jagger's sentence is reduced to a conditional discharge. In a separate case, Brian Jones is sentenced to three months, reduced on appeal to three months' probation. Even *The Times* voices disquiet over the apparent police witch hunt against the Stones.

Brothers in harmony

24th February 1967 The Bee Gees arrive from Australia sounding very like their Beatle idols. Managed by Brian Epstein associate Robert Stigwood, harmonising brothers Barry, Robin and Maurice Gibb debut with *New York Mining Disaster 1941* and close out the summer with the chart-topping *Massachusetts*.

Engelbert emerges

4th March 1967 Keeping the Beatles' *Penny Lane* off No. 1 and staying there for six weeks is *Release Me* by Gerry Dorsey – or, as he has renamed himself, Engelbert Humperdinck. His country-tinged ballads are aimed squarely at an older female audience. He has more weeks on the chart in 1967 than any other artist.

MY FIRST 18 YEARS — TOP 10 — 1967

1. **Paper Sun** *Traffic*
2. **See Emily Play** *Pink Floyd*
3. **Respect** *Aretha Franklin*
4. **Heroes and Villains** *The Beach Boys*
5. **Matthew and Son** *Cat Stevens*
6. **Excerpt from a Teenage Opera** *Keith West*
7. **Waterloo Sunset** *The Kinks*
8. **Don't Sleep in the Subway** *Petula Clark*
9. **Itchycoo Park** *Small Faces*
10. **Flowers in the Rain** *The Move*

Open | Search | Scan

Otis killed in air crash

10th December 1967 Five months after winning legions of hippie fans at Monterey, Otis Redding is killed with four members of his backing group the Bar-kays in an air crash in Wisconsin. His last record, made just three days before his death, is *Sittin' on the Dock of the Bay*, a departure from his usual style and a sign of his wish to develop a broader audience.

EMI think pink

July 1967 One of EMI's first 'progressive' signings, Pink Floyd enjoy a meteoric rise. Originally a blues band, they surface in London's underground clubs with an expansive, electronics-driven approach and eccentric Syd Barrett songs. They record debut LP *The Piper at the Gates of Dawn* at Abbey Road with ex-Beatles engineer Norman Smith, though by year end there is increasing concern about Syd's mental state and LSD intake.

SPORT

Manchester United best in Europe
On 29th May, Manchester United face Benfica of Portugal in the European Cup final at Wembley Stadium. Three goals in extra time, from George Best, Brian Kidd and Bobby Charlton, secure a 4-1 victory and make Manchester United the first English team to win the title. On 24th December, Best is awarded the Ballon D'Or as European player of the year.

What a flop
American high jumper Dick Fosbury revolutionises the high jump event at the Olympic Games by adopting a 'back first' technique which will become known as the Fosbury Flop.

Tragedy at Hockenheim
32-year-old Scottish farmer and racing driver Jim Clark, Formula One World Champion in 1963 and 1965, and winner of 25 Grand Prix races, is killed at Hockenheim race circuit when his Lotus-Cosworth somersaults off the track and into woods at 170 mph.

Hemery hurdles to gold
David Hemery wins the Olympic gold medal in 400m hurdles in Mexico City on 15th October. Commentator David Coleman (photo), in a frenzy of excitement as Hemery nears the finish line, neglects to notice his GB teammate John Sherwood gets bronze, and utters words he will long regret: 'Hemery takes the gold, in second place Hennige and who cares who's third? It doesn't matter.'

Winning on equal terms
Billie Jean King wins her third Wimbledon ladies' singles title, her first of the Open era, and receives a cheque for £750 compared to the £2,000 received by the men's champion, Rod Laver. The disparity triggers King's crusade to achieve parity of earnings for women in the game.

Black Power salute at Mexico Olympics
On 16th October, during the medal ceremony for the men's 200 metres at the Mexico Olympic Games, American athletes Tommie Smith and John Carlos, who have won gold and bronze medals respectively, each raise a black-gloved fist during the playing of the *Star Spangled Banner*.

---

15 JAN 1968
'Irretrievable breakdown of marriage' becomes legal grounds for divorce in the UK.

13 FEB 1968
Escaping discrimination in newly independent Kenya, up to 1,500 Kenyan Asians are arriving in Britain each week.

21 MAR 1968
Road deaths in the UK have fallen by 23% after introduction of breathalyser tests in January 1966.

DOMESTIC
NEWS

Ford launch the Escort
January 1968 Ford announce their replacement for the Ford Anglia, the 'Escort', which, like the Anglia, will be manufactured at the Halewood plant. The two-door base model features rear-wheel drive, but headlights are an additional extra, included in the De Luxe model.

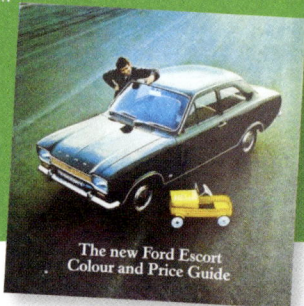

The new Ford Escort Colour and Price Guide

Dagenham ladies strike!
7th June 1968 Sewing machinists go out on strike to protest their classification as 'unskilled' workers. Labelled as such, they earn only 85% of what male 'skilled' employees at the plant earn. The strike is successful, leading to their pay being increased to 92% of the men's earnings, and sets in motion events that will lead to the 1970 Equal Pay Act.

DO YOU REMEMBER THIS?

Vacuum cleaner

Mining ends in Black Country
2nd March 1968 300 years of coal mining in the Black Country come to an end as the Baggeridge Colliery near Sedgley closes. Whilst a handful of open-cast mines survive, the way of life that had fuelled the Industrial Revolution, and earned the area its nickname, is on the decline in what was once its heartland.

Dust falls
1st & 2nd July 1968 England and Wales are struck by severe 'dust' storms that combine mineral dust from the Sahara with cold and wet weather. Some areas are thrown into near total darkness by the clouds, and the UK suffers one of its worst and most widespread hailstorms on record. Three people are struck by lightning and one person drowns in flood water.

Five and ten pence
23 April 1968 The country wakes with new coins in its pockets, as it moves toward the decimalisation of the currency. New five and ten pence pieces are introduced, replacing the shilling and the florin, in an attempt to get the public used to the new currency before the process is completed in 1971.

18 APR 1968
New London Bridge, opened 1831, is sold to US millionaire Robert McCulloch for £1 million.

16 MAY 1968
15-year-old Alex Smith becomes Britain's first lung transplant patient but dies 12 days later.

24 JUN 1968
Comedian Tony Hancock dies in Sydney after taking an overdose, aged 44.

Last steam service
11th August 1968 The very last of British Rail's steam locomotives makes its final journey from Liverpool to Carlisle, signalling an end to the age of steam. From now on the only operating steam trains in the UK are on heritage railways or special services.

The Great Flood of 1968
15th September 1968 Severe storms lead to the worst floods in the Home Counties in over 100 years as large parts of the south east are affected. In Edenbridge Railway Station, the service from London's Charing Cross become stranded by flood water, with passengers stuck on board for 12 hours.

Second-class post
16th September 1968 The General Post Office launches a change in services, splitting post into first and second class for the first time. New second-class stamps cost 4d, while first class is 5d.

4D
5D
From September 16th
Choose your post
The Post Office

Derry march
5th October 1968 400 people gather to march through Derry in protest at discrimination in housing. They are supported by the fledgling Northern Ireland Civil Rights Association and the march is attended by several prominent MPs. Trouble breaks out when the Royal Ulster Constabulary use batons to drive the crowd across the river and engage violently with young people. Many are injured, and the extensive media presence leads to images of police brutality being shared widely across the country.

Race Relations Act
26th November 1968 Building upon the Race Relations Act of 1965, the new Act makes it illegal to discriminate against people on racial grounds in issues relating to employment, housing, or public services.

Hong Kong flu
December 1968 Cases of the Hong Kong flu, present in Britain since August, begin to rise in the country. The pandemic will last into 1970, claiming millions of lives globally and around 80,000 within the UK.

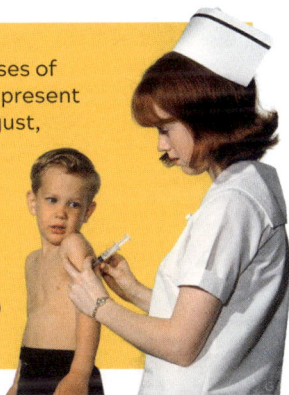

9 JUL 1968	8 AUG 1968	1 SEP 1968
The Queen opens the Brutalist Hayward Gallery on London's South Bank.	Princess Margaret makes the inaugural journey on board the Mountbatten-class hovercraft from Dover to Boulogne.	The first section of the London Underground's Victoria line opens between Walthamstow and Highbury & Islington.

ROYALTY & POLITICS

Anti-Vietnam demo
In a year characterised by protests around the world, on 17th March, demonstrators protesting against the United States, involvement in the Vietnam War, and Britain's support of US action, converge on Grosvenor Square where many clash with riot police outside the American embassy.

Rivers of Blood
20th April 1968 Shadow Secretary for Defence Enoch Powell makes his infamous 'Rivers of Blood' speech when addressing a meeting of the Conservative Political Centre in Birmingham. The speech is in opposition to the proposed Race Relations Act and immigration from the Commonwealth and proves enormously controversial both for its theme and its rhetoric.

Death of Princess Marina
Princess Marina, Duchess of Kent, dies at Kensington Palace on 27th August aged 61, a month after being diagnosed with an inoperable brain tumour.

FOREIGN NEWS

Prague Spring
4th January 1968 In Czechoslovakia, newly appointed Communist Party secretary Alexander Dubček pushes for 'socialism with a human face'. His political and social reforms are too much for the country's Soviet masters whose tanks invade on the night of 20th August. Dubček is replaced by hardliner Gustav Husak and 'the Prague Spring' comes to an abrupt end as.

Thatcher on track
Margaret Thatcher gives her first House of Commons speech as shadow transport minister this year, arguing for investment in British Rail. More than two decades later, in a premiership that had implemented the privatisation of most state-owned services, when Thatcher resigns as Prime Minister, British Rail is the only one that remains. It too is finally privatised under John Major's government.

18 OCT 1968
US athlete Bob Beamon sets an astonishing world record of 8.90m in the long jump at the Mexico Olympics.

28 NOV 1968
Death of prolific children's author Enid Blyton.

30 DEC 1968
Judy Garland begins a residency at the Talk of the Town in London in what will be her final performances.

Horror photo

1st February 1968 The most horrifying photograph of the Vietnam War is published, catching the moment a Viet Cong prisoner is executed by a South Vietnamese police chief.

Gagarin killed

27th March 1968 Yuri Gagarin, the first man in space, is killed on a training flight near Kirzhach in Russia. His ashes are interred in the walls of the Kremlin.

Baader-Meinhof

2nd April 1968 A new anarchist group announces itself with bomb attacks on department stores in Frankfurt. Andreas Baader and Ulrike Meinhof give their name to the gang, which is soon regarded as the biggest terrorist threat to mainland Europe. Also known as the Red Army Faction, these anti-imperialist urban guerrillas will get progressively more daring - and lethal - with assassinations and kidnappings before the leaders' capture in 1977.

King and Kennedy

4th April 1968 Martin Luther King Jr is murdered in Memphis, Tennessee. The killing of the most articulate and charismatic of civil rights leaders ignites days of rioting across the US. In Indianapolis, New York Senator Robert Kennedy calms his audience with a call for peace between the races. Presidential candidate Kennedy is cultivating young and disaffected voters with a promise to end the Vietnam War and plans for deep rooted social change. Two months later, following victory in the Californian Democratic primary, he is shot by Palestinian immigrant Sirhan Sirhan. He dies in hospital the next day. Millions line the route as a funeral train brings his body west for burial in Arlington Cemetery, Washington DC, where his brother was laid to rest five years before.

DO YOU REMEMBER THIS?

Slide projector

May '68 revolt

3rd May 1968 Inspired by a global wave of anti-war and anti-capitalist dissent, student protests erupt and bring France close to revolution. On 13th May, a million march through the streets of Paris. By the last week of May, two-thirds of French workers are on strike in sympathy, paralysing the world's fifth largest economy. On 30th May, with the government on the brink of collapse, President de Gaulle dissolves the National Assembly, promises reforms and calls an election. His gamble works: some normality returns and de Gaulle's party increases its majority. But while he holds the country together (just), his own days as leader are numbered.

Pope rejects birth control

25th July 1968 In an encyclical that dismays many, Pope Paul VI signals no change to the Catholic Church's position on artificial birth control. Catholics are advised to exercise abstinence and restraint. Sex is for procreation not recreation.

Nixon is President

5th November 1968 Republican candidate Richard Milhous Nixon, who after losing the presidential election to John Kennedy in 1960 told reporters that they 'won't have Nixon to kick around anymore', finally wins the race for the White House. His election marks a decisive turn to the right in US politics.

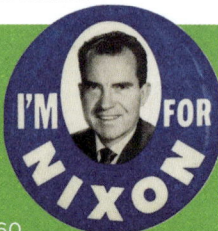

I'M FOR NIXON

Greetings from the Moon

25th December 1968 Apollo 8 is the first manned spacecraft to orbit the Moon. On Christmas Day a quarter of the world's population, at this point the largest television audience ever, watch the three astronauts deliver a seasonal message. Apollo 8's mission is to search for landing sites for future missions to the Moon. President Kennedy's promise that the US will put the first man on the Moon before the end of the decade is close to being realised.

ENTERTAINMENT

One for sorrow, two for joy

Magpie airs for the first time on 30th July as ITV's answer to the BBC's *Blue Peter*. *Magpie* is a bit more hip than its wholesome rival. It covers music and fashion, has a rock-tinged theme song based on the traditional rhyme about magpies and presenters like Mick Robertson (who joins in 1972 and looks a bit like Brian May) and Jenny Hanley find their faces pinned up on teenage bedroom walls.

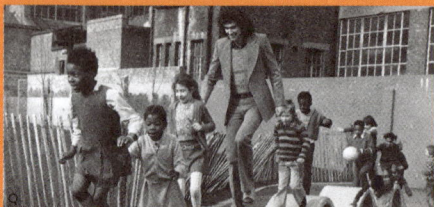

Garden greats

TV gets out in the garden this year. The first episode of *Gardener's World*, presented by Ken Burras from the Oxford Botanical Gardens, is broadcast on 5th January. The following year, Percy Thrower (photo) takes over as presenter with filming taking place in his own garden, The Magnolias in Shrewsbury. *The Herbs*, which debuts on BBC1 on 12th February, has Parsley the Lion, Dill the Dog, Tarragon the Dragon et al living in the walled kitchen garden of a country house. The magical password to gain entry to this horticultural wonderland? Herbidacious.

Home front humour

The members of Walmington-on-Sea's Local Defence Volunteers make their first appearance on 31st July. *Dad's Army*, penned by David Croft and Jimmy Perry, is a comic tribute to those who served in the Home Guard during the Second World War. Arthur Lowe plays pompous bank manager and self-appointed leader of the group, Captain Mainwaring, who heads a superb cast that deliver Croft and Perry's lines with immaculate timing and create some of British comedy's finest moments. The interaction between Mainwaring and Ian Lavender's hapless innocent, Private Pike ('You stupid boy') is particularly memorable.

Going ape

Hollywood make-up artist John Chambers is given a budget of $50,000 to transform Roddy McDowell, Maurice Evans and cast into unnervingly convincing simian overlords for the film, *Planet of the Apes*, adapted from Pierre Boulle's novel *La Planète des singes*. Charlton Heston, who spends most of the film in a loin cloth, is in the minority as a human, one of three astronauts who crash land on a planet where they discover, to their alarm, man is subjugated by monkey. Chambers is awarded an honorary Oscar for his work on the film.

Twinkle

The first issue of *Twinkle*, 'a picture paper for little girls', comes out on 27th January, with a free bracelet and St. Christopher charm on the cover to tempt buyers.

Hair **at last**

The 1968 Theatres Act is given royal assent on 26th July and finally ends censorship in the theatre. One of the first shows to benefit from the lifting of restrictions is the rock musical *Hair*, which contains nudity and pro-fanities. Hair opens at the Shaftesbury Theatre on 27th September with a cast that includes Paul Nicholas, Elaine Paige, Marsha Hunt, Tim Curry and Richard O'Brien. *Hair* runs for 1,997 performances, closing when the roof of the Shaftesbury Theatre collapses.

Chocs away

Cadbury's Milk Tray show their first TV advertisement in which actor and model Gary Myers is the thoughtful action man who thinks nothing of beating avalanches or plunging into waves in his bid to secretly deliver a box of chocolates, 'all because the lady loves Milk Tray'.

Chitty Chitty Bang Bang

After a heart attack in 1961, Ian Fleming's wife confiscates his typewriter in an attempt to force him to rest. So he simply writes a children's novel, *Chitty Chitty Bang Bang - The Magical Car* in longhand. In 1967, Albert R. Broccoli decides the story has potential as a film and recruits Dick Van Dyke to play inventor Caractacus Potts, while Sally Anne Howes stars as Truly Scrumptious. But perhaps more terrifying than any Bond villain is ballet dancer Robert Helpmann as the evil Childcatcher. *Chitty Chitty Bang Bang* goes on to become a children's classic.

1968

It's *The Basil Brush Show* - Boom boom!

After appearances of the garrulous Basil Brush on magician David Nixon's shows, *The Basil Brush Show* begins on BBC on 14th June. Basil is a talkative fox with an upper-class accent, a terrible habit of interrupting, and a tendency to laugh hysterically at his own jokes. In his traditional tweeds and cravat, he's a typical English gent (if you don't count the fact he's actually a fox AND a puppet) and charms the guests who willingly appear on his show. Ivan Owen, who provides Basil's voice, models it on the actor Terry-Thomas.

Wacky Races

Hanna-Barbera's latest cartoon features the wackiest motor racing competition in the world as an unusual set of competitors line up on the grid every episode, with some using more underhand means to win than others. *Wacky Races* introduces us to miniature gangsters the Anthill Mob, pink-loving southern belle Penelope Pitstop and moustache-twirling arch-villain Dick Dastardly and his snickering asthmatic sidekick Muttley.

(Morecambe and) Wise move

Eric and Ernie's move to the BBC, after seven successful years in ATV's *Two of a Kind*, is driven by the comedy duo's desire to have their show in colour at a time when BBC2 is still the only channel transmitting in colour. The first episode of the *Morecambe and Wise Show* airs on 2nd September, and soon becomes the jewel in the BBC's light entertainment crown, with up to 28 million people settling down to watch their annual Christmas Day shows.

Festival first

A year before Woodstock happens, 10,000 people descend on Ford Farm, Godshill for the first Isle of Wight festival. Among the acts on the bill are Jefferson Airplane, the Move, Smile and Fairport Convention. The following year, Bob Dylan plays the festival after a long absence and in 1970, the festival has swelled to such a size, the island is overrun with 100,000 festival-goers.

Hop to it

The Spacehopper hits UK shops in the spring of this year. Originally called 'Pon-Pon', this large inflatable with ball with ribbed horns to use as handles is manufactured by Corgi-Mettoy in the UK and soon streets, driveways, parks and cul-de-sacs are overrun with kids hopping about on them. The fact the Spacehopper has a fearsome face etched on its front and is possibly the most exhausting and inefficient way to get from A to B does little to dent its popularity.

Cilla
Cilla is broadcast on BBC1 on 30th January and marks the beginning of Cilla Black's transition from singing star to TV personality, in a deal brokered by Brian Epstein shortly before his premature death; *Cilla* will run for eight series until 1976.

Oliver!
Lionel Bart's 1960 stage musical comes to cinema screens in this big, loud and colourful adaptation of Dickens' *Oliver Twist*. Ron Moody, anxious to distance his character Fagin from the anti-semitic stereotype of the novel, plays the role with a light mischievous touch, while Jack Wild's Artful Dodger is full of chirpy confidence, Oliver Reed as Bill Sikes glowers with brooding menace and Mark Lester is guileless innocence in the title role. Add to that a bulging songbook of sensational tunes, and it's no surprise that *Oliver!* wins six Academy Awards.

MUSIC

Petula breaks a taboo
2nd April 1968 America's favourite British music star of the moment is former child star Petula Clark. Thanks to hits like *Downtown* and *Don't Sleep in the Subway* and the movies *Goodbye Mr Chips* and *Finian's Rainbow*, she now has a top-rated prime-time TV show. During a duet on the show with Harry Belafonte, she takes his arm and breaks an unwritten ban on interracial touching on US TV. The show sparks uproar but Petula is unrepentant.

Changes for the Beatles
15th May 1968 As the Beatles put the extravagances of *Sgt. Pepper* behind them to navigate life without Brian Epstein, they set up Apple Corps, to release Beatle records and promote new talent. George persuades the others to join him in India for a transcendental meditation course run by Mahirishi Mahesh Yogi. Although they no longer write collaboratively, a positive of the trip is the number of songs which John and Paul create. Many appear on a double album with a plain white cover simply titled *The Beatles*.

Small Faces, big sound
24th May 1968 A fine Mod band always slightly in the shadow of the Who and the Kinks, the Small Faces make Ogden's *Nut Gone Flake*, with a circular sleeve in the style of a tobacco tin. It includes *Lazy Sunday*, a comic take on their East London roots and a sequel to 1967's *Itchycoo Park*.

The king is back
3rd December 1968 Heralding Elvis Presley's re-emergence after years of so-so movies and records is the one-off television special *Elvis*. Singing live on stage for the first time since 1960, he looks lean and lithe and in great voice.

Cream goes sour
26th November 1968 After a productive but fretful year, Cream play their last gig to a packed Royal Albert Hall. Eric Clapton and Ginger Baker form another supergroup in Blind Faith (photo) with Stevie Winwood from Traffic.

Cliff does Eurovision

6th April 1968 The UK hosts the Eurovision Song Contest, with hopes pinned on Cliff Richard and the bouncy *Congratulations*. Cliff comes second by one point to Spain's entry, *La La La* by Massiel.

MY FIRST 18 YEARS

TOP10 1968

1. **Hey Jude** *The Beatles*
2. **Nights in White Satin** *The Moody Blues*
3. **What a Wonderful World** *Louis Armstrong*
4. **Classical Gas** *Mason Williams*
5. **Everlasting Love** *Love Affair*
6. **Fire** *The Crazy World of Arthur Brown*
7. **Where Do You Go to My Lovely** *Peter Sarstedt*
8. **The Mighty Quinn** *Manfred Mann*
9. **Cinderella Rockefella** *Esther and Abi Ofarim*
10. **Build Me Up Buttercup** *The Foundations*

Open | Search | Scan

Mary's opportunity

4th May 1968 Eighteen year old-Welsh folk singer Mary Hopkin appears on the ITV talent show *Opportunity Knocks* and is noticed by Paul McCartney, who's looking for artists to sign to Apple Records. He chooses a song for her based on a Russian folk tune, *Those Were the Days*, which is at No. 1 within weeks.

Here's to you, *Mrs Robinson*

1st June 1968 Contracted to supply songs to the movie *The Graduate*, Paul Simon writes one verse of *Mrs Robinson* for use on the soundtrack. Fully fleshed out and released as a Simon and Garfunkel single, the song is a satirical put-down of status-conscious middle America just as a wave of student protests hits its peak.

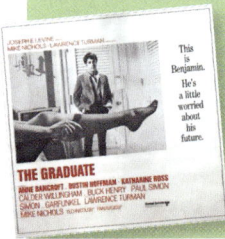

Led Zeppelin formed

7th July 1968 The Led Zeppelin story starts here with the break-up of the Yardbirds and Jimmy Page's formation of a new hard rock band - initially called the New Yardbirds - with Chris Dreja, John Paul Jones and Robert Plant. Debuting live in October and signing a massive deal with Atlantic Records, they record their hugely influential self-titled first album for release in January.

Fleetwood Mac

6th July 1968 Adding a third guitarist to an already much talked-about line-up is the most outstanding new British blues band in years, Fleetwood Mac. Danny Kirwan joins ex-John Mayall's Bluesbreakers Peter Green and Jeremy Spencer, drummer Mick Fleetwood and bassist John McVie completing the band.

Dusty in Memphis

24th November 1968 US TV's *Ed Sullivan Show* plays host to Dusty Springfield, fresh from recording in Memphis under top soul producer Jerry Wexler. It's a marriage made in heaven that yields the album *Dusty in Memphis* and possibly the greatest single ever by any white soul singer, *Son Of A Preacher Man*.

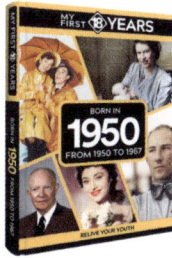

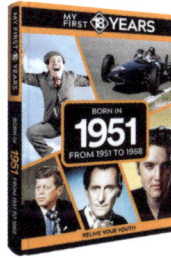

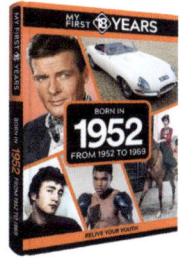

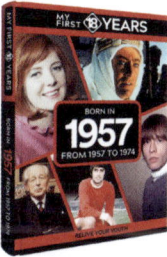

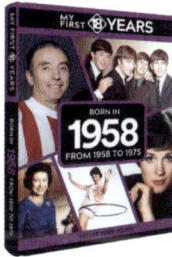

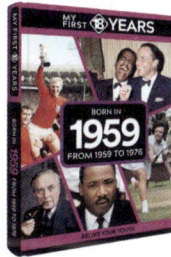

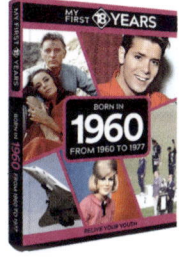

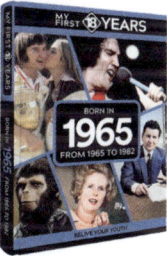

MY FIRST **18** YEARS

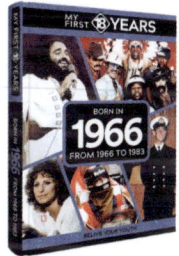

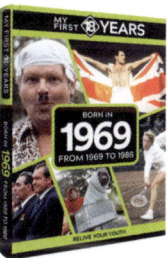

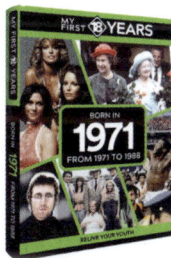

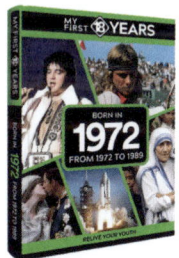

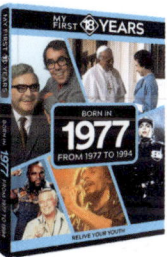

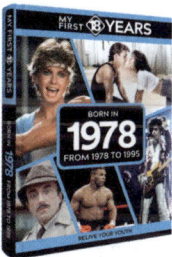

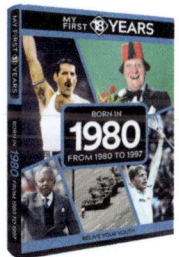

BORN IN 1949 — FROM 1949 TO 1966
BORN IN 1950 — FROM 1950 TO 1967
BORN IN 1951 — FROM 1951 TO 1968
BORN IN 1952 — FROM 1952 TO 1969
BORN IN 1957 — FROM 1957 TO 1974
BORN IN 1958 — FROM 1958 TO 1975
BORN IN 1959 — FROM 1959 TO 1976
BORN IN 1960 — FROM 1960 TO 1977
BORN IN 1965 — FROM 1965 TO 1982
BORN IN 1966 — FROM 1966 TO 1983
BORN IN 1969 — FROM 1969 TO 1986
BORN IN 1970 — FROM 1970 TO 1987
BORN IN 1971 — FROM 1971 TO 1988
BORN IN 1972 — FROM 1972 TO 1989
BORN IN 1977 — FROM 1977 TO 1994
BORN IN 1978 — FROM 1978 TO 1995
BORN IN 1979 — FROM 1979 TO 1996
BORN IN 1980 — FROM 1980 TO 1997

RELIVE YOUR YOUTH